Nordicism and Modernity

Gregers Einer Forssling

Nordicism and Modernity

palgrave
macmillan

Gregers Einer Forssling
Pitstone, UK

ISBN 978-3-030-61209-2   ISBN 978-3-030-61210-8   (eBook)
https://doi.org/10.1007/978-3-030-61210-8

This Palgrave Macmillan imprint is published by the registered company Springer Nature
Switzerland AG.
The registered company address is: Gewerbestrasse 11, 6330 Cham, Switzerland

For my family and friends

ACKNOWLEDGEMENTS

I would firstly like to thank Roger Griffin, Emeritus Professor at Oxford Brookes, and Martin Arnold, Emeritus Reader at the University of Hull, for their invaluable support and guidance in helping me to develop the PhD thesis on which this work is based. Their valuable expertise, in their respective research areas, and their encouragement through difficult times made this work possible. My thanks as well to Dr. Tom Crook and Charmian Hearne for their advice and support during my time at Oxford Brookes together with the staff and students of the Faculty of Humanities and Social Sciences who provided such a stimulating academic environment to work in. I would also like to thank those who assisted me in accessing research material at The British Library, Oxford Brookes University and my local library in Tring.

I am also grateful for those who spent time with me along the way, discussing my ideas and sharing their knowledge with me. My thanks to historian Roger Moorhouse for sharing his expertise on the Third Reich and translation skills; to Pastor Geir Waage of Reykholt Church, Iceland, for sharing his knowledge of Scandinavian history and Old Norse sagas during my visit and to Jens Peter Mortensen for his knowledge of Denmark under the occupation and for contributing artwork from his collection. I would also like to thank historian Matthew Glencross for his guidance and encouragement while I was preparing this work for publication. My thanks as well to Emily Russell and the editorial and production staff of Palgrave for their support in publishing this work.

Finally I would like to express my immense gratitude to my friends and family for their patience and understanding while I was busy and preoccupied with this work and for their encouragement to complete it.

Gregers Einer Forssling

Contents

LIST OF FIGURES

CHAPTER 1

Introduction: Nordicism, Myth and Modernity

Nordicism is more than a historical term that should be applied to a marginal group of Northern European and American racist thinkers of the early twentieth century. It is a living, evolving, cultural phenomenon rooted in the idealisation of the 'noble savage' during the late Enlightenment and Romantic periods. This later developed into a powerful racial fantasy through its fusion with the emerging fields of racial science and eugenics. This work attempts to shed fresh light on the nature and evolution of Nordicism and its relationship with modernity by examining it as a societal phenomenon which, in its variant forms, came into being as a source of psychological rootedness and identity with which to counter the disembedding, disenchanting impact of an ever-changing and accelerating state of modernity. This conceptual framework initially draws on Roger Griffin's model of modernism, as a reaction to the corrosive impact of modernisation, and later incorporates Zygmunt Bauman's parallel theory of the existential and socio-political dilemmas posed by reality's increasing 'liquefaction' under the impact of contemporary modernity. By using these perspectives to re-examine Nordicism, this work reveals its nature as a set of complex but coherent mythic strategies for establishing a sheltering home, a refuge from the relentless pace of progress. In this context, myth will be interpreted as the creation of narratives recounting the origins of a people, defining its characteristics and explaining its evolution.

© The Author(s) 2020
G. E. Forssling, *Nordicism and Modernity*,
https://doi.org/10.1007/978-3-030-61210-8_1

1

The historical development and dynamics of Nordicism will be analysed through this framework of sociological theory focusing on the role played by myth-making in protecting the individual and society from the challenges of an ever-changing state of modernity. This condition is characterised by ceaseless flux and endless liminality, denying the possibility of a stable, homogeneous and unitary culture of the sort that was believed to exist in pre-modern times. This study of its development will reveal how Nordicism has evolved since its emergence in the nineteenth century and the role of the Romantic Movement in laying the foundations for this development through its idealisation of a 'Golden Age' of the Nordic race, a time where life's dramas could still be lived out simply, powerfully and heroically. On the basis of this historical enquiry, this work will explore what fresh light can be thrown on Nazism's creation of an idealised image of the Nordic as the rationale for the 're-Nordification' of Germany and the purging of Europe of its Jewish communities. Through this lens, the process of myth-making will be approached as the manifestation of an innate human need to retain a sense of spirituality and social fixity to form a refuge from the disorientating effects of an ever-changing state of modernity that denies permanence or any sense of rootedness. In the words of Karl Marx, 'all that is solid melts into air, all that is holy is profaned, and man is at last compelled to face with sombre senses, his real conditions of life'.[1] A concluding section will study the way that adapted fragments of the failed project of Nordicism, both Romantic and Nazi, are manifested in contemporary society as part of our current society's eclectic appropriation of the historical and mythic materials of past cultures.

This study therefore combines academic strands. Firstly, it examines the history of Nordicism, which until now has been treated as a series of discreet episodes in the revival of Nordic myth with the main focus on either Romantic idealisation or Nazi revivalism. Secondly, it draws on a new interdisciplinary field of investigations into modernity that focuses on modernism as a bid to restore meaning and a sense of the sacred to modern society, not just through artistic innovation but in both socio-political and cultural initiatives of renewal. On the premise of this approach, existing studies of Nordicism in its three major manifestations (nineteenth-century Romanticism, Nazism and post-war identity politics) will be studied to create a continuous narrative of the evolution of Nordicism and its relationship with modernity.

LOCATING THIS INVESTIGATION INTO NORDICISM WITHIN EXISTING RESEARCH

This work builds primarily on two fields of research, modernity and Nordicism, and as such combines two areas of academic endeavour, which have often remained distinct within their respective disciplines of history and sociology. To develop a deeper understanding of the development and dynamics of Nordicism, I intend to draw on these complementary fields to examine its development in Northern Europe and the USA. This syncretic approach will encompass a range of primary and secondary sources examined through a theoretical framework drawn from the work of contemporary political, sociological and anthropological theorists. These academics have analysed the impact of modernity on society and the individual and propose that the 'disenchanting' impact on traditional culture constantly stimulates the countervailing force of myth-making to restore a sense of transcendence and rootedness to human existence.

Within the field of historical research, Nordicism has often been examined as a component of nineteenth-century new religions, racial science, eugenics, neo-paganism and Nazi occultism but less frequently as the single focus of a work concerned with it as a single entity with its own historical narrative and socio-cultural dynamics. This work draws on a number of published sources to present a chronological series of case studies that show the evolution of Nordicism from early to contemporary modernity. Notable in the limited research into the evolution of Nordicism and its relationship with modernity is the work of Christopher Hutton whose valuable insights have been cited herein. The aim of this study is to shed new light on the evolution of Nordicism by applying existing scholarship to a particular matrix of social theory and to reinterpret it as a distinct point in a cluster of reactions by the individual and society to modernity. In this way the inner cohesion and narrative continuity of Nordicism as a historical and contemporary phenomenon can be viewed from a fresh perspective.

In order to establish a theoretical matrix of analysis for the evolution of Nordicism as an aspect of modernity, this work will initially apply the theories of modernism and revitalisation movements of Roger Griffin. It will later dovetail this analysis with the theories of 'liquid modernity' and 'Retropia' proposed by Zygmunt Bauman, to examine how fragments of Nordicism can still be identified in our fast-paced contemporary society. Their work on the relationship between the individual, society and the endlessly shifting dialectic between the culture-fragmenting impact of modernity and the culture-recreating force of modernism forms a matrix of social theory for the analysis of the dynamics of Nordicism as more than a historical strand of marginal political, religious and scientific thought. Instead, it emerges as a social phenomenon which is present even in today's modern, increasingly secularised society and represents a significant strand of the constant struggle of human beings to re-imbue human life with some significance and sense of rootedness.

This work will also study the development of our reception of Old Norse culture and its transformation during the twentieth century. It draws, in part, on the research of academics such as Martin Arnold, Andrew Wawn, Margaret Clunies Ross, Lars Lönnroth, Heather O'Donoghue and Else Roesdahl who have made a significant contribution to our evolving reception and interpretations of Old Norse culture. Our perception and understanding of Old Norse culture is, however, still a work in progress as enhanced scientific techniques, applied to the field of archaeology, continue to provide us with fresh insights into this period, which have hitherto remained misunderstood or romanticised. This has led to a flourishing revision of this period, through interdisciplinary research in fields such as literature, history, anthropology, linguistics and archaeology, to create an increasingly realistic picture of daily life and consequently our overall understanding of Old Norse culture. These developments are vital to our understanding of the origins of the emergence of Nordicism during the nineteenth century. Much of the perceived image of the Nordic people at the time was based on semi-fictionalised and biased accounts, written with an authority that transformed it, in many cases, into historical fact. This lack of factual knowledge and empirical evidence allowed myth and history to be merged, during the eighteenth and nineteenth centuries, to create an idealised image of the Nordic race which Nordicists appropriated as worthy of protection and regeneration.

This proposed contribution to our understanding of Nordicism is therefore based on an interdisciplinary approach drawing on the complementary fields of history, literature, art, anthropology and sociology. It can be situated in the cluster of research which has surfaced in recent years into the development of various social, political and religious movements, which have emerged since the nineteenth century, in the form of revitalisation movements, seeking to re-establish a sense of rootedness and meaning in an ever-changing setting of modernity.

RECASTING NORDICISM

Before examining the historical development and dynamics of Nordicism as a socio-cultural phenomenon in its own right, this work will establish a working definition that distinguishes it from the various movements which have influenced our current perception of the term and which will be examined in more detail in later chapters. Since the late nineteenth century, movements such as National Romanticism, Aryanism, nationalism and Nazism have all interacted at various levels with Nordicism. Through this association, certain 'conceptual baggage' has accumulated which can often confuse any definition seeking to express the core of the movement. Scholarship by academics such as Nicholas Goodrick-Clarke and Christopher M. Hutton has done much to disentangle and differentiate the concepts of Pan-Germanism, Aryanism and Nordicism during the Third Reich, but in Hutton's own words, 'a considerable communication gap exists between specialist studies on Nazi Germany and the wider academic public'.[2]

The problematic nature of analysing any form of historical ideology is that we are often faced with what could be termed a 'composite definition'. This is formed by the actions and theories of notable personalities associated with a belief system and the reactions of the movement to a range of various historical events and influences. Ideologies therefore take on what could be termed an 'existential nature' defining themselves and being defined by observers and commentators, according to the various forms they have taken and the ideas, events and actions with which they have become associated. The result is a 'composite definition', a multi-layered ideological construct whose identity has developed and evolved over time and which, in many cases, is still in the process of being revised and defined.

A related factor, which further complicates any fixed definition of an ideological movement, is the fusion of both convergent and divergent shades of opinion within a movement at any given moment, even within totalitarian regimes such as Nazism. These elements create an ideological concept that is at the same time homogenous and heterogeneous, composed of a cluster of individual but generally compatible 'world-views', bound together by a core ideal and messianic leader. A key question raised by this issue of convergence and divergence within a movement is the extent to which any individual or group must conform to some or all of the definitional criteria of an ideology to qualify for inclusion in a movement. This is a problematic factor in any form of classification and has a significant bearing on any definition of Nordicism as an independent phenomenon and any subsequent identification of those considered Nordicists.

As a starting point in developing a working definition of Nordicism, it is useful to consider some established definitions of the terms 'Nordicism' and 'Nordicists'. The *Oxford English Dictionary* sums up Nordicism as a historical term used to describe 'the doctrine of or belief in the cultural and racial supremacy of the Nordic people' and a Nordicist as 'a person who believes in the supremacy of the Nordic people'.[3] Another description, proposed by A. James Gregor in the *Phylon* journal in 1960, also focused on biological and cultural supremacy but included an important element of the deterioration of the Nordic people, a pessimism that inspired the emergence of a range of modernist revitalisation movements:

> Nordicism involves the belief that men of the "Nordic Race"—tall, slender, fair skinned, blond, blue-eyed, narrow-faced, narrow-nosed, long-headed individuals—are qualitatively superior to the remainder of mankind. They are the creators of civilization, and their passing marks the passing of civilization.[4]

This definition appears to draw on the polemical works of writers such as American Nordicist Madison Grant whose 1916 publication, *The Passing of the Great Race*, listed these same Nordic characteristics and linked what he saw as the demise of the Nordic with the decline of civilisation.[5] A further description, proposed by historian Geoffrey G. Field in 1977, focused on Nordicists' appropriation of scientific theory to legitimise their theories and their relationship with völkisch ideologies that emerged in the years following the First World War:

> Nordicists argued that their achievement was to place the study of race upon a firm, unassailable basis, validated by careful research and free from the mystical yearnings and heavy-handed polemic pre-War writers. In fact, they largely tailored the already well-established Aryan myth to the circumstances of post 1918 Europe. Their thought was extremely derivative; often, they merely buttressed the standard shibboleths of romantic, völkisch ideology with more sophisticated "proofs" and data.[6]

This definition describes the development of Nordicism in Europe as a process of merging modern myth-making, nationalism and emerging scientific theories. From this perspective, it demonstrates how the 'conceptual baggage' of Aryan and völkisch thought of the late 1920s and early 1930s impacted on the development of the movement and consequently our 'composite definition' of the term. Another definition, focusing on the historical development of the movement and its association with Aryanism, can be found in the *Great Soviet Encyclopedia* (1973) in which the term Nordicism is described as a pseudoscientific theory of the superiority of the Nordic/Germanic race, later appropriated by Nazism as the legitimation of its state ideology:

> (Nordicism is) a variety of racism; a pseudoscientific theory based on the assertion that the northern (Nordic), or Aryan, race is superior to other human races. The French sociologists J. A. Gobineau and G. Lapouge are considered the founders of Nordicism. Apologists for Nordicism equate the northern race and the "Germanic," asserting that the latter constitutes the "highest" race, to which humanity owes all the achievements of civilization. Nordicism was used as a weapon by the "theorists" of German fascism, who made it the official ideology of Hitlerite Germany.[7]

These definitions collectively illustrate how Nordicism has evolved as a 'composite definition', with an emphasis on its function as a doctrine of racial supremacy, fused with that of Nazi Aryanism, which has for many years stood as the established definition of Nordicism. It is noticeable, however, that even the more recent of these definitions tend to suggest, through the omission of any post-war reference, that Nordicism's evolution ended as a concept and subsequently became fixed as a definition following the fall of the Third Reich. This approach fails to recognise, however, that ideologies do not disappear overnight but may continue in residual pockets for years even after they have become discredited by mainstream thought. These often re-emerge in adapted, resynthesised forms as marginal strands of extremism such as in many Northern European and American individuals and groups that will be examined in this work.

Since these definitions were proposed, considerable work has been carried out in the fields of anthropology, sociology and political theory. This has shed new light on the rise of many forms of nineteenth- and twentieth-century ideology as responses to the impact of modernity on traditional society. This research has examined a number of political and religious movements that have emerged as a reaction to a sense of social deterioration and disorientation caused by the erosion or destruction of traditional forms of society in the West. These revitalisation movements sought to regenerate or replace these eroded traditions and identities and thus combat the growing sense of crisis experienced as the degeneration or demise of civilisation.

With the aim of shedding new light on its nature and evolution, this work will apply the following description of the phenomenon of Nordicism, with an emphasis on revitalisation, rather than racial superiority:

> *Nordicism is a political, cultural or scientific movement that emerged during the nineteenth-century and had peaked in its influence by the mid-1940s, fragments of which can still be found in contemporary society. It is founded on the belief that it is possible to historically empathise with Nordic culture (Romantic Nordicism) or biologically identify and regenerate a pure Nordic type, based on scientific principles of taxonomy and eugenics (racial Nordicism). This racial type was based on an imagined, idealised sense of a superior physical, cultural and spiritual beauty and purity of the Nordic people. Whether as a literary, cultural, political or racial revitalisation movement, Nordicism seeks to combat the disenchanting and deracinating forces associated with modernity by presenting, to individuals who can identify with it, a vision of transcendence and rootedness located within their perceived, reconstituted Nordic identity.*

In conclusion, the recasting of Nordicism in a way which focuses on the concept of revitalisation, rather than just racial superiority, as the driving force behind this movement, is designed to enable this research to reveal the dynamics, development and continuity of Nordicism throughout the nineteenth and twentieth centuries and up to the present. This aims to view this phenomenon from a new angle, bringing to light new facets which only a shift in perspective will allow. This will enable Nazi Nordicism, the most notorious exploitation of Nordic myth, to be located within the longer and more diverse narrative of Nordicism as a whole and within a broader mythic response to the impact of modernity.

ROGER GRIFFIN'S THEORY OF MODERNISM

The theory that modernism should be redefined to embrace a wide range of phenomena emanating from the need to maintain or invent a sense of meaning, transcendental values and *communitas* in the face of an atomising modernity was developed by Roger Griffin in *Modernism and Fascism* (2007). In this work, he analysed modernism through the prism of what he terms a 'primordialist definition' proposing that modernism is an innate, multi-faceted set of reactions, emerging from the mid-nineteenth century onwards to the rapid modernisation of Western society and the concomitant loss of cultural homogeneity and sense of 'centre'.[8] In discussing the reactions of these revitalisation movements, Griffin points out that:

> Their common denominator lies in the bid to achieve a sense of transcendent value, meaning, or purpose despite Western culture's progressive loss of a homogenous value system and overarching cosmology (nomos) caused by the secularizing and disembedding forces of modernization. The modernists' rejection of or revolt against contemporary modernity was shaped by innate predispositions of the human consciousness and mythopoeic faculty to create culture, to construct utopias, to access a suprahuman temporality and to belong to a community united by a shared culture.[9]

In his framework of analysis, Griffin draws, in part, on Peter L. Berger's concept of the 'sacred canopy' (*The Sacred Canopy*, 1969) to describe a societal shield created against the terror of a seemingly meaningless state of rapid change. He also applies the terms *nomos* and *anomie*, originally used by sociologist Emile Durkheim, to define the 'solid' states of prevailing order and 'liquid' states of uncertainty and breakdown experienced by the individual and society. According to Griffin's theories, modern society has an innate need to maintain a sense of shared cultural rootedness and sense of transcendence, a 'sacred canopy' of externalised belief to avoid being pulled into an *anomic* state of existence devoid of meaning. One reaction has been the attempt to recreate lost connections through a process of more or less conscious myth construction through which individuals or segments of a society seek to regenerate their sense of identity and unity through the construction of new forms of belief, rooted in the past but adapted to be relevant and compatible with the contemporary setting. In his work, Griffin analyses this process of regeneration through Anthony F.C. Wallace and Kenneth Tollefson's model of the socio-cultural 'mazeway' (*Mazeway resynthesis; a bio-cultural theory of religious inspiration,* 1956). Griffin quotes Tollefson who describes cultural revitalisation as:

> an adaptive social response whereby the past and present values, customs, and beliefs – which produce dissonance arising from the distortions that exist between them – are analyzed and recombined into a new synthesis, a new mazeway, or a new Gestalt.[10]

Through this concept of 'mazeway resynthesis', Griffin describes how an individual or society reacts to a changing state of modernity, when past and present become misaligned, by creating new adapted belief systems allowing them to maintain a viable sense of rootedness and transcendence against a changing social landscape from which they feel detached and alienated. In a rapidly changing modernity, as one 'sacred canopy' becomes eroded, it is replaced by another reconfigured shelter or *nomos* against the terror of meaningless.

Griffin also draws on the work of French ethnographer Arnold van Gennep (1873–1957) who proposed the concept of liminality, which was refined and further developed by anthropologist and fellow ethnographer Victor Turner (1920–1983) in his work on rituals and rites of passage.[11] In Gennep's thesis, liminality represents an intermediate phase between two states of being which are often accompanied in both primitive and modern societies by a variety of rites of passage, which differ greatly in form and meaning but which perform the function of marking the transition into a new state of being. In an article, written for the *Journal for the Scientific Study of Religion* in 1991, sociologist Mathieu Deflem defines three distinct stages of this process. These are '*separation*, when a person or group becomes detached from an earlier fixed point in the social structure or from an earlier set of social conditions, *liminal*, when the state of the ritual subject is ambiguous and *aggregation*, when the ritual subject a new stable state with its own rights and obligations'.[12] These three stages, applied to the disembedding processes of modernity, describe how rapid change forces man to break away from eroded traditions and belief systems leaving both society and the individual in a disorientated state of 'limbo' which, if prolonged, can lead to a collective state of societal anxiety or *anomie*. To avoid such a condition, social groups periodically undertake a process of 'mazeway resynthesis' to regenerate and restore a sense of social order and meaningful existence, even if the ever-changing condition of the modern precludes any permanent mythic solution to the strain of *anomie*.

This study of the development of cultural, biological and political Nordicism will draw together these strands of sociological and anthropological theory to create a framework of analysis through which this work will analyse a series of historical case studies. These will highlight how Nordicism has emerged as complex and ambivalent forms of regenerative revitalisation movements reacting to aspects of modernity that have eroded the sense of the universe being imbued with meaning and sacrality. In other words, as attempts to reconstruct a sense of identity and rootedness using building blocks from the mythicised fragments of a past age of Norse culture.

To summarise these introductory reflections and methodological premises, Nordicism has emerged at distinct points in modern history when groups of individuals in Western society, who identify with their Nordic roots, have perceived that the continuance of their biological and cultural heritage has become threatened by phenomena associated with the unstoppable momentum of modernity. The erosion of shared traditions, belief systems and their perceived racial purity has driven them to attempt to reconstruct their mythical and biological origins in order to maintain a sense of social order and collective transcendence. Without this shield, they fear the terror of a prolonged *anomic* state of liminality and the eventual loss of their biological and cultural identity. This work will integrate into a single, composite history, the various narrative strands that constitute Nordicism as a constitutive element of modern culture by underlining their common genesis as a modernist reaction to the disenchantment of reality.

Overview

This introductory chapter has established the aims and objectives of this work and the theoretical matrix of analysis through which the narrative of Nordicism will be examined. Chapter 2 will examine the roots of Nordicism as they emerged from the National Romantic Movement's progressive appropriation, during the late nineteenth century, of the Nordic cultural revival as a nationalist ideological construct, notably in Germany and North America. Chapter 3 will examine the concurrently developing field of racial science and how this became entwined with the National Romantic Movement's mythologisation of the Nordic to develop into an agenda of biological Nordicism. It will focus on the emergence of this phenomenon, during the late nineteenth and early twentieth centuries, as a new form of programmatic political, cultural and biological ideology and examine its impact on both immigration legislation and its interaction with the developing field of international eugenics, with a particular emphasis on Germany and the USA. These case studies, and those in the following chapters, will analyse the evolution of Nordicism, from a conceptual ideology, into a political and scientific reality through the application of positive and negative Nordicist-inspired eugenics policies in these countries. Chapters 4 and 5 will study the assimilation of Nordicist beliefs into the racial ideology of Nazism, with a focus on Himmler's SS and its role in applying Nordicist theories which led to a programme of industrial-scale genocide. Chapter 5 will also examine the eventual demise of Nordicism in the collapse of Nazi Germany. In Chap. 6, the concluding chapter, this work will attempt to shed new light on our understanding and interpretation of Nordicism by extending the historical narrative to a series of contemporary case studies in Nordicism's survival into the post-Nazi era. These are intended to demonstrate the continued presence of aspects of Nordicist belief and will be examined through the cultural and political activities of right-wing groups and individuals, in Northern Europe and the USA, who seek to protect and regenerate what they perceive to be the purity and innate superiority of the Nordic race against the threat of globalisation. It will also consider the extent to which our enduring need of myth, in our state of rapidly evolving 'liquid modernity', as defined by Zygmunt Bauman, is reflected in our current reception of Norse history and culture and the relationship between this and the enduring phenomenon of Nordicism.

NOTES

1. Marx, Karl and Engels, Friedrich (1967) *The Communist Manifesto*. Penguin, London p 83.
2. Hutton, Christopher M. (2005) *Race and the Third Reich*. Polity Press, Cambridge p 3.
3. *The Shorter Oxford English Dictionary* (2002) Oxford University Press, Oxford.
4. Gregor, James A. (1961) *Nordicism Revisited*. Phylon Journal, 22 (4): 351.
5. Grant, Madison (1916) *The Passing of The Great Race*. C. Scribner's Sons, New York p 150.
6. Field, Geoffrey G. (1977) *Nordic Racism*. Journal of the History of Ideas, 38 (3): 524.
7. Prokhorov, A. M. and Waxman, Macmillan M. (eds.) (1973) *Great Soviet Encyclopedia*. New York: Macmillan. http://www.smartdefine.org/nordicism#!/nordicism/definitions/1826028 (Accessed 2/11/12).
8. See Chapter 4. Griffin, Roger (2007) *Modernism and Fascism – The Sense of a Beginning under Mussolini and Hitler*. Palgrave Macmillan, Basingstoke and New York.

9. Griffin, Roger *Modernism and Fascism*. p 116.
10. Tollefson, Kenneth quoted by Griffin, Roger *Modernism and Fascism*. p 106 The German term *Gestalt* means a configuration or pattern.
11. Notable works include *The Ritual Process: Structure and Anti-Structure Foundations of Human Behavior* (1969) and *Forest of Symbols: Aspects of Ndembu Ritual* (1967).
12. Deflem, Mathieu (1991) *Ritual, Anti-structure, and Religion: A discussion of Victor Turner's processual symbolic analysis*. Journal for the Scientific Study of Religion, 30 (1): 9.
    Quoted by Griffin, Roger in *Modernism and Fascism*. p 102.

BIBLIOGRAPHY

PRINTED WORKS

Deflem, M. (1991). Ritual, Anti-structure, and Religion: A Discussion of Victor Turner's Processual Symbolic Analysis. *Journal for the Scientific Study of Religion, 30*(1), 1–25.
Field, G. G. (1977). Nordic Racism. *Journal of the History of Ideas, 38*(3), 523–540.
Grant, M. (1916). *The Passing of the Great Race*. New York: C. Scribner's Sons.
Gregor, J. A. (1961). Nordicism Revisited. *Phylon, 22*(4), 351–360.
Griffin, R. (2007). *Modernism and Fascism – The Sense of a Beginning Under Mussolini and Hitler*. Basingstoke: Palgrave Macmillan.
Hutton, C. M. (2005). *Race and the Third Reich*. Cambridge: Polity Press.
Karl, M., & Friedrich, E. (1967). *The Communist Manifesto*. London: Penguin.
Roesdahl, E. (1998). *The Vikings*. London: Penguin Books.
Simek, R. (2007). *Dictionary of Northern Mythology*. Cambridge: D.S. Brewer.
The Shorter Oxford English Dictionary. (2002). Oxford: Oxford University Press.

WEBSITES AND DIGITAL PUBLICATIONS (WITH DATE ACCESSED)

Great Soviet Encyclopedia. New York: Macmillan. Accessed 2/11/12, from http://www.smartdefine.org/nordicism#!/nordicism/definitions/1826028

New Foundations: Nationalist and Romantic Visions of the Nordic in Northern Europe and America

This chapter opens this historical study of Nordicism by considering the emergence of the National Romantic Movement in Northern Europe and America during the late eighteenth and early nineteenth centuries as a cultural and later political trend that became, in certain countries, a foundation for the subsequent development of Nordicism. It will trace the revival and progressive idealisation of Old Norse culture across Scandinavia, Britain, North America and Germany and the subsequent development of what could be termed early forms of cultural and political Nordicism. It will also consider how the differing experiences of modernity in each country impacted on the emergence of Nordicism, notably in North America and Germany.

In 1872, Friedrich Nietzsche's image in *The Birth of Tragedy* described the *anomic* state of the modern 'mythless man', digging and grubbing for roots in the past for lost forms of mythology and identity. This articulated the need for modern man to re-establish and maintain a sense of cultural rootedness and *nomic* identity as a reaction to the seemingly unstoppable advancement of rationalist, secularising modernity:

> [...] the mythless man stands eternally hungry, surrounded by all past ages, and digs and grubs for roots, even if he has to dig for them in the remotest antiquities. The tremendous historical need of our unsatisfied modern culture, the assembling around one of countless other cultures, the consuming

© The Author(s) 2020
G. E. Forssling, *Nordicism and Modernity*,
https://doi.org/10.1007/978-3-030-61210-8_2

desire for knowledge—what does all this point to, if not to the loss of myth, the loss of the mythical home, the mythical maternal womb?[1]

This desperate nostalgic search of the 'mythless man' for roots in the past characterised the experience of many counties that underwent rapid and disorienting social change provoking a sense of liminality and emerging *anomie* as the 'solidity' of established traditions and institutions was washed away by the eroding forces of change. This prompted the search into the past of each nation for a sense of identity and rootedness that defined its uniqueness and provided a mythical homeland and sense of collective belonging for each national group.

The iconic storming of the Bastille in Paris on 14 July 1789 marked the eruption of a growing European social and ideological crisis, which manifested itself in the French Revolution. These pivotal events and the subsequent ebb and flow of revolution and counter-revolution that followed sent a series of political and cultural shock waves across Europe. These inspired and in many cases demanded new perceptions of our place in society and prompted the search for renewed forms of collective and individual identity. Many revolutionary thinkers and artists were inspired by the radical philosophies of thinkers such as Jean-Jacques Rousseau (1712–1778) whose seminal works, *Discours sur l'origine et les fondements de l'inégalité parmi les hommes* (1755) and *Du contrat social ou Principes du droit politique* (1762), presented his influential theories of the 'natural man'. It also described the corrupting effect of the civilisation that had enslaved him and a blueprint for future social regeneration based on the fundamental principles of freedom and equality.

Rediscovering National Roots in Northern Europe and North America

The significant political, academic and cultural changes that were taking place stimulated the need to seek out new national roots and mythology through a process of rediscovery and resynthesis of national history and culture. Out of this need for new, adapted forms of *nomos*, academics and artists across Europe began to seek out home-grown subjects that represented and promoted their perceived national identity in order to create a new sense of national rootedness for their imagined community. This gave rise to powerful blends of literary, historical and scientific fantasy reifying the nation or race until it became, for some, a sacralised entity with an organic life of its own to be celebrated in poetry, monuments and ceremonial rituals. In *Nationalism* (1984), Hutchinson and Smith define this mission of the National Romantic thinkers to recreate appropriate national roots and unity in both cultural and territorial terms. Their emphasis on the vital connection between the ancestral homeland and the people occupying it was to emerge later in Nazism's *Blut und Boden* (Blood and Soil) ideology and can still be traced in the ideological beliefs of certain right-wing groups today who express a nostalgic sense of belonging to an idealised homeland of racial purity. In their work, Hutchinson and Smith describe that from a nationalist perspective:

> The people must be united; they must dissolve all internal divisions; they must be gathered together in a single historic territory, a homeland; and they must have legal equality and share a single public culture. But which culture and what territory? Only a homeland that was 'theirs' by historic right, the land of their forebears; only a culture that was 'theirs' as a heritage, passed down the generations, and therefore an expression of their authentic identity.[2]

In *The God of Modernity* (1994), Josep R. Llobera discusses the National Romantic Movement's retrospective standpoint that brought about a new form of representing the past that he terms 'imperfect history'. This no longer had, as its sole aim, the acquisition of knowledge but the mission of seeking out periods of national prominence and iconic historical and mythological figures who were, through the work of historians, politicians and artists, transformed into symbols of national identity and greatness. Llobera's argues that:

> From the perspective of Nationalism, the nostalgia for the past took the form of looking back to a period in the history of a nation when it achieved literary fame, political success or had flourished culturally. Romantic historiography, whether to uncover the past of a forgotten country or to celebrate the past of a powerful nation was an unavoidable stage forming episodes through which all countries went.[3]

This nostalgic mission of Romantic historians to rediscover lost national roots, which would help to forge a common consensus on the mythic importance of key symbols of national pride and identity, led to a revival in Britain, Germany, Scandinavia and the USA, of the study of Old Norse culture. Facing both shared and individual challenges brought about by this new phase of modernity in Europe, certain influential groups of thinkers in these nations sought evidence of what they perceived to be the cultural and physical prominence of the Old Norse people. Initially this was intended to generate a renewed sense of national rootedness, but progressively it became entwined with the search to justify European and North American ascendency as dominant forces in the progress of civilisation. In certain conditions, this developed into forms of Nordicism in which the Nordic type became a signifier of national and even racial superiority in need of regeneration.

To understand the development of Nordicism out of the foundation of Romantic historians' interpretation and reconstruction of Old Norse culture, it is essential to consider the basis on which it was developed and the permeability of the membrane that separated the antiquarian and academic search for national roots and the idealisation of these as part of political and biological agendas. National Romanticism's historical representation of the Old Norse heritage of Northern Europe was largely based on the study of primary and secondary texts that, by contemporary standards, would be considered unreliable and biased. This was further confused by the often-inaccurate interpretation of historical sites and artefacts. In *The Vikings* (1991), Danish historian and archaeologist Else Roesdahl comments on the way in which distorted, often-idealised images of the old Scandinavian peoples and their culture were created on the basis of evidence that was originally flawed:

> The classic image of the Vikings, appearing on foreign shores in their ships, sword in hand, performing bloody deeds, plundering churches, extorting money, engaging in battle, murder and abductions, is a one-sided picture created originally by contemporary clerics in Western Europe, who tended to record only violent events, and elaborated by medieval story-tellers and historians, among them the Icelandic saga writers, in their search for a dramatic national identity.[4]

Roesdahl quotes Snorri Sturluson's *Heimskringla* (The Circle of the World c. 1230), Dudo of Saint-Quentin's *De moribus et actis primorum Normanniae Ducum* (c. 1020) and Saxo Grammaticus' *Gesta Danorum* (c. 1200) *The Anglo-Saxon Chronicles* and the numerous *Icelandic Sagas* of the thirteenth century as key sources for both Enlightenment historians and later Romantics. In her discussion of these sources, Roesdahl comments that the writings of these medieval scholars should not be considered as 'attempts to reproduce historical reality in the modern sense' but rather that they expressed the concerns and interests of their own age.[5] These sources therefore did not attempt to reconstruct objective reality in modern historical terms but to create suitably adapted national narratives and personalities for national posterity. Another significant point is the narrative perspective of the writers who were often from outside Scandinavia, or who wrote retrospectively, often hundreds of years after the events. On the basis of this often inconsistent and unreliable historiography, certain Northern European writers progressively created the image of the Viking as a representative symbol of Old Norse culture, an image which became increasingly radicalised and in Germany and North America became a foundation and symbol of later forms of Nordicism.

The following sections will examine this phenomenon across Scandinavia, Britain, Germany and parts of North America. It will also compare the way in which these nations sought to define their national identity by looking back into their past to create new future political and cultural identities and explore how the prevailing state of modernity in certain countries, notably Germany and North America, led to the emergence, in the late nineteenth century, of early forms of Nordicism.

Growing Apart Together: Scandinavian Romanticism and Nationalism

National Romanticism in Scandinavia was more than a reflection of the political, religious and social revolutions which were transforming Europe; it was an expression of the concerns and aspirations of Denmark, Norway and Sweden and their dependencies as a collective and, more significantly, as independent nations with inter-related but distinct national identities. The final dissolution of the *Kalmarunionen* (Kalmar Union) in 1523, which had united Scandinavia since 1397, brought to the fore the existing rivalry and differing interests of these nations, notably between Denmark and Sweden who both sought a more prominent role in Northern Europe. Central to this rivalry was the political and economic importance of control of the Baltic Sea, a significant military and trade route. This, together with disputes over territory, sovereignty and international alliances, led to a series of mutually destructive wars between these competing nations.

The most notable conflicts included the Northern Seven Years' War (1563–1570), the Kalmar War (1611–1613), the Torstenson War (1643–1645), the Dano-Swedish Wars (1657–1660), the Scanian War (1675), the Great Northern War (1700–1721) and the later conflicts between 1808–1809 and 1813–1814 which formed part of the Napoleonic Wars. Due to their strategic position as the gateway to the Baltic, the Scandinavian countries became embroiled in this European conflict resulting in the attack on 2 April 1802, led by Vice-Admiral Horatio Nelson, on the Danish-Norwegian fleet anchored off Copenhagen. This was followed by a further attack between 16 August and 5 September 1807 during which the city of Copenhagen was bombarded and attacked for two nights leaving the largely wooden city badly damaged and many dead.[6] This resulted in a loss of national standing, as Denmark had to concede its political and military vulnerability within Europe. External disputes over national territory also resulted in a further weakening of the Scandinavian states as Sweden was forced to cede Finland to Russia in 1809 and Denmark lost the duchies of Schleswig-Holstein firstly in 1848–1850 and then in 1864 when the territory was lost to Germany.

Economic and industrial modernisation was also slow to emerge in Scandinavia as the nations lacked the technology, capital and resources to move from rural to industrial activity. For instance in Denmark, agriculture still represented fifty percent of the nation's commercial production until 1870.[7] This lack of development, together with a significant increase in population and economic hardship, led many to leave their homelands, notably for America, to seek an improved standard of living. In *Scandinavia and the Great Powers* (1997), Patrick Salmon describes this process commenting that 'the symptoms of stagnation and rural overpopulation were evident in the massive emigration of Swedes and Norwegians to North America'.[8]

It is against this historical backdrop of inter-Scandinavian rivalry, loss of territory, diminished international status and late industrial development that National Romanticism emerged more as a reaction to the modernity of surrounding nations than its own. During this period Scandinavia needed, in many respects, to reinvent itself away from the image of the uncivilised North and its loss of international standing to create a renewed sense of national pride and identity. This led to a revival in interest in establishing a shared sense of national history, which promoted the historical and cultural uniqueness of each nation, its natural beauty and its status within European culture.

In *Thor: Myth to Marvel* (2011), Martin Arnold analyses the evolution and causes of this revival of interest in Old Norse culture, which progressively became more and more radicalised into political agendas and symbols of national identity and what could be termed early forms of political Nordicism. In this work, Arnold describes the increasing intensity of interest in the Old North as nationalist historians sought to appropriate Old Norse culture to further their political aims of establishing prestigious national roots, a process which he points out already had historical precedents in the thirteenth century:

> The scholarly interest in Old Norse myths and legends that persisted in Scandinavia beyond the retrospective fascinations of medieval writers was no more a matter of nostalgia for heathendom than it had been for Snorri Sturluson. Rather it was partly a case of patriotism and cultural pride, often defensively asserted in the face of those who considered the northern territories to be barbaric and culturally impoverished, and partly a case of continuing political rivalries between the Scandinavian countries.[9]

In his study of the reception of Norse history and literature during this period, Arnold also examines the cross-fertilisation of interest in Old Norse culture in Northern Europe which was appropriated by certain groups within the National Romantic Movement, to form the basis of a regenerated national identity. As part of this study, he considers how rivalries between the Scandinavian states and their collective need to reaffirm their status in Europe, expressed itself in the search for historical sources through which they could revise and reaffirm their collective and individual national identities. Arnold refers to the impact in Europe of the seminal works of Swiss-born Paul Henri Mallet (1730–1807) who, as professor of French at the Academy of Arts in Copenhagen, was commissioned by the Danish King Frederick V to produce a new history of Denmark. Mallet originally published this research in French (the language of the Danish Royal Court) in 1755, as the *Introduction à L'histoire du Dannemarc où l'on traite de la religion, des moeurs, des lois, et des usages des anciens Danois,* together with his 1756 publication entitled *Monuments de la mythologie et de la poésie des Celtes, et particulièrement des anciens Scandinaves.*[10] In these works, Mallet drew on the work of Roman historian Tacitus (56–117) as well as the work of a number of Icelandic and Danish scholars to present a study of the social, religious, military and legal customs of the Danish people and their mythological traditions. These included Saxo Grammaticus (c.1150–1220), Arngrímur Jónsson (1568–1648), Thormodus Torfæus (1636–1719), Ole Worm (1588–1655), Peder Hansen Resen (1625–1688) and Thomas Bartholin (1616–1680). In his work, Mallet attempted to revise and demystify previously written histories of the state of Denmark, rejecting the image of a cultural wilderness once inhabited by pagan barbarians, to present an early form of social history in which he described a primitive but well-ordered societal structure with a distinct ethnic culture.

In his attempt to create a new history of Denmark, distinguishing fact from fiction, Mallet was critical of previous histories, which bridged a lack of evidence with varying degrees of creativity and assumption. In his analysis, he quoted Icelandic scholar Thormodus Torfæus' comments describing Icelandic scholars' fusion of history with myth to present interesting and coherent narratives:

> For, in the first place, the Icelandic writers have left us a great number of pieces, which evidently show that their taste inclined them to deal in the marvellous, in allegory and even in that kind of narrations, in which truth is designedly blended with fable. Torfæus himself confesses that that there are many of their books in which it is difficult to distinguish truth from falsehood, and that there are scarce any of them, but what contain some degree of fiction.[11]

The Icelandic writers were products of their time, and their aim was not that of historians, in the modern sense of the term, but of storytellers recording the traditional sagas of their forefathers as a means of preserving their own national identity. Mallet was also however, like any historian, a product of his time. As an academic, he had limited sources at his disposal and would arguably have been influenced by the rise in National Romanticism and the political agenda of the Danish state that commissioned his work. It was, however, a significant attempt at revising the image of the Old North and had an impact on a number of later writers whose work explored the cultural heritage of Old Norse civilisation.

In 1763, Mallet published a six-volume edition of his work in which he revised much of his material and approach. In his analysis of this work, Arnold comments that 'it is from these latter volumes that the romance of the Old North can be properly dated, the enthusiasm for which spread beyond both the confines of Scandinavia and the provinces of scholarship'.[12] Arnold also identifies what he describes as the 'emerging principles of pre-romanticism'. He suggests that this influence came from the publication of works such as Montesquieu's *De l'Esprit des Lois* (1748), Edmund Burke's influential *A Philosophical Enquiry into the Origin of Our Ideas of the Sublime and Beautiful* in 1756 and Jean-Jacques Rousseau's *Discours sur l'origine des fondements de l'inégalité parmi les hommes* (1754). In his work, Mallet quoted Montesquieu's *L'Esprit des Lois* describing how the cold, harsh northern climate developed admirable characteristics of strength and independence in the Nordic people, a theory later developed by Nordicist thinkers. Montesquieu argued that:

> But how came these men to preserve themselves in so great a degree of liberty? This was owing to their climate and manner of life, which gave them such strength of body and mind as rendered them capable of long and painful labours, of great and daring exploits.[13]

This association of the northern climate with physical and psychological resilience prefigures Romanticism's and later Nordicism's fascination with the Nordic people's vital relationship with their natural environment and the need to re-establish and maintain this innate attachment. This was to emerge later in the more sinister form of Nazism's *Blut und Boden* (Blood and Soil) ideology and is still present in many forms of Northern European ultra-nationalism. In *The Norse Muse* (1998), Margaret Clunies Ross and Lars Lönnroth discuss the significance of Romanticism's concept of 'natural man' and in particular the concept of 'the sublime', on writers such as Mallet. Sublime art celebrated the awe-inspiring creative and destructive power of natural phenomena and the impact of this defining force on the human condition. According to Clunies Ross and Lönnroth, this literary and artistic mood laid the foundations on which writers such as Mallet could imbue their presentations of Old Norse literature with a primordial sense of the sublime, a concept that had considerable resonance for societies seeking to rediscover and reinvent their national roots. In the words of Clunies Ross and Lönnroth:

> Sublime too was the barbaric and ancient poetry of wild and primitive people not yet tamed, domesticated, and corrupted by modern civilization. It was this new aesthetics that made it possible for Mallet and his followers to present Old Norse poetry as particularly sublime.[14]

J-J Rousseau's pre-Romantic concept of the 'noble savage', uncorrupted by modernity and living in harmony with his environment, had a significant influence on literary and artistic thought in Europe, enabling Mallet and his followers to attract increasing European interest to their attempts to rehabilitate Old Norse verse and culture.

In his evaluation, Martin Arnold observes that the publication of Mallet's work was received with both hostility and enthusiasm in Northern and Western Europe but suggests that it was nonetheless 'extraordinary in its effect' and had a significant impact on the revival in interest in Old Norse culture in Britain, Germany and Scandinavia.[15] Mallet's work was translated into English as *Northern Antiquities* (1770) by Thomas Percy and translated into German between 1765 and 1769. In their analysis, Clunies Ross and Lönnroth describe the impact of Mallet's work both in terms of general public interest and as a basis on which writers developed their nations' sense of national identity: the Nordic 'natural man':

> In Germany and Britain the works of Mallet and Resen were chief sources for the reading public's knowledge of Old Norse poetry and myth, and Mallet provided, in addition, a holistic interpretative framework against which ordinary readers and creative writers could assimilate this new exotic primitivism to which they could claim an ancestral relationship.[16]

Mallet's work could therefore be considered significant in providing both a home-grown form of mythology and cultural origins in an attempt to rival the predominant Greek and Roman classicism of the period. This offered an attractive cultural heritage for the subsequent emergence of National Romantic writers in Denmark, as well as in Northern Europe and North America, who sought to appropriate Old Norse culture to provide new sources of national identity and symbols of historic national predominance.

Another influential literary figure that contributed to this Nordic Renaissance in Scandinavia and Germany was Friedrich Gottlieb Klopstock (1724–1803), a leading German romantic poet who, on the invitation of Frederick V, moved to Copenhagen in 1751 where he lived until 1770, before returning to Germany where he completed his major work *Der Messias* in 1773. Klopstock sought to create a form of poetry and culture that was inherently German and which celebrated the beauty of the German language, countryside and its people. During the 1760s he became an enthusiastic follower of Scottish poet James Macpherson

(1736–1796), whose *Ossianic* poetry was creating a sensation in Europe following the publication of his *Fragments of Ancient Poetry Collected in the Highlands of Scotland* in 1760, *Fingal* in 1762 and *Temora* in 1763. It was during this period that Klopstock came into contact with Heinrich Wilhelm von Gerstenberg (1737–1823), a former Danish cavalry officer from the Duchy of Schleswig, who published *Gedicht eines Skalden* (Poem of a Skald) in 1766. This was a romanticised interpretation of *Vǫluspá* (The Seeress' Prophecy) from the *Poetic Edda*, and according to Klopstock's correspondence of the time, it was this work that attracted him to draw on Old Norse mythology as a source of national culture and sense of rootedness.[17]

Notable amongst the literary circle, frequented and inspired by Klopstock and Gerstenberg, was the patriotic Danish poet and dramatist Johannes Ewald (1743–1781) whose operatic poem *Balders Død* (The Death of Balder), based on Saxo Grammaticus' *Gesta Danorum*, was premiered in the Royal Theatre in Copenhagen in 1778. This dramatic work comprised many features of early Romanticism in its portrayal of heightened passions and the struggle between good and evil, as in this dramatic verse from the concluding act in which *Þórr* (Thor) laments the loss of his brother as the Gods approach the apocalypse of *Ragnarǫk*:

Thor:
Gods of battle stern and glory
Weep ye o'er the hero slain
Balder, thou art the Aser's glory!
Love, base love, has prov'd thy bane.[18]

In his analysis, Martin Arnold interprets the nationalist elements of this work as encoded political messages through which Ewald expressed his early Pan-Scandinavian sentiment through symbolism and the figure of *Þórr* (Thor) as redeemer of the Scandinavian people. Pan-Scandinavianism was a movement that emerged during the late eighteenth century and was at its height in the mid-nineteenth century promoting political and economic cooperation between the Scandinavian nations. Arnold points out that:

In effect, Ewald's depiction of the Scandinavian past functions as a metaphor for the Scandinavian present, divided by ancient rivalries, oblivious of its shared destiny and on course for disaster. Yet, in Ewald's example of the conciliatory Thor, there is the possibility that such divisiveness could be set-aside in the recognition of common values and common cause.[19]

In 1778, Ewald added to his accomplishments as a nationalist artist when his work *Fiskerne* (The Fishermen) was staged at the Royal Theatre on the birthday of King Christian VII. This work celebrated the heroics of Danish sailors during the wars against Sweden in the seventeenth and eighteenth centuries, and in 1780, the first verse, *Kong Christian stod ved højen mast* (King Christian stood by the lofty mast), was adopted as the Royal Anthem. Ewald's contribution to the renewal of Danish poetry, both in artistic and political terms, was significant in laying the foundations for nineteenth-century Romantic writers such as Adam Oehlenschläger (1779–1850) who promoted their Old Norse heritage as a form of national identity and rootedness.

Oehlenschläger was influenced both by Ewald and by the Norwegian-born Danish philosopher, scientist and poet Henrik Steffens (1773–1845), whose studies and academic posts in Germany had brought him into contact with notable literary and philosophical figures such as Friedrich von Schelling (1775–1854), Johann Wolfgang von Goethe (1749–1832), Friedrich Schleiermacher (1768–1834) and Friedrich Werner (1768–1823). Their influence inspired Oehlenschläger to develop his own form of nationalist expression that was specifically Scandinavian. In 1803, he published *Guldhornene* (The Golden Horns), in which two highly decorated drinking horns, discovered in 1639 and 1734 in Jutland, were transformed into a symbol of Denmark's separation from its historical roots. This opening verse portrayed the poet's sense of decay and abandonment of the past:

> Upon the pages
> Of the olden ages,
> And in the hills where are lying
> The dead, they are prying;
> On armour rusty,
> In ruins musty,
> On Rune-stones jumbled,
> With bones long crumbled.[20]

Over the next twenty years, Oehlenschläger continued his considerable contribution to the revival of Old Norse literature, establishing himself as one of Scandinavia's leading Romantic poets. His works include *Thors Reise til Jotunheim* (Thor's Journey to Jotunheim, 1806), *Hakon Jarl* (Earl Hakon, 1807), *Baldur hin Gode* (Balder the Good, 1808), *Helge* (1814) and his major work, published in 1819, *Nordens Guder: et episk digte* (Gods of the North: An Epic Poem). In 1835, he was honoured by the nation when his patriotic poem *Der er et yndigt land* (There is a Lovely Land), written in 1819, was adopted as the state national anthem:

> There is a lovely land
> Where broad beeches grow
> Near the salty eastern beach
> Winding through hills and valleys
> Its called Old Denmark
> And it is Freya's hall
> There, in days gone by
> Armoured warriors sat
> Rested from battle
> Before setting out to face the enemy
> Now their bones lie
> Behind the mound's menhir.[21]

Oehlenschläger's verses, imbued with Nordic mythology, history and its relationship with the natural beauty of the Danish landscape, epitomised in many respects the nostalgic artistic focus of Scandinavian National Romanticism and its political aspirations during this period of European nation building and identity politics.

Another notable follower of Henrik Steffens, who sought to revive and resynthesise Old Norse mythology, was the Danish theologian, historian, poet, educationalist, Lutheran minister and politician, N.F.S. Grundtvig (1783–1872). Grundtvig's writings and activities were prolific and wide-ranging, covering a range of liberal reformist, Lutheran, political and educational issues of the day which were at the same time forward-looking and grounded in the need to establish a sense of 'Danishness' based on Denmark's history, traditions and mythology. This was in many ways a reaction against the dominant Latin and Catholic culture of Europe. Notable amongst his works on Norse mythology, which included many translations and commentaries, was his major work *Nordens Mythologi eller Sindbilled-Sprog, historisk-poetisk udviklet og oplyst* (The Mythology or Symbolic Language of the North, a historical and poetic exposition and explanation, 1808, revised and expanded in 1832). This work represented a new study of the *Eddas* and challenged the primacy of Latin classicism as a cultural foundation for Northern Europe. Through this work, N.F.S. Grundtvig sought to present Old Norse mythology as a framework for the growing sense of nationalism, which was growing in Scandinavia as a response to its loss of territory and international standing. In his analysis of Grundtvig, Martin Arnold argues that:

> The myths of the eddas are not just used to frame Grundtvig's argument—peppered as it is with references to Old Norse mythological personages and events—they are his argument, for what he perceives in northern myth is the symbology of a contemporary battle against all that is deleterious to the probity and power of the North, all that is alien to it.[22]

Although Denmark was arguably a significant driving force behind the Nordic revival of Scandinavian National Romanticism, this movement had its counterparts in Sweden, Norway and Iceland who also strove to establish their own national identities and relationship with Old Norse culture and mythology.

In Iceland, National Romanticism expressed a wave of nationalistic sentiment that emerged during the nineteenth century seeking to define a cultural and political identity for the nation. At this time, Iceland was part of the Danish Kingdom and remained so until it became an independent republic on 17 June 1944. During this period, the economy in Iceland was fairly stagnant, and the country's future prospects appeared bleak as it lagged behind modern industrialised nations. Iceland was a nation of farmers and fishermen and remained, in many ways, untouched by European modernity. It did, however, have a unique cultural heritage reaching back to the island's original Viking settlers who forged a new society and lives for themselves in this harsh volcanic landscape. Many of Iceland's leading academics and artists trained in Denmark where they came into contact with Danish and German thinkers who were seeking their own expression of national rootedness and who inspired them to seek out and develop their own unique Icelandic identity.

Notable in this movement was poet, author and naturalist Jónas Hallgrímsson (1807–1845), who founded the Icelandic journal *Fjölnir* in Copenhagen in 1835, together with fellow Icelandic students Brynjólfur Pétursson (1810–1851), Konráð Gíslason (1808–1891) and Tómas Sæmundsson (1807–1841). Together they formed a group leading a revival of nationalist thought in Iceland, expressed through Romanic verse, art and poetry drawing on the rich cultural heritage of Icelandic literature. The use of the Icelandic language also became an important expression of the nation's unique cultural and political identity within the Scandinavian nations. In the first volume of *Fjölnir*, Jónas published one of his most famous patriotic poems, *Ísland* (1835), in which he celebrated Iceland's natural beauty and lamented his countries loss of pride in its history and traditions, calling on the Icelandic people to reaffirm their national heritage and identity. In this poem, he uses the image of an overgrown and abandoned *Alþingi* at *Þingvellir*, the historical site of the Icelandic parliament, where Snorri was twice elected to the role of lawspeaker, to remind his nation of the greatness of its past and reawaken their sense of identity and national pride. Jónas also recalls the saga heroes: Þorgeir, Gissur, Gunnar, Geir, Njáll and Héðinn and their role in establishing a nation that once prospered both culturally and commercially.

Another significant contribution to the rediscovery of Iceland's national identity came from Jón Árnason (1819–1888), librarian of Reykjavik Cathedral, who published a collection of Icelandic folk tales entitled *Íslenzk Æfintýri* in 1852. This was later expanded and republished in two volumes, in 1862 and 1864, as *Íslenzkar Þjóðsögur og Æfintýri* (Icelandic Folktales and Legends) and, through translations, reached and influenced many European scholars, drawn to Iceland as a source of Nordic heritage.

Through this nostalgic mission of reconnecting with its past, Iceland sought to redefine itself through art and literature, to express a renewed sense of belonging to a unique historic identity which had developed in its harsh climatic conditions. Like many of its contemporary nationalist movements, Icelandic National Romanticism created a nostalgic, imperfect history to inspire the regeneration of a past 'Golden Age', of success and greatness. In this context, the Icelandic Sagas, the Eddas and Iceland's Viking heritage became part of the fabric of a reconstructed national identity aimed at creating a renewed sense of 'Icelandicness', national purpose and eventual political independence.

National Romanticism in Sweden began to emerge in the early nineteenth century through competing schools of nationalist thought who aimed to elevate and promote Sweden's historical heritage. In 1811 the *Götiska Förbundet* (Gothic League) was founded as a literary and social society for Swedish academics drawn to the revival of Old Norse mythology and the spirit of Olaus Rudbeck's patriotic *Gothicismus* movement under the leadership of antiquarian Jakob Adlerbeth (1785–1844). This society established the publication *Iduna* as the vehicle for its poems, translations, articles and reviews by notable literary and historical figures such as Esaias Tegnér (1782–1846), Erik Gustaf Geijer (1783–1847), Arvid August Afzelius (1785–1871), Karl August Nicander, Pehr Henrik Ling and Gustaf Vilhelm Gumaelius (1789–1877). In this journal, Esaias Tegnér, a founder member of the society, published his most famous work, drawn from the original Icelandic work, *Frithiof's Saga*. This paraphrase in verse was first published in *Iduna* in 1820, a work that he published in full in 1825 and which went on to make him famous throughout Europe. This work was translated into numerous languages throughout Europe, notably in Britain and Germany where the saga was a popular success.

Another founding member of the *Götiska Förbundet*, historian, poet and composer Erik Gustaf Geijer, who, together with Tegnér, made a considerable artistic and historical contribution to the emerging national identity of Sweden, published in *Iduna* one of his most famous poems, *Vikingen* (The Viking). In this poem, Geijer told the Romantic tale of a fifteen-year-old, living in cramped conditions with his family, who ran away to become a heroic Viking traveller and warrior, bravely conquering new lands. Geijer's historical works tracing the development of the Swedish people and the origins of its national culture included *Svea rikes häfder* (From the Records of Sweden, 1825) and *Svenska folkets historia* (The History of the Swedish People, 1832–1836).

In 1807, Per Daniel Amadeus Atterbom (1790–1855) established *MUSIS Amici* (The Friends of the Muses), renamed a year later as *Auroraförbundet* (The Aurora Society), and published much of his literary work and articles in the periodical *Fosforus*. Atterbom admired the work of Adam Oehlenschläger and was particularly influenced by the work of German Romantic poet Friedrich Schelling (1775–1854) after they met during his stay in Germany and Italy between 1817 and 1819.[23] In his writings, Atterbom sought to raise the standing of Old Norse mythology to that of the Greek, Hindu and Judeo-Christian faith systems and to create a form of Romantic poetry which was distinctively Swedish. In his analysis, Martin Arnold describes Atterbom's publication of *Skaldarmål* (The Speech of the Poet) in 1811, as 'a tribute to Scandinavian myth and legend, a repudiation of the declining standards of modernity, and a plea for a national Swedish poetry based on indigenous Scandinavian models'.[24]

National Romanticism in Norway emerged somewhat later than in Denmark and Sweden and is generally dated from the 1840s. It was during this latter part of the nineteenth century that the nationalist movement began to find its momentum with Norway finally gaining its full independence from its union with Sweden, after a national referendum in 1905. Notable literary figures whose work contributed to the development of a revised Norwegian identity and sense of cultural rootedness, away from that of Viking aggression and dark mystic paganism, were Peter Christen Asbjørnsen (1812–1885) and Jørgen Engebretsen Moe (1813–1882). These writers and academics travelled around Norway and gathered together a considerable number of folk tales, which they edited and adapted for popular readership as *Norske Folkeeventyr* (Norwegian Folk Tales). This collection was first published in 1842–1843, followed by a second volume in 1844 and a new expanded edition in 1871. Their work contributed not only to the cultural enrichment of Norway but also to the linguistic heritage of the Norwegian language through the preservation of local dialects and is comparable in many ways to the work of the Grimm brothers in Germany, Elias Lönnrot (1802–1884) in Finland and Jón Árnason in Iceland.[25] Significant in the field of linguistics and national identity in Norway was the work of Ivar Andreas Aasen (1813–1896), who developed *Nynorsk* to provide a Norwegian alternative to the Danish language, which was commonly written in Norway at the time.

Another key Norwegian literary figure was Bjørnstjerne Martinius Bjørnson (1832–1910) whose poems and dramas brought him considerable national acclaim; in 1903 he was awarded the Nobel Prize in Literature. Much of his early work centred on the lives of the Norwegian peasantry, and his major work was the poetic trilogy *Sigurd Slembe* (Sigurd the Bad), based on the twelfth-century Norwegian pretender to the throne, published in 1862. In 1859, Bjørnson published the verses entitled *Ja, vi elsker dette landet* (Yes, We Love This Land), which were adopted as the national anthem after 1864 when it was first performed at an event celebrating the 50th anniversary of the Norwegian constitution:

Yes we love this country
as it rises up,
rugged and weathered, above the sea,
with the thousands of homes.
Love, love it and think
of our father and mother
and the saga night that lays
dreams upon our earth.
This country was united by Harald
with his army of heroic warriors,

this country was protected by Håkon
while Øyvind sang;
In this country Olav painted
the cross with his blood,
from its heights Sverre spoke
up against Rome.[26]

These first two patriotic verses resemble the opening of Oehlenschläger's *Der er et yndigt land* and Jónas' *Ísland* in its Romantic celebration of Norway's natural beauty and glorious past. Bjørnson celebrates Norway's kings and their achievements which founded the nation, such as the unification of Norway by Haraldr Hálfdanarson (c 850–932), the prevention of civil war by Håkon Haraldsson (c. 920–961), the introduction of Christianity by Olaf II Haraldsson (995–1030) and the opposition to Rome of Sverrir Sigurðarson (c. 1145–1202). This revival of literary interest in Old Norse culture in Norway was also reflected in the work of one of Norway's most notable playwrights and poets, Henrik Johan Ibsen (1828–1906), who published *Kjæmpehøjen* (The Warriors Barrow) in 1850, *Hærmændene på Helgeland* (The Vikings at Helgeland) in 1858 and *Peer Gynt* in 1867.

This period, during which Norwegian academics and artists sought to establish their own national identity, saw the emergence of what became termed The Norwegian Historical School. This interpretation of Norway's prehistory was founded by Rudolf Keyser (1803–1864), professor at the Royal Frederick University in Oslo, and one of his students Peter Andreas Munch (1810–1863). Their theories suggested that the original Sami inhabitants of Norway had been displaced, firstly by Celtic tribes, who brought with them the Bronze Age, and secondly by Germanic tribes who founded the Iron Age. This theory suggested that Norway was a diffusion point of a superior culture and society founded originally by ancient Germanic tribes. This interpretation fitted with the current theories of Germanic racial superiority and Scandinavian settlement of thinkers such as Swedish academics Anders Retzius (1796–1860) and Sven Nilsson (1787–1883). In *Measuring the Master Race: Physical Anthropology in Norway 1890–1945* (2015), Jon Røyne Kyllingstad discusses the role played by a small but influential group of Scandinavian anthropologists in the later development of Nordicism. Kyllingstad argues that the emerging concept of Nordic racial superiority in Europe became a means of defining their own national standing in both a Scandinavian and international context:

Among Scandinavians themselves, the idea of Nordic racial superiority has a significant impact upon notions of national identity, and in the nineteenth and twentieth centuries Scandinavian scholars played an important part in creating and perpetuating the concept of a Nordic race. By imbuing the idea of the Nordic race with scientific legitimacy, these scholars also advanced its international recognition and standing.[27]

Kyllingstad suggests that Norway's struggle for independence and the recovery of its national identity and standing in the international community led some thinkers, such as Rudolf Keyser, to seek to locate the nation's pride in a mythical era of Germanic greatness. This association was disputed by many contemporary thinkers but had some influence on a marginal group of later Nordicists in Scandinavia who sought to regenerate a mythical former greatness. In his analysis of Keyser, Kyllingstad points out that:

> Keyser's theory implied that, despite the weak state of present-day Norway, the forefathers of the Norwegians had once dominated Scandinavia and were the true originators of the ancient Norse Culture [...] Keyser's narrative implied that the present-day Norwegian state embodied the reawakening of ancient Germanic traditions and modern ideas of liberty and democracy.[28]

In the visual arts, National Romanticism was reflected across Scandinavia in much the same way as its literature, in what came to be termed *Den danske guldalder* (The Danish Golden Age). In her analysis of this period, *In Another Light* (2007), Patricia G. Berman comments on the political motivations of these artists stating that the 'instability of this period gave rise to a consolidated effort in the visual arts to stabilize and magnify a sense of Danish identity'.[29] The proliferation in nationalist art during this period spanned a range of styles and media reflecting the European trend from neo-classicism through Romanticism towards realism.

The romanticised neo-classical images of Norse mythology reflected the revival of interest in Norse mythology as a rival to Greco-Latin subjects, depicting stunning scenes from the *Eddas*. Notable works were *Tors strid med jättarna* (Thor's Battle with the Giants, 1872) (Fig. 2.1), by Swedish painter Mårten Eskil Winge (1825–1896), *Åsgårdsreien* (The Wild Hunt, 1872) by Norwegian painter Peter Nicolai Arbo (1831–1892) and the numerous illustrations from the *Eddas* of Danish artist Lorentz Frølich (1820–1908).

Fig. 2.1 Mårten Eskil Winge—*Tors strid med jättarna* (Thor's Battle With the Giants). Reproduced with the kind permission of the National Museum, Stockholm, http://collection.nationalmuseum.se

Another popular strand of Romantic art was the development of landscape painting during this period depicting the beauty of the countryside, often featuring the rural population, historical buildings, menhirs and burial mounds as a reminder of the enduring presence of the nation's past. Notable artists and works of this genre from Denmark include *Frederiksborg Castle in the Evening Light* (1835) and *The Transept of Århus Cathedral* (1830) by Christen Købke (1810–1848), Johan Thomas Lundbye's (1818–1848) *Landscape at Arresø* (1838) and *Dolmen at Raklev* (1839) (Fig. 2.2). In Norway, this school of art was represented by Johan Christian Claussen Dahl (1788–1857) who became the leading painter of the Norwegian Golden Age with stunning landscapes such as *Megalithic Tomb in Winter* (1824–1825), *Shipwreck on the Coast of Norway* (1832) and *Stalheim* (1842).

In their creative work, the literary and visual artists of Scandinavia encoded the nationalist agenda of the period, reflecting the duality of their

Fig. 2.2 Johan Thomas Lundbye, *Dolmen at Raklev, Røsnæs*, 1839. Reproduced with the kind permission of the Thorvaldsens Museum, www.thorvaldsens-museum.dk

shared roots and overlapping interests as well as their individual struggles for independence as separate nations. What emerges strongly from this period is their need to establish a sense of national identity, rootedness and unity as a reaction to a European modernity, which was undermining their culture and national status. The Scandinavian Nordic revival was, however, hugely influential in Northern Europe and the Eastern States of America, providing inspiration and new sources from which many National Romantic writers and artists and later racial ideologists in these countries were to develop their own variants of this phenomenon, some of which could be considered early forms of cultural and biological Nordicism.

ROMANTICISM AND THE VIKING IN GEORGIAN AND VICTORIAN BRITAIN

In Britain, interest in Nordic culture was limited during the first half of the eighteenth century and had remained in the main antiquarian, literary or linguistic. It attracted however increasing public interest and popularity in the second half of the century, a period during which Britain experienced rapid change as the Industrial Revolution and Britain's growing international status began to transform society. This revival in interest in the Old North coincided with what has come to be termed the Celtic revival, a literary and cultural movement that, in many respects, took a similar and often convergent path into the developing field of nationalist identity politics.

In 1705, George Hickes provided the first translation into English of Norse poetry in his linguistic study *Linguarium veterum Septentrionalium thesaurus grammatico-criticus et archæologicus* which became an important source of later scholarship. Together with this, the influence of Paul-Henri Mallet's vision of old Scandinavian culture and society in *L'histoire du Dannemarc* was conveyed to a Georgian society through its translation, published in 1770 by Bishop Thomas Percy (1729–1811), as *Northern Antiquities*. Prior to this in 1763, Percy had published his *Five Pieces of Runic Poetry Translated from the Islandic Language*, in which he presented his translations of Old Norse poems by Olaus Verelius (1618–1682), Olaus Worm (1588–1654), Johan Peringskiöld (1654–1720) and Thomas Bartholin (1616–1680). These poems were imbued with dramatic tales of battle, revenge, courage, love, death and camaraderie, which plunged the reader into a primordial pagan world, free of the constraints, conventions and complications of modern life.

In *The Vikings and the Victorians* (2002), Andrew Wawn describes the vibrant, emotive themes of Percy's work in which 'readers could relish the zest for life, the sensuous thrill of battle, and the clear sighted way in which death is confronted'. Wawn adds, however, that the initial public reception of Percy's work was 'by no means ecstatic' and that it was his 1770 publication of *Northern Antiquities* that had a more significant impact on British interest in Old Norse culture.[30] In this work Percy revised and corrected many aspects of Mallet's earlier work and provided the most scholarly, comprehensive study available at the time, a work which future scholars such as J.A. Blackwell built on in his revised edition of *Northern Antiquities* (1847) which became an influential work amongst enthusiasts of the Old North throughout the nineteenth century.[31]

Notable amongst British poets who drew inspiration from translations of eddic poetry was Thomas Gray (1716–71) who published *The Fatal Sisters* and *The Descent of Odin* in 1768, enhanced in subsequent editions with illustrations by both William Blake (1757–1827) and Swiss-born artist Henry Fuseli (1741–1825). In this work, written in the emerging Gothic style of the period, Gray presents a dark, menacing, mythical world, as in this verse where *Oðinn* rides his horse *Sleipnir* into *Hel*, the realm of the dead, which is guarded by the monstrous wolf *Fenrir*. In *Hel, Oðinn* is to learn, from the prophetess, of the future fate of his son *Balder* and the approaching events of *Ragnarǫk*:

Uprose the king of men with speed,
And saddled straight his coal-black steed:
Down the yawning steep he rode,
That leads to Hela's drear abode.
Him the dog of darkness spied:
His shaggy throat he open'd wide,
While from his jaws, with carnage fill'd,
Foam and human gore distill'd:[32]

This Gothic treatment of Nordic subjects was also reflected in the field of the visual arts. The striking style of Fuseli's representation of Norse mythology offered dramatic, awe-inspiring images of the Norse pantheon, adding significant momentum to Romanticism's idealised portrayal of Norse culture and mythology. Notable amongst Fuseli's works is his famous *Thor Battering the Midgard Serpent*, which he completed in 1790. In this work, Fuseli's image of the naked God fused the established neo-classical style, usually associated with the portrayal of Greek and Roman gods, with Norse myth to create a dark, stunning representation of *Þórr's* battle with the serpent *Jǫrmungandr*. This trend of Romantic artists joining poets and novelists in depicting dramatic, heroic scenes drawn from Old Norse culture was followed by a number of later British artists such as W.G. Collingwood (1854–1932), Sir Frank Dicksee (1853–1928) and Charles Ernest Butler (1864–1933), whose works contributed to the formulation of a romanticised visual interpretation of the Old North.

In the literary field, *Letters Written During a Short Residence in Sweden, Norway, and Denmark* (1796), a travel narrative and personal autobiographical memoir, by writer and early advocate of woman's rights, Mary Wollstonecraft (1759–1797), was a popular success which brought Scandinavia and the natural beauty of its countryside to public and literary attention. Her work covered a range of social, economic and personal reflections, notably the relationship between society and individual subjective experience and inspired many to travel to Scandinavia to experience the sublime relationship with the beauty of the Nordic landscapes depicted in her work.

Another early influence on the Nordic revival in Britain and Europe was the work of Scottish poet James Macpherson who published *Fragments of Ancient Poetry Collected in the Highlands of Scotland, and Translated from the Gaelic or Erse Language* in 1760 and *Fingal* in 1761. Collectively these works became known as *The Poems of Ossian* and had a considerable impact on both the scholarly and popular readership in Britain and Europe. The success of Macpherson's dark, atmospheric tales, which described early Celtic and of Nordic culture, had an influence extending beyond Britain and was subsequently translated into twenty-six languages.[33] In his discussion of the significance of Macpherson's work, Martin Arnold suggests that it did much to stimulate subsequent artistic, literary and public interest across Europe in northern literature. In his biography *Heinrich Himmler—A Life* (2012), Peter Longerich describes how the nineteen-year-old Himmler included Macpherson's poems in a personal reading list and commented that 'this type of heroic saga suited his taste exactly'.[34] Collectively these early Romantic visions of Old Norse culture set the scene for the later Victorian fascination with Old Norse culture, a relationship with a romanticised distant past that defined what came to be known as the Viking Era.

The enduring popular image of the Viking as a 'noble savage' owes much to the Victorian idealisation of this period, which built on late eighteenth- and early nineteenth-century Romanticism to establish what could be termed a 'historical caricature' of Old Norse culture. In his study of the Victorians' relationship with the Vikings, Andrew Wawn comments that 'in many ways, the Victorians invented the Vikings', and it was arguably during this period that an enduring idealised image of the Vikings was cast.[35] In his analysis, Wawn points out that the term 'Viking' first appeared, in its current form, in the *Oxford English Dictionary* in 1807 and that it was during this period of rapid industrial growth and concomitant social change that many academics and the general public sought to embrace their Nordic roots.[36] This resulted in a proliferation of literature, both academic and aimed at a broader public readership, including children, in which the term Viking became associated with a plethora of idealised characteristics. In his discussion of use of the term, Wawn comments that:

> The ubiquity of the term 'Viking' masks a wide variety of constructions of Vikingism: the old northmen are variously buccaneering, triumphalist, defiant, pious, relentlessly jolly, or self-destructively sybaritic. They are merchant adventurers, mercenary soldiers, pioneering colonists, pitiless raiders, self-sufficient farmers, cutting-edge naval technologists, primitive democrats, psychopathic berserks, ardent lovers and complicated poets.[37]

This complex composite image of the Viking was developed by Victorian visual and literary artists and appealed to a Victorian society seeking to establish a sense of connection with an exciting and untamed cultural past, depicted as noble, bold and adventurous: all aspirational qualities of this period of international rivalry, conflict and empire building. Public interest in the Viking during this period produced an increasing division between academic research and popular literature aimed at exploiting the burgeoning publishing market for the novel.

In academic circles, the publication in 1835–1837 of the first translation into English of the Anglo-Saxon *Nowell Codex* manuscript, which came to be known as *Beowulf*, provided a new source of scholarly research into Norse culture. The text, which has been dated to between the eighth and early eleventh centuries, remained neglected for many years until it reappeared in 1563 as part of a collection of the antiquarian Laurence Nowell (c.1515–c.1571).[38] The text was translated into Latin in 1815, by

Icelandic scholar Grímur Jónsson Thorkelín (1752–1829), whose research was commissioned by the Danish government, and subsequently translated into Danish by N.F.S. Grundtvig in 1820. In 1835–1837 John Mitchell Kemble (1807–1857) published the first full English edition making this previously neglected work available to a broader public.

The *Beowulf* poem is set in pre-Viking Scandinavia and tells the tale of a heroic *Geat* warrior from Southern Sweden who crosses the sea to Denmark, where he rids the Danes of a grotesque man-eating demon called Grendel. Beowulf subsequently battles the mother of the beast to rid the region of this evil. In a later final scene, he battles a fire-breathing dragon, which inflicts a fatal wound on him bringing a dramatic end to this heroic tale. This epic poem is imbued with a fusion of Christian and pagan beliefs and values, depicting a newly established Christian society where, in times of difficulty, the villagers still fall back on their old pagan Gods for guidance and intervention. *Beowulf* is presented as a super-human hero, synthesising Christian virtues with the courage and humanity of *Þórr* who frequently undertook sensational, heroic trials in his battle against evil.

The scholarly and public interest generated by *Beowulf* is evident in the numerous re-editions and new translations, which were published during this period.[39] J.M. Kemble added to and improved his original translation in editions published in 1835 and 1837, and further translations were subsequently published by A. Diedrich Wackerbarth in 1849, Benjamin Thorpe in 1855 and 1875, Thomas Arnold in 1876, Lieut.-Colonel H.W. Lumsden in 1881 and 1883 and John Earle in 1892, together with numerous translations into other European languages.[40] Notable recent translations have also been produced by Irish poet Seamus Heaney in 2001 and J.R.R. Tolkien (published posthumously in 2016). Our enduring interest in *Beowulf* is also evident in the popular reception of director Robert Zemeckis' modern CGI interpretation of *Beowulf* (2007). It is also interesting to note the ideal Nordic physical appearance of the computer-generated character conforming to the received image of the blond, blue-eyed Nordic hero.

Victorian society's fascination with its Viking past was particularly evident in the public response to the 1861 publication of *The Story of Burnt Njal* by Sir George Webbe Dasent (1817–1896). Dasent's pre-publication sales of a thousand copies indicated a readership eagerly awaiting his latest work.[41] Wawn comments that it was through this tale of Old Icelandic honour codes and prolonged blood feuds 'that Dasent won his Victorian celebrity'.[42] Contemporary reviewers described his work as 'unequalled in European poetry' and 'unsurpassed by any existing monument in the narrative department of any literature, ancient or modern', and his work has been regularly republished.[43]

Another popular Victorian work was *Thrithiof's Saga*, which was first translated into English in 1833 by Rev. William Strong. This Icelandic saga, about the son of a Norwegian King, was subsequently republished in sixteen different versions during the Queen's reign, and its themes of dark magic, love, treachery, perdition, violence and adventure must have appealed to a Victorian readership as a form of entertaining escapism.[44] On another level, it also invited the reader to empathise with its hero and to connect on an emotional level with an Old Norse experience. The concluding Christian redemption of its hero must have appealed to the moral sensibilities of a Victorian society who could enjoy a feeling of Viking kinship whilst still celebrating their sense of civilisation and morality through Christ. Its popularity as a literary work and its idealisation of the Viking was enhanced by the illustrations, added by Thomas Heath Robinson (1869–1950) whose impressive artwork contributed to the image of the Viking warrior-figures wearing horned helmets attacking from their terrifying ships of war, the type of image that became engrained in the Victorian collective imagination. Other notable publications during this period include William Morris' *The Saga of Gunnlaug Worm-Tongue* and *Grettis Saga* in 1869 and the *Story of the Volsungs and Niblungs* in (1870), Rider Haggard's *Eric Brighteyes* (1891), J.F. Hodgetts' *The Champion of Odin* (1885) and *Kormak the Viking* (1902).

In the emerging academic disciplines of history and archaeology, the nineteenth century saw many developments such as the foundation of the British Archaeological Association in 1843, the Royal Historical Society in 1868 and the Viking Society for Northern Research in 1892, a group dedicated to the study and promotion of the Scandinavian culture. History as a social science was, however, still defining its role and methodology and was often forced to bridge a lack of factual evidence with varying degrees of assumption. Archaeology or antiquarianism, in particular, become a fashionable field of research across Europe, and many historical grave sites were opened and areas of Viking occupation were excavated in order to recover evidence of this period and understand more about their everyday lives. Scandinavia and particularly Iceland became sites of interest for British historians and artists who wished to immerse themselves in

Nordic culture and seek out historical evidence of the heroic sagas, recover artefacts and study the runic inscriptions which appeared on standing stones, buildings and personal objects throughout Scandinavia. Notable in this field was the work of George Stephens (1813–1895), an archaeologist and philologist, who conducted research in Scandinavia on the interpretation of runic inscriptions. His works included *The Old-Northern runic monuments of Scandinavia and England*, published in four volumes (1866–1901), *Old Norse fairy tales* (1882) and *The runes: whence came they* (1894).

The relationship between Victorian society and the Vikings was a complex one. Despite early descriptions of Vikings, in sources such as the *Anglo-Saxon Chronicles*, as primitive, brutal and violent heathen invaders, the depiction of the Viking became progressively 'domesticated' to suit Victorian sensibilities. This image, created by a burgeoning market in popular literature, came to dominate the public imagination and over-shadow serious academic research. Through this process, which Martin Arnold describes, as 'a bourgeois populism bordering on what might be called Viking kitsch', the public embraced this ennobled image of the Viking as a source of national identity and pride.[45] This relationship was articulated on the final page of R.M. Ballantyne's *Erling the Bold: A Tale of Norse Sea-Kings* (1869), in which the author expressed his belief in the virtues that the British had inherited from their Viking ancestors with a sense of heightened nationalist fervour:

> Yes, there is perhaps more of Norse blood in your veins than you wot of, reader, whether you be English or Scotch; for these sturdy sea-rovers invaded our lands from north, south, east and west many a time in days gone by, and held it in possession for centuries at a time, leaving a lasting and beneficial impress on our customs and characters. We have good reason to regard their memory with respect and gratitude, despite their faults and sins, for much of what is good and true in our laws and social customs, much of what is manly and vigorous in the British Constitution, and much of our intense love of freedom and fair play, is due to the pith, pluck and enterprise, and sense of justice that dwelt in the breasts of the rugged old sea-kings of Norway![46]

This was a period of national prosperity and international power during which Britain sought to export its culture to its expanding colonies and Victorian society sought to mould its perception of the Viking in this context. A strong sense of national cultural and religious identity had pre-viously been established, notably during the Tudor period, and patriotism was promoted as an essential social value throughout Georgian and Victorian society. This sense of 'Britishness' centred on the nation being an island race that, through absorbing Celtic, Roman, Anglo-Saxon, Viking and Norman influences, had already established a sense of rooted-ness and stability. This acted as a cultural and biological foundation for the British people.

This cultural mix also meant that there was no particular group within Britain that sought to lay claim to a pure Nordic heritage. This sense of cultural identity provided a stable *nomos* against the eroding forces of modernity, and there was therefore no apparent need to establish a rela-tionship with an Old Norse past other than for scholastic interest and public entertainment. The British also had other, more outward-looking preoccupations as Heather O'Donoghue argues in *From Asgard to Valhalla*: 'Britain was far less concerned with gathering itself together than with furthering the imperial project. Imperialism was in many ways the opposite of Romantic Nationalism'.[47]

Interest in the Viking and his kinship to the British, which endured into the early twentieth century, tended therefore to remain either populist or academic and did not have a significant influence on mainstream political thought in Britain at the time. These socio-cultural conditions meant that, apart from a few isolated cases, the Victorians' relationship with their Viking heritage did not become radicalised or politicised as in Germany and America during the late nineteenth and early twentieth century. Although it could be argued that traces of early cultural and biological Nordicism can be identified in Britain, they did not evolve into any signifi-cant form of nationalist or racial agenda. Britain was, however, significant in contributing to the cultural foundations from which Nordicism was to emerge in other nations, creating a nostalgic, idealised image of Old Norse culture which was adaptable to emerging ideologies of Northern European supremacy.

Born in the USA: The Vínland Myth

The *Declaration of Independence* on 4 July 1776 and the war with Britain that lasted until 1783 marked the political rupture of the thirteen east coast British colonies from the rule of George III.[48] It also established the basis of a new republican social order, whose rationale was epitomised in Thomas Jefferson's proclamation that 'all men are created equal, that they are endowed by their Creator with certain unalienable Rights, that among these are Life, Liberty and the pursuit of Happiness'.[49] These iconic words became the founding principles of the new nation, which sought to cast off established institutions of class, monarchy and nobility to embrace the revolutionary spirit of National Romanticism that was sweeping across Western civilisation. The act of severing the links with the Mother Country and the Old World also inaugurated an era in which the newly formed state was forced to achieve its own sense of independent cultural identity.

Many Europeans considered the newly established American nation a 'land of plenty' looking across the Atlantic for the promise of a new homeland away from the corruption, hardship and disorienting impact of modern European industrialisation and urbanisation. During the nineteenth century, the USA spread rapidly westwards as the result of state railroad expansion and opened its doors to mass immigration as increasingly large passenger liners made international travel accessible to a much wider public. European immigrants left their countries of origin for a range of social, religious, political and economic reasons, attracted by the promise of land, enterprise, social equality and religious tolerance.

Settlers from Northern Europe had created communities in areas such as New England since the early seventeenth century, notably the large group of German immigrants who settled in the Pennsylvania area between the 1680s to 1760s and who, by 1775, constituted about one-third of the population of the state. Immigration increased rapidly during the nineteenth century as America offered unprecedented opportunities for new settlers, and between 1820 and 1870, German immigrants accounted for one-third of the 7.5 million immigrants from Northern and Western Europe, who poured into America to escape the political turmoil and economic hardship of their native countries. By 1890, an estimated 2.8 million German-born immigrants lived in the USA, many of whom were located in the 'German triangle' between Cincinnati, Milwaukee and St. Louis. It is estimated that, by 1894, about 800 German-language journals were being printed in the USA.[50]

The Homestead Act of 1862 provided a considerable stimulus to this immigration by offering free land to any settler who cultivated and developed an allocated plot for a period of five years.[51] During this period, immigration from Scandinavia also increased significantly as overcrowding, the scarcity of land, a number of crop failures and subsequent economic hardship caused Danish, Norwegian and Swedish citizens to emigrate from Scandinavia, many to the USA.[52] These settlers set up home primarily in the Midwest, often clustered in communities across states such as Minnesota, Wisconsin, North Dakota, Iowa and Illinois and had an increasing impact on the development of American culture.

The creation of a new, unified nation out of the expanding socio-economic and multicultural melting pot of the USA also required the creation of a sense of national rootedness and cohesion through the con-struction of a shared history and traditions. The history of the nation, through the lens of National Romanticism, provided heightened, inspira-tional representations of the nation's founding; its natural beauty, the lives of early settlers and their struggle for independence. American Romantic literary and visual artists expressed the sense of renaissance, optimism and individualism that was spreading across the nation. They expressed the search for new unifying spiritual roots and the sense of the sublime inspired in them by the untamed beauty of the American land-scape. One of the most influential elements of this movement was the Hudson River School, inspired by the work of its founder Thomas Cole (1801–1848) and influenced by the Düsseldorf Academy, where many of them had trained. The work of this group reflected the American experi-ence of discovery, exploration and settlement, showing Native Americans living in harmony with nature. In this context, the Hudson River School associated Rousseau's 'noble savage' with the Native American portrayed in romanticised representations of America's unspoilt natural wilderness. The work of Thomas Cole, in particular, expressed the pastoralist view that the spread of settlers across America would ultimately lead to the devastation of its natural beauty and native population. Between 1833 and 1836, Cole created his powerful five-part series of paintings entitled *The Course of Empire* in which he depicted the same landscape over gen-erations from its untouched natural state to its civilisation, decline and eventual destruction.

Within this search for national roots and identity, many first and subse-quent second-generation Germanic and Scandinavian Americans became increasingly attracted to their own foundation myth based on Vínland, the original discovery of American soil by Leifr Eiríksson around the year 1000. This mythologising of Vínland originated in scholarly interest in the *Vínland Sagas* during the eighteenth century and progressively took on an increasingly political and cultural dynamic as it spread to a much wider public during the nineteenth century. The *Grœnlendinga saga* (The Saga of the Greenlanders) and *Eiríks saga rauða* (Eirík the Red's Saga) were originally written in Iceland during the thirteenth centuries and represent a composite account of the discovery and colonisation of Greenland, the subsequent discovery of North America and attempts by early Norse settlers to inhabit this new land. Collectively, the sagas recount the discovery and settlement of Greenland by Eiríkr rauði, the first accidental sighting of the American coast by Bjarni Herjólfsson, Leifr Eríksson's first expedition and subsequent exploration and attempts to settle the new lands by Leifr's brothers Þórvaldr Eríksson, Þorfinnr Karlsefni and Freydís Eiríksdóttir. These accounts originated from a range of Icelandic sources and were recopied and edited over centuries until they reached their established form, as Icelandic scholar Magnus Magnusson points out in his introduction to the sagas:

> It must always be borne in mind that the Icelandic sagas were never museum pieces, embalming for all time a literary act; they were living things, and later generations thought nothing of adapting or rewriting them to suit changing tastes.[53]

These sagas evolved as organic literary works, a process that reflected the aspirations and concerns of their successive writers as much as it reflected the reality of the original expeditions. Although an imperfect history, the sagas stimulated considerable scholarly interest, as evidence of the early Norse discovery and attempted settlement of America. This led to a revision of Leifr's discovery and naming of the rocky Helluland, the wooded Markland and the land where they remained for the winter that he named Vínland.[54] These regions became a focus of interest as historians and enthusiasts attempted to identify a Nordic homeland where wild grapes grew, where rivers teemed with Salmon and where the climate was so mild that there was no winter frost and livestock could graze all year round.[55]

These texts were opened to European scholarship by the publication of a Latin paraphrase of the sagas in *Historia Vinlandiæ Antiquæ* (1705) by Icelandic historian Þormóður Torfason. In 1837, Danish antiquarian Carl Christian Rafn (1795–1864) published his account of early Viking expeditions to *Vínland* entitled *Antiquitates Americanae*. This work, published in Latin and Danish, provided translations and notes on the sagas and a commentary in English on a range of historical sites and artefacts, which Rafn presented as evidence of early Norse occupation of the Eastern States of America. Notable amongst Rafn's archaeological evidence was his claim that the Newport Tower on Rhode Island, a stone tower resting on eight archways, was part of a Church built by early Norse settlers. Rafn also suggested that the Dighton Rock, a large boulder, originally located in the riverbed of the Taunton River at Berkley, Massachusetts, bore Old Norse inscriptions. His identification of these artefacts attracted, however, considerable criticism from academics in Europe and America who dismissed his interpretations.

Rafn's work, however, provided one of the first scholarly works on early Norse settlement on American soil and generated considerable interest in America and Northern Europe. In her analysis of Rafn in *Viking America: The First Millennium* (2001), Geraldine Barnes describes how the reception of *Antiquitates Americanae* was mixed, both in terms of criticism of its methodology and its challenge to the popular foundation narrative of Christopher Columbus. His work was, however, of particular interest amongst those seeking evidence of a Viking heritage in the USA and who continued to present, throughout the late nineteenth and early twentieth centuries, a considerable number of now discredited artefacts as evidence of a Viking past and the geographical location of Vínland. Noteworthy amongst these finds was the Kensington Runestone, found in 1898 in Solem, Douglas County, Minnesota, and Thorwald's Rock in Hampton, which was claimed to mark the burial site of Þórvaldr Eiríksson, brother of Leifr.

In 1832, the discovery of a skeleton with metal, bark and fabric artefacts in Fall River, Massachusetts, sparked considerable attention and a range of theories as to its origin. This find inspired Romantic poet Henry Wadsworth Longfellow (1807–1882), one of the popular groups of New England poets who later became known as the *Fireside Poets*, to publish *The Skeleton in Armor* in 1841, in which the ghost of a Viking tells of his life in Norway, his love for a Norwegian princess and their journey to America. In *Longfellow and Scandinavia* (1970), Andrew Hilen examines Longfellow's relationship with Scandinavia and suggests that he had planned a heroic poem about the Norse discovery of America for some time and that the discovery of this skeleton, together with a recent visit to the Newport Tower, provided him with the ideal material to compose this ballad. The poem enjoyed considerable public success, which according to Hilen 'reemphasised the fact, for Longfellow, that Scandinavian history and tradition offered fresh and diverting subjects for romantic poetry'.[56]

Hilen describes Longfellow as a well-travelled scholar who became significantly influenced by the European National Romantic Movement and who developed a keen interest in Nordic literature and culture, notably during his stay in Copenhagen in 1835. During this two-week trip, he studied the works of Johannes Ewald, Adam Oehlenschläger and N.F.S. Grundtvig and came into contact with a circle of Danish academics, including Carl Christian Rafn who was working on his *Antiquitates Americanae*. Hilen also describes how they developed a close working relationship as Rafn saw Longfellow as a 'likely representative in America'.[57]

In 1863, Longfellow published a series of poems based on Norse history and mythology as part of his *Tales of a Wayside Inn*. In his analysis, Martin Arnold suggests that many of these were inspired by his reading of Samuel Laing's 1844 translation of Snorri Sturluson's *Heimskringla*, notably his series of poems, published in 1863, based on tales of the late tenth century Norwegian King, Olaf Tryggvason.[58] Amongst these narrative poems, *The Challenge of Thor* became one of his best known works in which Þórr confronted Christ challenging him to combat. Arnold also suggests that the themes of Longfellow's work convey the *Zeitgeist* of the era as Northern European immigrants sought to adapt to a new nation whilst still seeking to create their own sense of national identity, mythology and rootedness:

> Taken by itself, the Challenge of Thor could also be read as a compound metaphor for the mixed feelings of US-Scandinavian immigrants, whereby, on the one hand, the redemptive image of Christ correlates with the immigrant's hopes for a better future in the US, while on the other, the ancient claims of Thor correlate with their nostalgic yearnings for their homeland.[59]

This creation of a Northern European foundation myth, based primarily on the *Vínland Sagas*, but increasingly disseminated through literature and popular history, challenged the established history of the discovery of the Americas by Christopher Columbus. Through a process of Romantic historicism, *Vínland* became transformed into what Martin Arnold terms 'an imagined space', a mythologised homeland for Germanic and Scandinavian Americans, and what he describes as 'a stage setting for a wide range of contemporary concerns for over a hundred and fifty years: politics, race, religion, and gender'.[60] The debate over the first European to set foot on American soil intensified, during the nineteenth century, and took on political and religious overtones raising in particular the issue of cultural, religious and physical differences between Northern and Southern European immigrants. This issue became increasingly polemical in the years leading up to the Columbus quarter centenary in 1892, producing works such as *America Not Discovered by Columbus* (1874) by Ramus Anderson. His fundraising and campaigning, with the support of the *Fireside Poets*, made a considerable contribution to the cost of a bronze statue of Leifr Eríksson in Boston, unveiled in 1887. This debate also became increasingly radicalised through the work of a marginal but increasing number of influential scholars who proposed the Nordic type as the apex of the European race. In his analysis of this debate, Arnold comments that:

> As the nineteenth century progressed, those of Anglo-Saxon, German and Scandinavian descent became less comfortable with the idea of Columbus as the founding father for two main reasons: first, Columbus was a Catholic (...) and second according to the Gobineau-style race theories cherished by some Anglo-Nordic Americans, Columbus' Italian origin meant that he belonged to a lower caste of Europeans.[61]

This growing nativist belief in the concept of Nordic racial primacy, concentrated in influential pockets such as the New England States, progressively developed *Vínland* into an 'imagined space' of racial superiority and purity. Arnold argues that underlying the debate over America's foundation was a fundamental religious, cultural and racial divide, 'which among New Englanders usually meant pro-Puritan and which could also signify Teutonic racial supremacy'.[62]

This growing racial element within the American Nordic revival is evident in the works of Ottilie Liljencrantz (1876–1910), one of the most successful American writers of Nordic fiction. Liljencrantz published a highly popular trilogy of fiction works based on the Vínland sagas entitled *The Thrall of Leif the Lucky* (1902), *The Vinland Champions* (1904) and *Randvar the Songsmith: A Romance of Norumbega* (1906). Liljencrantz's work differed from previous Scandinavian historical fiction in America and Victorian Britain, through her interest in the developing field of racial science. This element is discussed by Geraldine Barnes who comments that 'her stories are informed by an ideology very different from the popular imperialist ideals of the superiority of Northern efficiency, masculinity, and race that underpin the Vínland fiction of the late Victorian and early twentieth century British writers'.[63] There is a striking contrast in her work, between the primitive baseness of the native inhabitants of *Vínland* and the physical and the moral beauty and strength of the Christian Nordic settlers. In her analysis, Barnes suggests that this was influenced by the racial Aryan views of British academic and writer Charles Kingsley (1819–1875) pointing out that Kingsley was listed as a source of inspiration in the acknowledgements of *The Thrall of Leif the Lucky*.[64]

The *Vínland* foundation myth attempted to place Northern Europeans at the heart of their new homeland's history. Through this process, the *Vinland Sagas* and 'imagined space' of *Vínland* were progressively appropriated as an element of the National Romantic Movement, as evidence of Nordic primacy and national identity in America. In his work on Longfellow, Hilen comments that:

> Just as Bjarni Herjólfsson and Leifr Eríksson found themselves off course in territory west of Greenland in *Grœnlendinga saga* and *Eiríks saga rauða,* so the *Vínland sagas* were removed from their Scandinavian provenance and stranded on the cultural map of America, on whose physical landscape Vínland was erratically positioned.[65]

Through this process of displacement, the search for national roots, mythology and worship emerged as a form of National Romanticism during the early nineteenth century. This became increasingly radicalised as it merged with religious, cultural and racial concerns of the day and progressively formed the foundation for the emergence of forms of cultural, political and later biological Nordicism in the USA during the late nineteenth and early twentieth centuries.

Establishing a Home-Grown Mythology: German Romanticism, Myth and National Unity

The emergence of interest in Old Norse culture in Germany during the late eighteenth and nineteenth centuries was a significant strand of National Romanticism which was later appropriated by certain Nazi ideologists as a rationale for their racial political agenda. As in Scandinavia, Britain and North America, National Romanticism in Germany was more than just a reflection of the Romantic Movement that was flourishing throughout Europe. It was an individual response to the concerns and aspirations of a nation seeking unification and a new sense of collective identity, rootedness and spirituality, as it rapidly transformed itself over a century from a fragmented collection of small territories into a unified, powerful, modern, industrialised nation.

As a result of the disunity and lack of a centralised government to develop cohesive national economic policies during the first half of the nineteenth century, German industrialisation had lagged behind that of Great Britain. From the middle of the century onwards, Germany experienced a phase of rapid industrial and economic growth, which, by the 1900s, placed it amongst Europe's leading industrial nations. This was accompanied by considerable population growth, which rose from 22.4 million in 1816 to 67 million in 1913 and a marked shift from rural to urban living.[66] In the industrial Ruhr valley, the population in 1831 numbered some 200,000, increasing dramatically to nearly 3,000,000 by 1910. Small towns such as Duisburg, Dortmund, Bochum and Essen were rapidly transformed into large cities.[67] The population of Berlin also grew from 412,000 in 1849 to 1.84 million in 1914 making it Europe's most densely populated city.[68] This 'growth spurt' transformed the German nation pushing it, within two generations, into the heart of European modernity. This phase of rapid industrialisation and urbanisation confronted the population with a dramatic shift in the political, economic, social and cultural landscape, the upheaval of which is described by George L. Mosse in his analysis of the growth of *völkisch* movements during this period in *The Crisis of German Ideology* (1964):

> Stimulated or shocked—depending upon one's partisanship—by the recurring revolutions in France, surrounded by an encroaching industrial society, men and women looked for a deeper meaning in life than the transitory reality of their present condition. The rapid process of European industrialization was indeed bewildering to them, accompanied as it was by the dislocation of the population, by the sudden obsolescence of traditional tools, crafts, and institutions, and by social maladjustment and political upheaval.[69]

It was against this turbulent political and social backdrop of progressive national unification, rapid industrialisation and international rivalry that the National Romantic Movement in Germany defined its mission of creating a new sense of German cultural identity, mythology and sense of rootedness. Emerging from the earlier literary movements of *Sturm und Drang* (Storm and Stress) and *Weimarer Klassik* (Weimar Classicism) of the second half of the eighteenth century, Romanticism emphasised humanism, subjectivity and emotions as a reaction to the constraints of Enlightenment rationalism and secularisation. Through this process, Germany arguably became one of the driving forces of the National Romantic movement in Northern Europe. Notable thinkers such as Johann Wolfgang Goethe (1749–1832), Johann Gottfried Herder (1744–1803), Friedrich Schiller (1759–1805), Christoph Martin Wieland (1733–1813) and Friedrich Gottlieb Klopstock (1724–1803) defined the movement's early nationalist agenda of celebrating and promoting the German language as a shared national heritage. This became increasingly relevant as a reaction against the growing cultural and political predominance of French across Europe. Linguistics became a vital source of national identity and cohesion for academics such as Wilhelm von Humboldt (1767–1835) and Herder whose early psycholinguistic theories proposed that language determined thought processes and hence both self and national identity.

Published in 1772, Herder's *Über den Ursprung der Sprache* (On the Origin of Language) became fundamental to the development of linguistics and philology as academic disciplines in Germany. In his poetry, Herder also called for the German people the *Volk* to regenerate its sense of national identity and pride through language as in these patriotic and Francophobic lines from *An die Deutschen* (To the German People):

> And you German alone, returning from abroad,
> Wouldst greet your mother in French?
> O spew it out, before your door
> Spew out the ugly slime of the Seine
> Speak German, O you German![70]

Herder's focus on language and cultural traditions, as the essential historical links that create and bind a nation, also included folklore, dance, music and art. In his analysis of Herder's work and nationalist aspirations, *Herder and Modern German Nationalism* (1976), Robert Ergang suggests that both the Ossianic poetry of James Macpherson and the publication of Thomas Percy's *Reliques of Ancient English Poetry* (1765) had a direct influence on Herder. These works inspired him to explore the potentially rich stock of German culture encoded in the folklore, customs and traditions of the German *Volk*.[71] Herder's work was published in two volumes as *Volkslieder* (Songs of the People) between 1778 and 1779 and was a possible source of inspiration for Jacob and Wilhelm Grimm in their collection of German folk tales, initially published in 1812 as *Kinder-und Hausmärchen* (Children's and Household Tales), a literary project which they continued to develop throughout their writing careers.

In her analysis of the nationalist mission of Herder and his contemporaries, in *The Anti-Enlightenment Tradition* (2010), Zeev Sternhell concludes that within Herder's circle there was a sense of 'a special mission to accomplish in history'.[72] For Herder, this futural project lay in the concept of Germany, as a young nation from which a generation of unified Germans would bring about the fulfilment of the nation's destiny. In her analysis, Sternhell argues that it was Herder who invented the idea of young people who would 'appropriate the heritage of other peoples who were exhausted'.[73] Sternhell quotes Herder's *Letters for the Advancement of Humanity* in which he expressed his optimism in the nation's potential to achieve greatness and eclipse the others' European nations whose culture and civilisation were in decline. In this work, he described the German nation as 'latecomers on the scene' with a renewed sense of national energy and unity, 'while other nations enter into their rest, having produced all they can'.[74] This sense of renewal and national awakening was later to become a central theme of Nazism's project of national regeneration with its slogan of *Deutschland erwache!*

Alongside this development in what could be termed linguistic and literary nationalism, the National Romantic movement in Germany also sought to establish a 'home-grown' mythology to create a truly Germanic form of rootedness, *nomos* and sense of collective transcendence. This led many National Romantic philosophers and writers to seek out relevant and authentic forms of Germanic faith that predated Christianity. In 1796, G.F.W. Hegel (1770–1831) expressed this growing anti-Christian mood and the need to find and regenerate a mythology from what he perceived as the subjugated collective memory of the *Volk*. In an essay entitled *The Positivity of the Christian Religion*, Hegel argued that:

> Christianity has emptied Walhalla, felled the sacred groves, extirpated the national imagery as a shameful superstition, as a devilish poison, and given us instead the imagery of a nation whose climate, laws, culture, and interests are strange to us and whose history has no connection whatever with our own ... all that we have is the remains of an imagery of our own, lurking amid the common people under the name of superstition.[75]

Hegel's references to the Old Norse 'Hall of the Dead', the Sacred Groves and the superstitions of the *Volk* reflect what was becoming a growing movement in Germany which sought to re-establish the legends of the Old Norse and Germanic Gods as a source of 'home-grown' spirituality and rootedness in a culture which was distinctly Northern European. The challenge facing this movement was to locate and develop a national mythology, drawing on a virtuous and inspirational Germanic past, to create a sense of national cohesion and spirituality. This 'mazeway resynthesis' was prompted by the liminal state of transition that prevailed, as industrialisation and urbanisation rapidly eroded traditional ways of life, communities and social cohesion. This description by George S. Williamson of this search for sources evokes the image of Nietzsche's mythless man digging desperately for roots in the past:

> Undaunted by the paucity of sources, they attempted to recover the traces of a lost Germanic mythology, translating the medieval epics, gathering folk songs and fairy tales, excavating pagan burial mounds, and reinterpreting the Nordic gods in such a way that they became evidence of an earlier pre-Christian religion.[76]

In *The Longing for Myth in Germany*, George S. Williamson provides an analysis of the development of the diverse elements of this movement and described what he termed 'a publication mania'[77] as academics and artists searched for evidence of a lost Germanic culture from which a new mythology could be constructed. This search through Germany's *Vorzeit* for the scattered fragments of Germany's cultural and mythical essence became a form of 'mazeway resynthesis' as scholars and romantic writers sought to select and rewrite elements of German mythology, predating the material and political complications of the modern era, but which were still relevant to the state of modernity. This *Vorzeit* represented a romanticised 'sacred space', 'mythic home' or *óðal* outside the fragmented and deracinating contemporary world. This aimed to create a new path of national identity, cohesion and spirituality in the modern era which was uniquely German and which corresponded to the aspirations of a new nation. In his analysis, Williamson explains that:

> In the Vorzeit, it was maintained, the German heroic myth had supplied a psychological substrate, filling each phase of life with religious significance. Since then, however, it had split into a thousand fragments, which were now

scattered across the German landscape. Each scrap of evidence was a potential piece of the lost mythology and thus worthy of collection and
preservation.[78]

The rediscovery, during the eighteenth century, of the previously lost
and neglected fragments of medieval manuscripts recounting the
Nibelungenlied (The Song of the Nibelungs) had a significant impact on
this search for sources of national myth. This epic poem, written during
the thirteenth century, was considered a truly Germanic epic. It fused
aspects of the Old Norse legend of *Sigurðr Fáfnisbani* (Sigurd the dragon
slayer), *Brynhildr* (Brynhild the outcast Valkyrie), *Guðrún* (Gudrun) and
Hogni from the Icelandic sagas, with the medieval Germanic context of
the fall of the kingdom of Burgundy in the fifth century. The *Nibelungen
Saga* was turned into a major play by Friedrich Hebbel and was first performed in 1861.[79] This was especially appealing to the growing number of
thinkers who were attracted to the concept of *Rittermythologie*, a knightly
mythology, through which writers, such as A.W. Schlegel, sought to rehabilitate what they considered the noble, heroic era of medieval Germany,
as a resynthesised form of national rootedness and spirituality. In *Über das
Mittelalter* (1803), Schlegel described his vision of the greatness of this
Rittermythologie, which fused native German attributes with the spread of
Christianity to form a synthesis through which Catholicism would experience a rebirth in modernity:

> The knightly spirit emerged from the combination of the robust and honest
> bravery of the German North with a completely spiritual greatness coming
> from the Orient—Christianity, an occurrence that was not just brilliant but
> truly enchanting, and hitherto without parallel in human history.[80]

Schlegel's attempted rehabilitation of the era of knightly Christian values, which was intended to displace the secularising impact of the French
Revolution and the influence of French language and culture in Europe,
met with a mixed reception and provoked considerable debate. Writers,
such as Joseph Görres, were inspired by this concept to publish, in 1807,
a number of popular stories and folk tales from the sixteenth century entitled *Die teutschen Volksbücher*. Others, such as Jacob Grimm, rejected the
concept of *Rittermythologie*, believing that the actual origins of a national
Vorzeit and mythology lay further back in time, during the early period of

migration of the Germanic people from the East to Northern and Central Europe.

Despite this debate, the rediscovery of medieval works such as *Parzival*, the *Nibelungenlied* and the subsequent emergence of this school of Romantic medievalism became, as George S. Williamson describes, 'quite fashionable in the salon culture of Berlin', and the *Nibelungenlied* was republished a number of times in popular editions in the early nineteenth century.[81] It was however, as Williamson argues, 'poorly suited for the role it was chosen to play in German history' in that being neither explicitly pagan nor Christian, it presented a spiritually ambiguous epic 'in which greed, lust, and treachery predominate and God is strangely absent'.[82]

The expanding search for suitable material amongst the fragmented and scarce sources on German territory led academics to broaden their definition of the Germanic to include the Scandinavian countries, which like Germany had resisted the spread of Roman influence and Christianity. Philology had established the shared linguistic roots of a Germanic/ Scandinavian culture spreading from the East into Northern Europe, and Romantic Nationalism developed this concept to broaden the geographical extent of their cultural search. In *Wagner and the Volsungs* (2003), Árni Björnsson describes the influence of philosopher and nationalist Johann Gottlieb Fichte (1762–1814). In a series of speeches delivered in 1808, entitled *Reden an die deutsche Nation* (Addresses to the German Nation), Fichte defined the German people and therefore, by implication, Germanic territories as those that had remained culturally and linguistically untouched by the influence of Roman rule and the Latin language. In his analysis, Björnsson argues that according to this Pan-Germanic theory, 'all Nordic peoples could be counted as parts of the Germanic cultural heritage'.[83]

This Pan-German cultural perspective broadened the geographical scope of German academics and writers who sought a sense of rootedness and national identity in the contemporary interest in Scandinavian history. This interest was also emerging in Britain, Scandinavia and the Northern states of the USA and drew on sources from the recently published translations and commentaries of early medieval Icelandic sagas. The publication of Mallet's *Introduction à l'histoire de Dannemarc* and its translation into German in 1765 by Gottfried Schütze had a significant impact on the work of early Romantic writers, such as Herder and Klopstock, offering a new source of inspiration for those seeking to create a new national mythology founded on Pan-Germanism. This interest in incorporating

Scandinavian myth and culture into the search for Germanic rootedness progressively took on a momentum and dynamic of its own. In 1811, Wilhelm Grimm published his account of traditional Danish tales and ballads in *Altdänische Heldenlieder, Balladen und Märchen* (*Old Danish heroic songs, ballads and fairy* tales), and in 1815, the brothers published *Lieder der alten Edda* (Tales from the Old Edda). In *Aryan Idols—Indo-European Mythology as Ideology and Science* (1968), Stefan Arvidsson discusses the cultural and political significance of the brothers' investigations of rural Germanic folklore:

> The purpose of their famed project of collecting folktales from the German peasant population was primarily to (re-) create a strong German culture that could free itself from dependence of "foreign" cultures. One step in this project was to show that there existed a rich "German" mythology that could successfully compete with classical and Judeo-Christian traditions.[84]

In 1819, Jacob Grimm developed his linguistic analysis of Northern European folklore publishing the first of his three-part philological study of the German language, *Deutsche Grammatik*. This was a groundbreaking comparative linguistic analysis of Germanic, Anglo-Saxon and Norse texts, in which Grimm presented his evidence to support the theory that the Scandinavian languages were rooted in an ancient Germanic *Ursprache* or prehistoric root-language. The methodology established by this work had a significant influence on the progressive fusion of Germanic and Nordic mythology by later Pan-Germanic scholars. The essence of this work was the theory that became known as 'Grimm's law' whereby the similarities and differences between Germanic and Latin/Greek language were analysed to reveal their historic relationships and shared origins. The application of this theory, by subsequent scholars, made a considerable contribution to the emerging field of racial science and the development of Aryanism and Nordicism by providing a linguistic rationale for emerging Pan-Germanist theories.

In developing his theory, Jacob Grimm was influenced by the research of Danish scholar and philologist Rasmus Christian Rask (1787–1832), notably his analysis of the historic connections between Nordic/Germanic languages and their relationship with the Classical and Eastern languages. In 1809, Rask completed his first work, the *Introduction to the Grammar of the Icelandic and other Ancient Northern Languages*, which he published in Danish in 1811. In 1814, he completed an essay, which he submitted to the Danish Academy of Sciences entitled *Investigation of the Origin of the Old Norse or Icelandic Language*, in which he presented his evidence linking Old Norse with other Germanic and Slavic languages which he further linked to Latin and Greek. In his analysis of Grimm's work in *A Revolution Reconsidered: Mythography and Mythology in the Nineteenth Century* (2005), Tom Shippey describes Grimm's research as a 'paradigm shift' in attitude and theory in the field of humanities, creating the new discipline of comparative philology.[85] In this work, Shippey analyses the significant impact of this shift, which transformed the field of linguistics and, through the elaboration of Grimm's research, the growing interest in the discovery and creation of a national mythology.

In 1835, Jacob Grimm extended this theory and methodology in another seminal work, *Deutsche Mythologie*, in which he undertook the comparative study of Classical and Northern European deities in the search to discover and reconstruct a lost Germanic national mythology compatible with Germany's search for a unifying sense of national identity and transcendence. A notable feature of this work is Grimm's attempt to connect traditional Germanic folklore with ancient Indo-European oral tradition predating Christianity, which had suppressed and eroded old pagan mythology and traditions. Through his research, Grimm attempted to discover traces of a 'Golden Age' of Germanic mythology, inherited from the nobility of the Aryan, that he could resynthesise into a mythological model capable of providing a truly Germanic creation myth for the developing nation. Tom Shippey discusses this nationalist, political dimension of Grimm's research, which attracted much criticism of his work at the time and places Grimm's work in the socio-political and cultural context of the progressive creation of the German nation state. He also points out the role of Grimm in creating a scientific rational for the development and promotion of Pan-Germanism:

> When Grimm wrote the *Deutsche Grammatik* and the *Deutsche Mythologie*, there was no political entity known as *Deutschland*, only the many independent German-speaking states. For such an entity to be formed, an idea of "Germanness" had to be created, and Grimm, born in 1787 and profoundly affected by the weakness of the German states during the Napoleonic wars, set himself to do it, in ways which were contested at the time (notably by Scandinavian scholars) and have been more so ever since.[86]

Shippey examines the opposition of a number of Scandinavian and German scholars, such as Grundtvig and Johann Ludwig Uhland (1787–1862), to what they perceived to be Grimm's Pan-Germanic appropriation of Nordic culture and its potential implications as a hidden political agenda to create a greater Germanic empire. This was a particularly sensitive issue to the Danish people, whose military conflict with Germany over the Schleswig-Holstein territories concluded in 1864, with the loss of territory in Southern Jutland. In his analysis, Martin Arnold highlights Grimm's nationalistic views towards his Scandinavian neighbours, by quoting the address he made in 1848, during the first phase of the Schleswig-Holstein conflict, to the Frankfurt National Assembly in which he declared that 'other nations would not tolerate even a sod to be taken off the dwelling place of their renowned ancestors'.[87] Hence, Jacob Grimm was increasingly at odds, both politically and culturally, with his Scandinavian counterparts who viewed his appropriation of the Old North with some suspicion, as discussed by Shippey in his analysis of the reaction to Grimm's often ambiguous use of the term *Deutsch*:

> Grimm wanted above all to have a mythology, which was specifically German or Deutsch. Unfortunately for him, most of the surviving sources were not German but Scandinavian, written in Old Norse and preserved in Iceland. He tended therefore to use *deutsch* to mean (a) German, but (b) Germanic, a term which included all the Scandinavian languages as well as the Low German ones (Dutch and English among them). Scandinavian scholars especially saw this as a "takeover bid", which implied furthermore that German was, so to speak, the central or master-form of all the Germanic languages.[88]

Grimm's appropriation of Nordic culture as a strand of a greater Germanic literary and mythological foundation threatened both the cultural and political ambitions of surrounding nations whose scholars opposed Grimm's theories. An example of European scholarship's opposition to this 'takeover' of Nordic culture by Pan-Germanists was expressed in the work of George Stephens (1813–1895) who published, in 1878, *Thunor the Thunderer, Carved on a Scandinavian Font of About the Year 1000: The First Yet Found God-Figure of Our Scando-Gothic Forefathers*, a work based on the discovery of old inscriptions and carvings on a font found in the ruins of an old church at Ottrava in Våstergotland, Sweden. In his analysis of this work, Martin Arnold discusses how Stephens' passionate presentation of Þórr constituted a statement of ownership of the Norse god as an ever-present defender of the people against evil. Arnold quotes Stephens' poetic presentation of Þórr as 'the dread of every Bug and Ogre; the "Bani tröll-quenna", the relentless slayer of Troll and Hag and Witch-quean, whether tripping winsome in guise of Light-angel fair, or stiffly striding with scowling fire-red balls and matted snake-hair, her crooked fingers grasping the torch and dagger of destruction and despair'.[89] Arnold further suggested that Stephens was aware of the cultural and political significance of defending and gaining possession of Northern Europe's mythological roots against the advance of the 'crooked fingers' of Pan-Germanism arguing that:

> In short, what Stephens saw in the Thor font was a racial, moral and political ideology that united the northern peoples, among whom he included the English, and from which he excluded the Germans. The Thor font spoke for pan-Scandinavianism and against pan-Germanism, and when Stephens rails against the 'crooked fingers' of trolls, he is signalling, among other things, German ambitions to arrogate the heritage of the Old North and political ascendancy over its inheritors along with it.[90]

The philological research of Jacob Grimm could therefore be considered a fundamental turning point whereby cultural interest in the literature and mythology of the Old North was progressively incorporated into the nationalist agenda of Pan-Germanist thinkers and into what could be interpreted as early forms of cultural and political Nordicism. Through the influence of the Grimm brothers, the field of comparative philology became a significant element of the field of racial science attempting to locate the original homeland of the prehistoric Indo-Germanic/Nordic descendants of the original Aryan people.

In his analysis of this period, George S. Williamson points out that, despite continued academic debate concerning the validity and relevance of sources, the basic foundations of a national mythology had been re-established in Germany by the 1830s amongst the educated classes and, to a lesser extent, in a popular context:

> An epic literary tradition had been uncovered, the folktales were widely read, and the outlines of a Germanic pantheon had been reconstructed. Artists had begun to produce paintings, songs, and stories based on the *Kaiser* legends, the oak tree, and the *Nibelungenlied*. Moreover the ele-

ments of this mythology had been connected to the geography of Germany: The Rhine River, the Teutoburg Forest, and the North Sea.[91]

This cultural 'solidification' of a national mythology, in the visual and literary arts, fused Norse mythology with the eclectically reassembled elements of traditional Germanic folklore to create a cohesive framework for the development of a national *völkisch* creation myth, which would bind together the fragmented German nation. This was particularly evident in the emergence of a number of thinkers at the end of the nineteenth century who sought to develop new forms of religion as a reaction what they considered to be the failing project of modernity.

In the visual arts, as in the field of literature, there was a significant degree of cultural interaction and influence with the emerging schools of National Romantic art in Scandinavia, Britain and America. The Düsseldorf School of painting, a group of painters who taught or studied at the Düsseldorf Academy in the 1830s and 1840s and who drew inspiration from earlier National Romantic artists such as Caspar David Friedrich (1774–1840), and many Scandinavian artists such as Peter Nicolai Arbo (1831–1892), Mårten Eskil Winge (1825–1896) and Hans Dahl (1849–1937). These artists trained at the academy and made a significant impact on what has been termed the 'Golden Age' of Scandinavian Romantic art. Notable amongst those considered to be the founders of the Düsseldorf School was Andreas Achenbach (1815–1910), a German landscape and seascape painter whose work influenced many others, inspired by his dramatic Romantic style, which portrayed the sublime power and beauty of nature. Many of Achenbach's most striking seascapes depicted violent storms in which man struggled against the forces of nature (Fig. 2.3).

The Düsseldorf School had a considerable influence on National Romantic art throughout the nineteenth century depicting dramatic, idealised landscapes of notably the German and Scandinavian countryside. This visual expression of nationalist aspirations included ruins of medieval buildings, images from the *Nibelungenlied* and, as the influence of the Pan-Germanic cultural movement developed, prehistoric Scandinavian features such as dolmens and figures from Norse mythology.

The culmination of Nordic influence on the arts was epitomised in *Der Ring des Nibelungen* (*The Ring of the Nibelung*) of Richard Wagner (1813–1883). This epic operatic work, composed between 1848 and 1874, combined the literary, visual and musical arts to create a

Fig. 2.3 Andreas Achenbach (1815–1919) Ein Seetrurm an der norwegischen Küste (Storm at sea on the Norwegian coast) painted in 1837. Städelsches Kunstinstitut und Städtische Galerie, Frankfurt. Photo by Martin Kraft reproduced with his kind permission

Gesamtkunstwerk, a total work of art, that synthesised Germanic and Nordic elements, to create a monumental visual, musical and lyrical interpretation of Germany's *Vorzeit*. *Der Ring des Nibelungen* follows the struggles of gods, heroes and mythical creatures over a powerful magic ring that grants domination over the entire world and was first performed, in its entirety, over three days at the first Bayreuth Festival in 1876. At this acclaimed première, Wagner created a visual and auditory 'sacred space' imbued with Nordic mythology that transported the audience into a highly stylised, Romantic world of the Norse pantheon. In 1872, Friedrich Nietzsche published *Die Geburt der Tragödie aus dem Geiste der Musik* (The Birth of Tragedy), in which he celebrated Wagner's 'total work of art', which he saw as providing the heroic myth that modern man desperately needed.[92] The stage costumes with winged helmets, designed by artist Carl Emil Doepler (1824–1905), created an enduring image of the Norse gods that emphasised their powerful warrior image and which has influenced popular representations of the Norse pantheon throughout the twentieth century up to the modern times. The four phases of this epic opera, *Das Rheingold* (*The Rhine Gold*), *Die Walküre* (*The Valkyrie*), *Siegfried* and *Götterdämmerung* (*Twilight of the Gods*), collectively represent in many ways the most enduring and influential cultural fusion of the Germanic and the Nordic in a spectacle that still attracts audiences today.

In *Wagner and the Volsungs*, Árni Björnsson analyses Wagner's use of sources from the *Eddas, Vǫlsunga saga, Þiðreks saga, the Heimskringla, Egil's saga, Gísla saga* and the *Nibelungenlied*, which stemmed from his readings of heroic legends by historian Franz Josef Mone (1796–1871). Björnsson quotes Wagner's acknowledgement of Mone's influence in his autobiography *Mein Leben* (1911) in which Wagner described his growing attraction to Nordic mythology as a source of inspiration for his artistic work:

> I now tried to get to know the Eddas as well as the prose fragments comprising the basis for large parts of these legends. Viewed in the light of Mone's comments, the Wälsunga saga exerted a decisive influence on the manner in which I began to form my material for my own purposes. The consciousness of the close primeval kinship of these old myths, which had been shaping within me for some time, thus gradually gained the power to create the dramatic forms, which governed my subsequent works.[93]

Building his influential opera on the historical and literary foundations of earlier National Romantic writers and their evolving cultural Pan-Germanism, Wagner created a powerful national myth, which expressed both National Romanticism's search for national identity and unity and the cultural aspirations of the newly founded German nation following the unification of 1871. In this socio-political context, Wagner's work represents a significant threshold between German National Romanticism's attraction to Nordic mythology and the later emergence of Nordicism as a cultural, political and scientific movement during the late nineteenth and twentieth centuries. As Martin Arnold explains:

> After Wagner's reworking of Old Northern myth and legend, spotted with prejudice and elitism, and composed in tribute to the glory of the German Volk and their history, whatever previous analyses of the gods of Nordic antiquity there had been, soon became fodder for the appetites of German national self-assertion. So it happened that an increasingly powerful Germany, a politically enfeebled Scandinavia, a theory of linguistic purity,

and a proposition regarding Germanic origins that hinted at supremacism were gradually articulated under a single heading: *völkisch*.[94]

Many critiques of Wagner's work have underlined the anti-Semitic, Pan-Germanic and elitist themes and their influence on early Nordicist and *völkisch* thought, a movement which was to include one of Wagner's most significant and influential supporters, Adolf Hitler. The *Führer* admired and promoted Wagner's opera as a source of national identity, unity and racial prominence in the Third Reich. Wagner's work was significant in providing, for future generations, a powerful artistic composite of the spirit of National Romanticism, which consolidated and solidified the appropriation of Nordic culture within a larger Pan-Germanic cultural context, which in turn was integrated into the fields of racial science and politics.

Notable amongst other Pan-Germanists seeking to establish home-grown forms of national mythology in which to root the growing *völkisch* movement was Austrian journalist, playwright, novelist and occultist Guido von List (1848–1919), who became one of the principal founders of what came to be termed the Ariosophy movement in Germany and Austria. List and his influence on later Nazi occultism, notably within Heinrich Himmler's SS, are a subject of Nicholas Goodrick-Clarke's influential work *The Occult Roots of Nazism* (2004). In this work, Goodrick-Clarke describes how List rejected his Catholic upbringing to claim that the ancient Germanic tribes of Northern Europe had practised a gnostic faith system, which he termed *Armanism* and *Wotanism*. In formulating a modern resynthesis of this old religion, List drew on a number of works from twelfth- and thirteenth-century Icelandic scholars together with the burgeoning Pan-Germanic literature of the period to develop a resynthesised form of new religion rooted in native Northern European mythology. Goodrick-Clarke explains how List developed the thesis that prior to the spread of Christianity throughout Northern Europe, there had once been a culturally unified Germanic civilisation spread across much of Europe and which had been eroded and divided by the spread of Christianity. Persecuted for their pagan beliefs by Christian civilisation, the original Wotanists had sought refuge in Scandinavia, where they continued and preserved their traditions and customs. In the development of his theories, List was also influenced by current thought from the emerging fields of racial science and philology that linked these ancient Germanic tribes with the once superior Aryan race that had migrated from the east.

In his analysis, Goodrich-Clarke describes List as 'disenchanted with modernity', proposing an alternative futural vision based on a reconnection with what he perceived to be the spirituality of the ancient Nordic/Germanic tribes. Goodrich-Clarke argues that for List, the erosion of established values and identity by 'evil powers' constituted an 'apocalyptic model' for the Germanic race within Austria:

> It is evident that List's description of contemporary Austria amounted to a fundamental devaluation of the present. The entire industrial-urban complex together with its emergent social and political institutions was utterly condemned. List followed the apocalyptic model even further by claiming that this situation was due to the domination of evil powers. The dissolution of traditional social practices and institutions posited, in List's view, a simpler and more conscious agent of change than the play of market forces, social circumstances, and structural changes of the economy.[95]

Goodrick-Clarke considers List a 'cultural pessimist' who rejected what he perceived to be the failed project of modernity, which had eroded the *nomos* of local traditions and communities, and allowed foreign influences to destroy the unity and spiritual essence of the Germanic people. In List's view, this loss of Germanic spirituality and sense of community was the essence of the malaise of the era. Goodrick-Clarke further argues that the significance of occultism in the doctrine of Ariosophists such as List was 'principally explicable as a sacred form of legitimation for their profound reaction to the present and their extreme political attitudes'.[96] In this context, the emergence of Ariosophy during the late nineteenth century constituted a marginal but significant strand of reaction against modernity and its deracinating, secularising impact on society prompting the reconstruction of ancient belief systems as shelters from the storm of progress.

Together with the emerging Pan-Germanist movement, which sought the *Anschluss* of Austria into a greater Germanic nation, List was influenced by the theories of the growing Theosophical Society. This group was officially formed in November 1875, in New York, by Helena Petrovna Blavatsky (1831–1891) and an influential group of her followers, including American journalist and lawyer Colonel Henry Steel Olcott and lawyer William Quan Judge who both had a profound interest in the occult. This movement sought, through the study of comparative religion (notably eastern religions), philosophy and science, to explore the basis of human development and spirituality. Blavatsky originally set down the basic principles of this movement in her major work, entitled *The Secret Doctrine* (1888), in which she attempted to reconcile ancient eastern esoteric wisdom with modern science. According to Goodrich-Clarke, List also drew on the writings of German theosophist Max Ferdinand Sebaldt von Werth (1859–1916), who combined Theosophy with his own interpretations of Germanic mythology, racial theories and its application to the emerging field of eugenics. Werth claimed, in his 1897 publications, *Wanidis* and *Sexualreligion*, that the sexual religion of the ancient Aryan tribes was based on a sacred practice of positive eugenics, a selective breeding ritual designed to maintain and strengthen the purity of the race and its superior physical and mental traits.[97]

One of the key elements of List's developing belief system lay in his belief that the foundations of Wotanism were to be found in the runic alphabet, believing that they could be deciphered by linking these letters with particular runic spells contained in the Old Norse *Hávamál* of the *Poetic Edda*. In his description of List's background, Goodrick-Clarke described how, in 1902, List suffered an eleven-month period of blindness during which his occult insight revealed to him the linguistic and spiritual meaning of runes. Following this experience, List produced a manuscript which he later published, in 1908, as *Das Geheimnis der Runen*, detailing what he regarded to be a proto-language of the Aryan race, in which he claimed to be able to interpret the letters and sounds of both runes and glyphs found on old inscriptions. This interpretation, based on a runic alphabet, which was partially invented by List himself, became the foundation of his later Ariosophical beliefs. List referred to these runes as the *Armanen Futhark*, a series of eighteen runes, closely based on the historical Younger Futhark whose origins date back to the seventh and eighth centuries. In his decoding of the runes, List revealed the significance of these sacred runic symbols of the Aryan faith such as the swastika, sun and eagle that were to feature prominently in later Nazi and notably SS iconography.

List termed the resynthesised belief system that he proposed Armanism after the *Armanen*, an elite group of high-ranking priests of the ancient Aryo-Germanic nation who, according to List, worshipped the sun and who collectively formed the *Armanenschaft*. According to List's theories, their religious belief and its transmission functioned on two levels. The esoteric doctrine (*Armanism*) contained secret spiritual knowledge and was reserved for the initiated elite, while the exoteric doctrine (*Wotanism*) took the form of popular myths and traditions intended for the lower social classes. List's theories, however marginal and esoteric, had considerable resonance amongst Pan-Germanists both within and outside Austria, who were disenchanted with nineteenth-century modernity and rationalism. These Romantic thinkers rejected Enlightenment thought and its culture-eroding forces, to seek out new forms of mythology at the end of the nineteenth century, a period which historian George L. Mosse describes in his 1964 work *The Crisis of German Ideology*. In this work, Mosse examines the emergence of the mystic strand within National Romanticism in Germany as a reaction to the disenchanting conditions of modernity, which had provoked a state of spiritual crisis during which 'romantics sought to find the larger, all encompassing unity outside the prevalent social and economic condition of man'.[98] Mosse describes how:

> Bewildered and challenged, men attempted to re-emphasize their own personality. But, since the rate of industrial transformation, as well as its effects, seemed to evade the grasp of reason, and men could not easily make themselves part of the new social order, many turned from rational solutions to their problems and instead delved into their own emotional depths.[99]

Significant amongst Pan-Germanic thinkers who were influenced by the work of Guido von List was Austrian political and racial theorist Lanz von Liebenfels (1874–1954). Liebenfels promoted and developed the Ariosophical theories of List and, together with an influential group of supporters, founded the *Guido-von-List-Gesellschaft* (Guido von List Society) in 1908. A former Cistercian monk, initially influenced by *Rittermythologie*, Lanz left the order in 1899 to develop the principles of his religio-scientific theory of *Theozoölogie* which he published fully in 1905 as *Theozoölogie oder die Kunde von den Sodoms-Äfflingen und dem Götter-Elektron* (Theozoology or the Lore of the Sodom-Apelings and the Electron of the Gods). This synergic work fused his interpretations of recent developments in the fields of the humanities and natural sciences with nationalist politics, neo-paganism and occultism that Goodrick-Clarke describes as a form of 'radical theology, an idiosyncratic view of history and abstruse scientific speculation'.[100]

In his publication, Lanz developed his theory that ancient Aryan tribes had diluted their superior gene pool through interbreeding with 'love-dwarves' (*Buhlzwerge*), reared for sexual pleasure. He also claimed that the

Gods, an earlier superior form of life, had possessed advanced sensory organs for the reception and transmission of electrical signals, giving them the power of omniscience and telepathy.[101] According to Lanz, the miscegenation of this once superior race could be restored to its blond, blue-eyed, Northern European, Aryan origins through a process of segregation and selective breeding in 'eugenic convents' together with an enforced programme of sterilisation. In 1905, Lanz founded the magazine *Ostara* or *Ostara, Briefbücherei der Blonden und Mannesrechtler* (*Ostara*, newsletter of the blonde and masculists) in which, together with like-minded collaborators, he wrote a number of articles concerning the classification of racial types, sex, women and prostitution, the spiritual and physical comparisons between blonds and dark-skinned, religion and the occult.[102] Although it is difficult to determine the actual publication figures or readership of this publication, it is reasonable to conclude that it was an influential but marginal element of the melting pot of Romantic, nationalist, pseudo-scientific and religious 'New Age' thought which was emerging at the time. To support and promote his philosophy, Lanz founded his own esoteric organisation, the *Ordo Novi Templi* (Order of the New Templars) in 1907.

Amongst List's other influential admirers was nationalist politician Theodor Fritsch who, together with fellow followers of List and Pan-Germanists, founded the List-inspired *Germanenorden* (Germanic Order) in 1912, a *völkisch* anti-Semitic secret society set up to monitor Jewish activity, support *völkisch* occultist research and promote the concept of Pan-Germanic supremacy. According to Goodrick-Clarke, application forms for the Order requested details of the applicants' hair, eyes and skin colour and information regarding their parents and grandparents. The subsequent selection process favoured the ideal Nordic type and excluded the physically handicapped or those deemed 'unpleasant looking'.[103] The Order also used an early form of the swastika (with curved arms superimposed on a cross), which was displayed, from 1916, on the front cover of its official newsletter *Allgemeine Ordens-Nachrichten*. This symbol was also used, together with designs incorporating runic inscriptions, on a number of *völkisch* personal items such as jewellery, which were advertised in the newsletter.[104] Another *völkisch* religious society, which used the swastika as a symbol together with the *Mjöllnir* (Thor's hammer) in its publications, was the *Germanische Glaubens—Gemeinschaft* (Germanic Faith Society), founded in 1907 by writer and artist Ludwig Fahrenkrog (1867–1952).

The swastika was also used to represent the *Thule-Gesellschaft* (Thule Society), established in Munich by Rudolf Freiherr von Sebottendorff (1875–1945), in 1917. This offshoot of the *Germanenorden* took its name from the legendary island in an unknown far-northern location, featured in classical European literature and cartography, which many including Sebottendorff believed to be Iceland. As its main emblem, the society used the powerful image of a vertical long dagger surrounded by oak leaves superimposed on a radiating swastika sun symbol. The society also used the eagle and List's Ar-rune as symbols of their Aryan origins. The Thule Society was significant in the development of the later Nordicist element of Nazi ideology through the interaction of this society with the early *Deutsche Arbeiterpartei*, later reorganised by Hitler into the National Socialist German Workers' Party. Although historians have debated the actual membership role of the *Thule-Gesellschaft*, it is generally agreed that many founder members of the NSDAP and Nazi ideologues had been associated, to varying degrees, with the group as members, speakers or guests. In his biography of Hitler, Sir Ian Kershaw describes the membership of the Thule Society as a 'Who's Who of early Nazi sympathizers and leading figures in Munich'.[105]

Another disciple of List who, according to Goodrich-Clarke, was associated with members of the Thule Society was Rudolf John Gorsleben (1883–1930), who founded the *Edda-Gesellschaft* (Edda Society) in 1925, an Aryan mysticism study group that published the journal *Deutsche Freiheit* (German Freedom), later renamed *Arische Freiheit* (Aryan Freedom). Gorsleben was one of a number of List's followers who, in the years following the First World War, founded his own new religion, described by Goodrich-Clarke as based on 'Social Darwinism and eulogies of the Aryan type', elements which later emerged in strands of Nazi ideology.

Nordic culture, fused with the myth of the Aryan, was an integral component of the Ariosophy movement inspired notably by the work of Austrian occultists and Pan-Germanic nationalists Guido von List and Lanz von Liebenfels. The term Ariosophy, coined by Liebenfels in 1915, described knowledge of the mythical ancient Aryan civilisation and became an important part of his political/religious doctrine during the 1920s. This nationalist strand of the numerous new religions that emerged in Germany and Austria at the end of the nineteenth century fused the National Romantic Movement's appropriation of Old Norse culture and mythology with a developing nationalist and racial agenda out of which early forms of Nordicism began to emerge, promoting the protection and regeneration of the Nordic race. In his analysis of the Ariosophy movement, Goodrick-Clarke describes it as politically marginal but nonetheless influential through a process of the transmission of their cultural and religious beliefs into the field of racial politics by those early Nazi party members whose interests straddled the fields of religion and politics:

> As romantic reactionaries and millenarians, the Ariosophists stood on the margin of practical politics, but their ideas and symbols filtered through to several anti-Semitic and nationalist groups in late Wilhelmian Germany, from which the early Nazi Party emerged in Munich after the First World War.[106]

The progressive appropriation of Nordic mythology by German National Romanticism, as a basis for its reconstruction of the nation's *Vorzeit*, was significant in forming an idealised Pan-Germanic foundation for the later emergence of Nordicism within Nazi ideology. This development and elaboration of a heroic and inspirational foundation myth responded to the need to bring together a fragmented collection of *Länder* into a new modern nation state adapted to the wave of modernity spreading across Europe. In this context, the Romantic Movement, which had initially emerged as a reaction to the secularising and deracinating impact of Enlightenment thought, progressively became the cultural basis of a modern unified German state and, through its fusion with the developing field of racial science, the foundation of the later emergence of Nordicism.

In *The Anti-Enlightenment Tradition* (2010), Zeev Sternhell argues that the rejection of the Enlightenment by the Romantic Movement stemmed from a revolt against rationalist thought that emerged during the late eighteenth century. Sternhell describes this as an alternative modernity, lasting from the second half of the eighteenth century to the age of the Cold War, during which rationalist thought was constantly challenged. Sternhell proposes that by the turn of the twentieth century, 'the cultural victory of rationalism was eliciting a violent response and that a different political culture was emerging'.[107] She further argues that 'at the beginning of the twentieth century, a comprehensive attack upon the essence of the Western rationalist and universalist tradition was coming to maturity'.[108] In her concluding comments, Sternhell assesses the later emergence of Fascism in Europe as 'an extreme expression of the

Anti-Enlightenment tradition' and Nazism as 'a total assault on the human race' through its rejection of universal values and humanism.[109]

Conclusion: National Romanticism as a Foundation for Nordicism

The Nordic cultural revival of the late eighteenth century, which became a significant strand of the National Romantic Movement in Northern Europe and North America, took comparable but progressively divergent paths through the varying states of modernity in these nations. This divergence reveals how early forms of Nordicism, as modern forms of nationalist myth-making, emerged as a response to the distinctly unique conditions and aspirations of certain nations as they adapted to the prevailing forces of modernity. It also reveals the cultural nostalgic core from which Nordicism began to proliferate into its variant forms, fragments of which are still present in today's society.

In Scandinavia, this revival became the inspiration for national regeneration away from established European preconceptions of an uncivilised North and the assertion of the inter-related but distinct cultural and political identities of the individual kingdoms of Norway, Denmark and Sweden. Britain already had an early multicultural sense of its national heritage and had become a driving force of the Age of Industry and Empire. Victorian society transformed the Viking into an expression of the bold, adventurous but noble spirit of the expanding influence and territorial expansion of Britain around the world. In fin-de-siècle Austria, notably in Vienna, the occultist revival drew on a Pan-Germanic political agenda that appropriated Old Norse culture, notably runes and the belief that Nordic culture contained the remnants of Aryan civilisation. It was, however, in Germany and Northern America that the Nordic revival grew into a significant dimension of more radicalised forms of nationalism, rooted in Old Norse culture, as these nations sought to establish suitably adapted foundation myths onto which they could graft the future development of their rapidly developing modern nations. This stimulated the appropriation of Old Norse mythology to form the basis of 'home-grown' national mythologies and a sense of Nordic biological identity, which corresponded to the individual needs of these nations to generate their own sense of nation rootedness and collective spirituality.

In America, increasing levels of immigration from nations around the world, notably from Latin and Eastern countries, together with rapid industrialisation and expansion to the West, threatened the perceived primacy of the Germanic and Nordic settlers of the original thirteen eastern colonies and their claim to be the descendants of the founders of the American nation. This progressively led to the transformation of their sense of Northern European heritage and rootedness into a biological political agenda. In Germany, the search for national unity against the backdrop of rapid industrialisation, social turmoil, religious division and cultural and political rivalry with the French led to the appropriation of Old Norse culture as the foundation of a romanticised *Vorzeit*. This resynthesised past represented the end product of the National Romantic search for the cultural greatness of Germany's past and opened the path to the transformation of this historically orientated cultural movement into a futural political and racial agenda of national identity and racial predominance which was later to be appropriated as a rationale for Nazi racial policies. From its origins as a national cultural phenomenon, its mutation into the murderous modernist ideology of the twentieth century became a reality through its interaction with the concurrently emerging fields of racial science and eugenics, during the late nineteenth century. These scientific and pseudo-scientific fields provided a scientific rationale and eventually the means to transform Nordicist theory into practice.

NOTES

1. Nietzsche, Freidrich (Trans. Kaufmann W. 1967) *The Birth of Tragedy and the Case of Wagner*. Random House, New York p. 135
2. Hutchinson J, Smith Anthony D. (1994) *Nationalism*. Oxford University Press, Oxford p 5.
3. Llobera Josep R. (1994) *The God of Modernity - The Development of Nationalism in Western Europe*. Bloomsbury, London p 172.
4. Roesdahl, Else (1998) *The Vikings*. Penguin Books, London p 292.
5. Ibid. 4 p 370.
6. Jespersen, Knud J.V. (2011) *A History of Denmark*. Palgrave Macmillan, Hampshire (Digital edition) p 570.
7. Jespersen, Knud J.V. *A History of Denmark*. p 2975.
8. Salmon, Patrick (1997) *Scandinavia and the Great Powers*. Cambridge University Press, Cambridge p 22.

9. Arnold, Martin (2011) *Thor – Myth to Marvel*. Continuum Books, London p 77.
10. During this period it was common for French to be spoken in the Danish Royal Court, state officials used German, and the population of rural communities generally used Danish. The subsequent movement during the nineteenth century to generalise the use of Danish was a significant affirmation of Danish national identity.
11. Mallet, Paul Henri (Trans. Percy Thomas et al. 1847) *Northern Antiquities*.
Henry G. Bohn, London p 76.
12. Ibid. 9 p 88.
13. Mallet, Paul Henri, Percy, Thomas et al. *Northern Antiquities*. p 125.
14. Clunies Ross, Margaret, Lönnroth, Lars (1998) 'The Norse Muse' *International Research Project* (9): 3–28. http://userpage.fu-berlin.de/~alvismal/9muse.pdf (Accessed 20/03/13).
15. Ibid. 9 p 91.
16. Ibid. 14 p 16.
17. Ibid. 9 p 103.
18. Ewald, Johannes (Trans. Borrows G. 1889) *The Death of Balder*. Jarrold & Sons, London http://www.gutenberg.org/files/13879/13879-h/13879-h.htm (Accessed 20/07/13).
19. Ibid. 9 p 100.
20. Oehlenschläger, Adam (Trans. Borrow, George) (1913) *The Golden Horns, Act III*. Wise, London http://www.gutenberg.org/files/29124/29124-h/29124-h.htm (Accessed 21/07/13).
21. Oehlenschläger, Adam *Der er et yndigt land (1819)*. My translation.
22. Ibid. 9 p 112.
23. Atterbom, Per Daniel Amadeus poethunter.com http://www.poemhunter.com/per-daniel-amadeus-atterbom/biography/ (Accessed 23/07/13).
24. Ibid. 9 p 110.
25. Elias Lönnrot compiled the *Kalevala*, the national epic of Finland from national folk tales, first published in 1835. *The Kalevala* played an instrumental role in the development of the Finnish national identity and its linguistic breakaway from Swedish.
26. Bjørnson, Bjørnstjerne Martinius (1859) My translation.
27. Kyllingstad, Jon Røyne (2014) *Measuring the Master Race: Physical Anthropology in Norway 1890–1945*. Open Book Publishers, Cambridge p xiv.

28. Kyllingstad, Jon Røyne *Measuring the Master Race.* p 19.
29. Berman, Patricia G. (2013) *In Another Light - Danish Painting in the Nineteenth Century.* Thames and Hudson, London p 17.
30. Wawn, Andrew (2002) *The Vikings and the Victorians; Inventing the Old North in Nineteenth Century Britain.* DS Brewer, Cambridge p 25.
31. Wawn, Andrew *The Vikings and the Victorians.* p 26.
32. Gray, Thomas (ed. Sharpe, J. 1821) *The Descent of Odin - The Poetical Works of Thomas Gray.* G. Cawthorn, London. Google books (Accessed 14/03/13). p 37.
33. Ibid. 9 p 92.
34. Longerich, Peter (2012) *Heinrich Himmler - A life.* Oxford University Press, Oxford p 29.
35. Wawn, Andrew *The Vikings and the Victorians.* p 3.
36. In his work Wawn also provides a detailed account of the linguistic evolution of the term Viking.
37. Ibid. 31 p 4.
38. Bates, Catherine (2010) *The Cambridge Companion to the Epic.* Cambridge University Press, Cambridge p 64.
39. An authoritative analysis of the reception history of *Beowulf* is provided by Shippey Tom A. (1998) *Beowulf: the critical history.* Routledge, London.
40. See Tinker, Chauncey B. (2008) *The Translations of Beowulf - A Critical Biography.* Yale University, Connecticut http://www.gutenberg.org/files/25942/25942-h/25942-h.htm (Accessed 03/03/13).
41. Ibid. 31 p 142.
42. Ibid. 31 p 148.
43. Ibid. 31 p 157 Wawn quotes *The Guardian* and *Saturday Review.*
44. Wawn, Andrew. *The Viking Revival* BBC History On-Line http://www.bbc.co.uk/history/ancient/vikings/revival_01.shtml (Accessed 11/04/13).
45. Ibid. 9 p 127.
46. Ibid. 44.
47. O'Donoghue, Heather (2008) *From Asgard to Valhalla.* I.B.Tauris, London p 131.
48. Delaware, Pennsylvania, New Jersey, Georgia, Connecticut, Massachusetts Bay, Maryland, South Carolina, New Hampshire,

Virginia, New York, North Carolina, and Rhode Island and Providence Plantations.

49. Jefferson, Thomas *The Declaration of Independence* http://www.ushistory.org/declaration/document (Accessed 01/06/13).

50. *'German Immigration to the USA'* http://www.loc.gov/rr/european/ (Accessed 25/03/18).

51. *The Homestead Act.* http://www.ourdocuments.gov/doc.php?flash=true&doc=31 (Accessed 15/06/13).

52. Figures show: 1,000,000 Swedes (1868–1914), 800,000 Norwegians (1825–1925) and 300,000 Danes (1820–1920) *Scandinavian Immigration.* http://ocp.hul.harvard.edu/immigration/scandinavian.html (Accessed 15/06/13).

53. Magnusson, Magnus (1965) (Trans.) *The Vinland Sagas.* Penguin Books, London (Digital edition) p 48.

54. Now identified as Baffin Island, Labrador, Newfoundland and the north-east coastline of the USA.

55. Magnusson, Magnus (Trans.) *The Vinland Sagas.* p 83.

56. Hilen, Andrew (1970) *Longfellow and Scandinavia, A study of the Poet's Relationship with the Northern Languages and Literature.* Archon Books, Hamden, CT p 93.

57. Ibid. 56 p 24.

58. Ibid. 9 p 140.

59. Ibid. 9 p 104.

60. Arnold, M (2013) *Imagining Vinland - George Mackay Brown and the Literature of the New World.* Journal of the North Atlantic, Special volume 4, pp. 199–206.

61. Ibid. 9 p 139.

62. Ibid. 9 p 144.

63. Barnes, Geraldine (2001) *Viking America - The First Millennium.* D.S.Brewer, Cambridge p 137.

64. Ibid. 63 p 135.

65. Hilen, Andrew *Longfellow and Scandinavia.* p 58.

66. Martinsson Örjan, *Population of Germany* https://www.tacitus.nu/historical-atlas/population/germany.htm (Accessed 31/07/13).

67. Griffin, Emma (2010) *Short History of the Industrial Revolution.* Palgrave Macmillan, London p 164.

68. Schnurr, Eva-Maria *The late nineteenth century saw the birth of Berlin.* http://www.spiegel.de/international/germany/the-

late-19th-century-saw-the-birth-of-modern-berlin-a-866321.html (Accessed 31/07/13).

69. Mosse, George L. (1964) *The Crisis of German Ideology - Intellectual origins of the Third Reich.* Howard Fertig, New York p 13.

70. Herder, Johann Gottfried *An die Deutschen* quoted by Oakes, Leigh (2001) *Language and National Identity - Comparing France and Sweden.* John Benjamins, Philadelphia p 22.

71. Ergang, Robert Reinhold (1976) *Herder and the Foundations of German Nationalism.* Octagon Books, New York p 202.

72. Sternhell, Zeev (Trans. Maisel, David) *The Anti-Enlightenment Tradition.* Yale University Press, New Haven & London p 301.

73. Ibid. 72 p 301.

74. Ibid. 72 p 301.

75. Hegel, G.W.F. quoted by Williamson, George S. (2004) *The Longing for Myth in Germany.* Chicago University Press, Chicago p 72.

76. Williamson, George S. (2004) *The Longing for Myth in Germany.* Chicago University Press, Chicago p 73.

77. Ibid. 76 p 76.

78. Ibid. 76 p 76.

79. See Gruener, Gustav. *The Nibelungenlied and Sage in Modern Poetry.* PMLA 11 (2): (1896): pp. 220–257.

80. Schlegel, A.W. Quoted by Williamson George S. *The Longing for Myth in Germany.* p 77.

81. Ibid. 76 p 86.

82. Ibid. 76 p 84.

83. Björnsson, Árni (2003) *Wagner and the Volsungs - Icelandic Sources of Der Ring des Nibelungen.* Viking Society for Northern Research, London p 90.

84. Arvidsson, Stefan (2006) *Aryan Idols - Indo-European Mythology as Ideology and Science.* University of Chicago Press, Chicago p 131.

85. *A Revolution Reconsidered: Mythography and Mythology in the Nineteenth Century.* Shippey, Tom (ed.) *The Shadow-Walkers: Jacob Grimm's Mythology of the Monstrous,* Medieval and Renaissance Texts and Studies Volume 291 (2005) Arizona Center for Medieval and Renaissance Studies, Tempe p 1.

86. Shippey, Tom. *A Revolution Reconsidered.* p 8.

87. Ibid. 9 p 119.

88. Ibid. 85 p 11.

89. Ibid. 9 p 116.

90. Ibid. 9 p 117.
91. Ibid. 76 p 112.
92. http://notesonnotes.org/2013/02/14/wagner-nietzsche-a-gesamtkunstwerk-relationship/
93. Wagner, Richard quoted by Björnsson, Árni *Wagner and the Volsungs - Icelandic Sources of Der Ring des Nibelungen* p 99.
94. Ibid. 9 p 130.
95. Goodrick-Clarke, Nicholas (2009) *The Occult Roots of Nazism.* Tauris Parke, London p 83.
96. Ibid. 95 p 2.
97. ibid. 95 p 51.
98. Mosse, George L. (1964) *The Crisis of German Ideology - Intellectual origins of the Third Reich.* Howard Fertig, New York p 14.
99. Mosse, George L *The Crisis of German ideology.* p 13.
100. Ibid. 95 p 51.
101. Ibid. 95 p 95.
102. Ibid. 95 p 51.
103. Ibid. 95 p 129.
104. Ibid. 95 p 129.
105. Kershaw, Ian (2000) *Hitler 1889–1936: Hubris.* Penguin Books, London pp. 138–139.
106. Ibid. 95 p 5.
107. Sternhell, Zeev (Trans. David Maisel) *The Anti-Enlightenment Tradition.* Yale University Press, New Haven & London p 1.
108. Ibid. 107 p 441.
109. Ibid. 107 p 441.

BIBLIOGRAPHY

PRINTED WORKS

Arnold, M. (2013). Imagining Vínland - George Mackay Brown and the Literature of the New World. *Journal of the North Atlantic*, Special Volume 4.

Arnold, M. (2011). *Thor – Myth to Marvel.* London: Continuum Books.

Arvidsson, S. (2006). *Aryan Idols - Indo-European Mythology as Ideology and Science.* Chicago: University of Chicago Press.

Bates, C. (2010). *The Cambridge Companion to the Epic*. Cambridge: Cambridge University Press.

Berman, P. G. (2013). *In Another Light - Danish Painting in the Nineteenth Century*. London: Thames and Hudson.

Björnsson, Á. (2003). *Wagner and the Volsungs - Icelandic Sources of Der Ring Des Nibelungen*. London: Viking Society for Northern Research.

Ergang, R. R. (1976). *Herder and the Foundations of German Nationalism*. New York: Octagon Books.

Goodrick-Clarke, N. (2009). *The Occult Roots of Nazism*. London: Tauris Parke.

Gray, T. (1821). *The Descent of Odin - The Poetical Works of Thomas Gray*. London: John Sharpe.

Griffin, E. (2010). *Short History of the Industrial Revolution*. London: Palgrave Macmillan.

Herder, J. G. (2001). An Die Deutschen Quoted by Oakes, L. *Language and National Identity - Comparing France and Sweden*. Philadelphia: John Benjamins.

Hilen, A. (1970). *Longfellow and Scandinavia, A Study of the Poet's Relationship with the Northern Languages and Literature*. Hamden, CT: Archon Books.

Hutchinson, J., & Smith, A. D. (1994). *Nationalism*. Oxford: Oxford University Press.

Jespersen, K. J. V. (2011). *A History of Denmark*. Hampshire: Palgrave Macmillan.

Kershaw, I. (2000). *Hitler 1889–1936: Hubris*. London: Penguin Books.

Kyllingstad, J. R. (2014). *Measuring the Master Race: Physical Anthropology in Norway 1890–1945*. Cambridge: Open Book Publishers.

Llobera, J. R. (1994). *The God of Modernity - The Development of Nationalism in Western Europe*. London: Bloomsbury.

Longerich, P. (2012). *Heinrich Himmler - A Life*. Oxford: Oxford University Press.

Longfellow, H. W. (1864). *The Challenge of Thor - Tales of a Wayside Inn*. Boston: Ticknor and Fields.

Macpherson, J. (1801). *The Poems of Ossian*. Vienna: R. Sammler.

Magnusson, M. (1965). (Trans.) *The Vinland Sagas*. London: Penguin Books.

Mallet, P. H. (1847). (Trans. Percy, T., et al.) *Northern Antiquities*. Henry G. London: Bohn.

Mosse, G. L. (1964). *The Crisis of German Ideology - Intellectual Origins of the Third Reich*. New York: Howard Fertig.

Nietzsche, F. (1967). (Trans. Kaufmann, W.) *The Birth of Tragedy and the Case of Wagner*. New York: Random House.

O'Donoghue, H. (2008). *From Asgard to Valhalla*. London: I.B. Tauris.

Pois, R. (1986). *National Socialism and the Religion of Nature*. London: Croom Helm.

Salmon, P. (1997). *Scandinavia and the Great Powers*. Cambridge: Cambridge University Press.

Shippey, T. A. (1998). *Beowulf: The Critical History.* London: Routledge.
Shippey, T. A. (2005). *A Revolution Reconsidered: Mythography and Mythology in the Nineteenth Century. The Shadow-Walkers: Jacob Grimm's Mythology of the Monstrous. Medieval and Renaissance Texts and Studies* (Vol. 291). Tempe: Arizona Center for Medieval and Renaissance Studies.
Sternhell, Z. (Trans. Maisel, D.) *The Anti-Enlightenment Tradition.* New Haven: Yale University Press.
Tinker, C. B. (2008a). *The Translations of Beowulf - A Critical Biography.* Connecticut: Yale University.
Wawn, A. (2002). *The Vikings and the Victorians; Inventing the Old North in Nineteenth Century Britain.* Cambridge: D.S. Brewer.
Von List, G. (1988) (Stephen E. Flowers ed.) *The Secret of the Runes.* Vermont: Destiny Books.
Williamson, G. S. (2004). *The Longing for Myth in Germany.* Chicago: Chicago University Press.

WEBSITES AND DIGITAL PUBLICATIONS (WITH DATE ACCESSED)

Clunies Ross, M., & Lönnroth, L. (1998). The Norse Muse. *International Research Project* (9), 3–28. Accessed 20/03/13, from http://userpage.fu-berlin.de/~alvismal/9muse.pdf
Ewald, J. (1889). (Trans. Borrows, G.) *The Death of Balder.* London: Jarrold & Sons. Accessed 20/07/13, from http://www.gutenberg.org/files/13879/13879-h/13879-h.htm
German Immigration to the USA, Library of Congress Online Accessed 25/03/18, from http://www.loc.gov/rr/european/
Longfellow, H. W. *The Skeleton in Armor.* University of Pittsburgh. Accessed 22/06/13, from http://www.pitt.edu/~dash/longfellow.html#skeleton
Martinsson, Ö. *Population of Scandinavia.* Accessed 31/07/13, from http://www.tacitus.nu/historical-atlas/population/scandinavia.htm
National Anthem Lyrics - Ja, Vi Elsker Dette Landet. Accessed 24/07/13, from https://www.lyricsondemand.com/n/nationalanthemlyrics/norwaynation-alanthemlyrics.html
Oehlenschläger, A. (1913). (Trans. Borrow, G.). *The Golden Horns, Act III.* London: Wise. http://www.gutenberg.org/files/29124/29124-h/29124-h.htm
Oehlenschläger, A. *Der er et Yndigt Land* (1819). *Not One But Two National Anthems.* Denmark.dk. Accessed 23/07/13, from http://denmark.dk/en/quick-facts/national-anthems/
Per Daniel Amadeus Atterbom. Accessed 23/07/13, from http://www.poem-hunter.com/per-daniel-amadeus-atterbom/biography/

Scandinavian Immigration. Harvard University Library Open Collections. Accessed 15/06/13, from http://ocp.hul.harvard.edu/immigration/scandinavian.html

Schnurr, E-M. *The Late Nineteenth Century Saw the Birth of Berlin.* Accessed 31/07/13, from http://www.spiegel.de/international/germany/the-late-19th-century-saw-the-birth-of-modern-berlin-a-866321.html

Jefferson, T. *The American Declaration of Independence.* Accessed 01/06/13, from http://www.ushistory.org/declaration/document

The Homestead Act. Accessed 15/06/13, from http://www.ourdocuments.gov/doc.php?flash=true&doc=31

Tinker, C. B. (2008b) *The Translations of Beowulf - A Critical Biography.* Yale University, Connecticut. http://www.gutenberg.org/files/25942/25942-h/25942-h.htm (Accessed 03/03/13).

Wawn, A. *The Viking Revival.* Accessed 11/04/13, from http://www.bbc.co.uk/history/ancient/vikings/revival_01.shtml

CHAPTER 3

Regeneration: Racial Science, Eugenics and the Emergence of Nordicism

Descending from his ten-year retreat in a mountain cave, Nietzsche's prophet Zarathustra arrived in a nearby town to announce, to a largely indifferent crowd gathered in the market place, that God was dead. The true meaning of life on earth now lay in humanity's mission to surpass his current state to evolve into a spiritually higher level of humanity, the Superman.[1] Nietzsche had already announced his belief in the death of the Christian God both as a real, living entity and as a meaningful myth in his 1882 work, *Die fröhliche Wissenschaft* (The Gay Science). It was, however, through the testimony of Zarathustra that he proposed his philosophy of man as 'a rope stretched between the animal and the Superman—a rope over an abyss' as Zarathustra announced:[2]

> The Superman is the meaning of the earth. Let your will say: The Superman shall be the meaning of the earth! (…) Once blasphemy against God was the greatest blasphemy; but God died, and therewith also the blasphemers. To blaspheme the earth is now the dreadfulest sin, and to rate the heart of the unknowable higher than the meaning of the earth![3]

Without God and the constraints of the Christian creationist belief system, modern man was free to perceive his condition as a developmental phase through which mankind could aspire to reach an ultimate stage of human development, that of a supreme being 'beyond man'. The rationalist project of scientific enquiry, initiated by the Enlightenment phase of early modernity, had progressively challenged and eroded the role of God

© The Author(s) 2020
G. E. Forssling, *Nordicism and Modernity*,
https://doi.org/10.1007/978-3-030-61210-8_3

as the omniscient, omnipotent creator of all in the cosmos. By the end of the nineteenth century, Nietzsche attempted to make mankind aware of his transitory state in nature and, through this awakening, strive for greater heights of existence. Nietzsche was arguably anticipating the academic and popular response to his modernist vision through his description of the indifferent reaction of the market place to Zarathustra's prophecy but was, nevertheless, announcing both the emergence of a new deracinating, nihilistic phase of modernity and the solution, in a new vitalistic form of ethics and attitude to life. This period was to present an increasingly god-less society with the challenge of defining a renewed sense of purpose and meaning to its existence, that of understanding its own creation and potential to control its evolution and destiny through transcending the present liminal phase of history and bringing about the inauguration of a new, heroic *nomos*.

Against the countervailing, 'culture-regenerating' background of the Nordic revival of the late eighteenth century, this chapter will examine how Nordicism emerged from the fusion of this cultural and later political movement with the concurrently developing field of racial science to offer an alternative, purportedly more rational and empirically grounded *nomos* to the Nietzschean 'higher self'. It will then examine its relationship with the developing eugenics movement through which nations sought to improve and perfect the human race by encouraging the reproduction of 'valuable' human types whilst purging it of elements that they considered degenerate and detrimental to the future development of mankind. It will also consider the complex relationship between Nordicism and modernity as some Northern Europeans sought to regenerate the mythical purity of their historical racial origins as a response to what they perceived to be the modern era's neglect of superior races, a modernist reaction expressing a man's need to establish new forms of meaning and purpose to his existence.

THE GENESIS QUESTION: THE WORD OF GOD AND HUMAN DIVERSITY

It was through the developing scientific fields of philology and anthropology that early Enlightenment thinkers sought to align the word of the Bible with the evident diversity of human beings which had, throughout history, been the source of conflict, segregation and domination of one people over another. According to the word of the Old Testament, God had created mankind in his own image to rule over the world, and early scientific thought attempted to investigate and explain how humans could be so diverse whilst remaining, according to the biblical paradigm, an image of God. European culture had progressively established the figure of Adam as a white European, an image epitomised by Michelangelo's iconic representation of the birth of mankind in *The Creation of Adam* on the ceiling of the Sistine Chapel in 1501. From this vital and fundamental question emerged two fields of thought: monogenism and polygenism. These two schools of academic thought drew on anatomical observations, early philology and biblical sources to determine how man had evolved and become diversified.

Monogenists drew largely on the creation myths of the Abrahamic religions of Judaism, Christianity and Islam to propose the theory of a single, common point of human creation and the subsequent metamorphosis of this original human type through a process of geographical dispersal into a range of formative climactic conditions. This biblical model was supported by early academics such as Robert Morton (1627–1691), Robert Boyle (1627–1691), John Mitchell (1711–1768), author of *An Essay upon the Causes of the Different Colours of People in Different Climates*, and J.A.L. Montriou. In his 1787 work, *Elements of Universal History*, Montriou described the linguistic division and subsequent geographical dispersal of Adam and Eve's descendants into geographically and hence racially developmental zones:

> Noah's descendants multiplied greatly, and attempted to build the stupendous tower of Babel as a monument of their power, and a safe retreat in case of any new inundation, 2247 BC. God punished their presumption by producing diverse languages amongst them: they spoke, yet they no longer understood each other; whereupon they parted, and dispersed over the whole earth: Japhet settled in Europe, Shem in Asia, and Ham in Africa, about 2287 BC.[4]

This monogenist interpretation of creation and the subsequent linguistic dispersal of the original human race was popular amongst those who attempted to defend the teachings of the Church against the eroding forces of early modernity.

Polygenists posited the theory that instead of originating from a single source, that of Adam, mankind originated from a range of geographical origins that had determined, through a process of adaptation to varying climactic conditions, the diversity of human races. This theory marked for many a significant point of departure from the acceptance of Abrahamic and particularly Christian doctrine as an unquestionable literal source of knowledge and understanding of the human condition. Initially criticised by many, notably the Catholic Church, as a form of heresy, polygenism threatened deep-rooted creationist beliefs of Christian society. In response to this growing division between the field of science and the word of God, many Christian scientists adopted 'natural theology' as a belief system based on observation and physical evidence that reconciled their personal Christian beliefs with the emerging contradictions between science and the word of the Bible.

Taxonomy: Measuring and Classifying a Race

Alongside this on-going debate over the origins of human diversity, the emerging scientific field of taxonomy sought to establish an empirical basis on which these differences in mankind could be identified, compared and potentially explained. During the eighteenth century, the work of Swedish physician, botanist and zoologist Carl Linnaeus (1707–1778) was fundamental to the development of racial science. He created an analytical framework for studying the variety of life on the planet and their complex interrelationships, research that was to form the basis of modern taxonomy, the science of classifying and naming biological organisms according to shared characteristics. His research into biological classification was to become the core of his major works, *Systema Naturae* (1735) and *Species Plantarum* (1753). In these works, Linnaeus developed a standardised binomial order (using one name for genus and a second for species) for animal and plant species. This system formally categorised plant and animal life on the planet for the first time. A Christian monogenist, Linnaeus believed in the biblical paradigm of a single source for mankind and was an early supporter of the theory that geography played a vital role in racial determination. He also initially believed in the 'fixity of species', the theory that God had created the animal world in its existing form and that '*Unitas in omni specie ordinem ducit*' (the invariability of species is the condition for order).[5] He later revised these beliefs, however, as he saw evidence of plant hybridisation.[6] In his work, Linnaeus controversially linked mankind to the animal world and divided humans into five human taxa or races based mainly on variations in skin colour and what he perceived as behavioural characteristics, a system of classification which was to have a significant influence on the development of racial science and later forms of racist ideology, such as Nordicism.[7] Linnaeus used skin colour and geographical origin to determine and classify human *taxa*. He also applied descriptors to each race that were to become a prominent feature of later works on racial science. Linnaeus described the *Asiaticus* as 'yellow-skinned, avaricious, and easily distracted', whereas the *Africanus* were 'black-skinned, relaxed, and of negligent character' and the *Europeanus* were 'white-skinned, of gentle character, inventive mind, and bellicose'.[8]

Linnaeus' racial descriptors placed the *Europeanus albus*, the white European, at the apex of the human species with superior intellect, beauty and leadership qualities. This provided, for those involved, a scientific rationale for colonialism and the flourishing slave trade of the period. Linnaeus believed that God had created the world in a divine order with mankind at the apex and his purpose in creating his taxonomical system was arguably as much a religious as scientific. In his preface to a later edition of *Systema Naturae*, Linnaeus stated that '*Creationis telluris est gloria Dei ex opere Naturae per Hominem solum*' (The purpose of Creation is the glory of God, as can be seen from the works in nature by man alone).[9] Linnaeus believed that God had created a biological order in nature and that it was the role of the naturalist to discover and reveal this act of divine creation.

Another significant contribution to racial science was the research of Swedish professor of anatomy, anthropologist and polygenist Anders Retzius (1796–1860) who is credited with the development of the cephalic index. This system measured the dimensions of the heads of mammals to establish a means of categorising the diversity of animal species. The cephalic system divided humanity into dolichocephalic (long headed), mesaticephalic (moderate headed) or brachycephalic (short headed). This system, which is still used in modern medicine and particularly in the field of animal breeding, provided another scientific means for naturalists and anthropologists, of recording and analysing the variations in human anatomy. This system was later used by racial prehistorians to determine the physical characteristics and development of racial diversity and complimented the field of philology by establishing a scientific means of identifying and linking the origins of the Aryan and Nordic races with their modern descendants. Retzius' system of racial classification was highly influential and shaped racial thought throughout the late nineteenth and early twentieth centuries. The work of American racial theorists William Z. Ripley (1867–1941) and Madison Grant (1865–1937) was based on the cephalic index, and later Nazi scientists adopted this system to determine racial origins and various degrees of Nordic racial purity. Retzius' theory proposed that the measurements of the skull from different races indicated different levels of cerebral development, which in turn could be used to establish the intellectual superiority of certain races over others. In *Measuring the Master Race* (2015), Jon Røyne discusses how Retzius linked behavioural and social attributes to measurable physical features that he had categorised as racial indicators. Røyne concludes that according to Retzius:

> It was a 'universally acknowledged fact' that Celtic and Germanic peoples possess the strongest intellectual facilities. This corresponded to their low, narrow and long skulls, with their strongly protruding occipital, and was in contrast to the inferior Slavs and Lapps with their broad skulls and weakly developed occiput [...] Short-skulled peoples had more primitive brains and more primitive cultures than long-skulled peoples.[10]

Through his analysis, Retzius laid a significant foundation on which future linguists and anthropologists developed their theories on the racial superiority of the Nordic/Germanic race and the theories of subsequent Nordicists who perceived that the greatness of their prehistoric superiority needed protection and regeneration.

One of the most significant scientific breakthroughs that impacted on the developing field of the science of race, largely through its appropriation and distortion to align with racial and nationalist agendas during the early nineteenth century, was the research of evolutionists, notably that of Charles Darwin (1809–1882). Theories concerning the evolution and transmutation of species, and in particular mankind, were gathering pace amongst academics during the eighteenth century. This became a significant strand of enquiry emerging from the debate between traditionalist monogenists and the increasing number polygenists, who argued that the diversity of the human race was a result of adaptation over time to a range of formative geological locations and climatic conditions which had produced differing physical and behavioural characteristics. These theories of evolution had, however, never been fully explored due not only to a lack of evidence and scientific methodology but also to the fact that they contradicted the established creationist doctrine of Christianity. Notable amongst these early thinkers was French naturalist and taxonomist Jean-Baptiste Lamarck (1744–1829), who posited the theory that later became termed *Lamarckism* in his work *Philosophie zoologique* (1809). In this work, Lamarck established what he considered to be two principal laws of nature: firstly, that environmental changes affect the biological functions of an animal anatomy and hence their size and, secondly, that these characteristics were inheritable producing a continuous and gradual evolutionary process.[11]

The Evolution of the Races: The Impact of Darwinism

Darwin's publication of *On the Origin of Species* (1859) in which he first proposed his theory of evolution through the process of natural selection and *The Descent of Man* (1871), which applied this theory to humankind, were both seminal works that collectively had an immense impact on man's perception of his place within nature. Darwin's work scientifically established that all species had evolved and that *Homo sapiens* had not been created in its current form but had developed from primates. Before its publication, Darwin was aware that his work would cause considerable academic and public controversy. In a frequently quoted letter to J.D. Hooker of 11 January 1844, he discussed the potential impact of his work:

> I have read heaps of agricultural and horticultural books, and have never ceased collecting facts – at last gleams of light have come, and I am almost convinced (quite contrary to the opinion I started with) that species are not (it is like confessing a murder) immutable. [...] I think I have found out (here's presumption!) the simple way by which species become exquisitely adapted to various ends.[12]

Darwin was aware that the publication of his evolutionary theory would constitute a significant erosion of the word of the Bible. The naturalist's inner conflict, between his personal Christian beliefs and the evidence of evolution that was confronting him, is expressed in his feelings of 'confessing a murder'. Darwin's empirically grounded research was hugely influential and effectively repositioned humankind in relation to the cosmos established by Old Testament doctrine, which had for centuries provided the core nomos of Christian society. Darwin's work arguably contributed significantly to the part played by natural science in what Nietzsche described later in the century as the 'death of God'.

Although Darwin alluded to the possible application of his work to *Homo sapiens* in this work, it was not until the publication of *The Descent of Man* in 1871 that he took the step of applying his developing theories to humans and the nature of different races. In this work, Darwin asserted that differing races shared a common ancestry and that the differences between people of varying geographical origin should be considered part of a continuum of human variation rather than separate races or species.[13] Through his work, Darwin scientifically established natural laws, those of natural selection, or the 'survival of the fittest' as it came to be termed.[14] This process of evolution, favouring the strongest, was appropriated and distorted by later academics and nationalists to support, legitimise and promote their claims of Northern European and Nordic supremacy. Darwin's research also had a significant impact on the emergence of the eugenics movement, as certain scientists sought to apply Darwinian evolutionary principles to the improvement of mankind and later to the refinement and protection of the superiority of the Northern European, Nordic/Germanic race.

From Genesis to Racial Science

As a lasting consequence of the Darwinian revolution, the debate between monogenists and polygenists, and later between creationists and evolutionists, defined modernity's challenge to the traditions and teachings of established religion and is still active today.[15] Although many academics within this debate did not intend to contribute to nationalist claims of European racial superiority, the field of science provided nonetheless empirical evidence to support developing racial theories. This modernist project of establishing the origins of man contributed to the progressive erosion of traditional Christian beliefs consolidating a new era of rationalism. This mood was expressed by popular American historian Charles Morris who, at the turn of the century, criticised the impact of what he described as the academic obstacle of the man-made narrative of Genesis in *Man and his Ancestor—A study in Evolution* (1900):

> It might have been better for civilized mankind if the opening pages of Genesis had never been written, since they have played a potent part in checking the development of thought. As the case now stands, the cosmological doctrines they contain can no longer claim even a shadow of divine authority, since they have distinctly traced back to a human origin.[16]

By the end of the nineteenth century, modern science had liberated many influential thinkers from the academic constrictions of creationism, placing man within nature, establishing that humans could be classified into different racial types and could potentially take control of their biological destiny. This process, however, also negated the creation myth of the Bible, a sense of origin that had provided Western society with a sense of identity and destiny. The process of natural selection, based on scientific rationalism and empiricism, was replacing the established creation narrative, based on scripture and revelation. This was part of the process whereby modernity's thirst for material progress and knowledge progressively secularised society, causing a sense of deracination from time-honoured traditions and perceptions of the cosmos. Entwined with the development of the cultural and political movement of European National Romanticism, the field of racial science provided a significant source of legitimation in support of emerging racial theories of Aryan and Northern European primacy.

The Aryan and the Nordic

Alongside the rapidly developing fields of biology, taxonomy, anthropology, history and archaeology, the field of philology became a significant element in the later development of Nordicism through its thesis of a once superior Aryan race. The concept of the Aryan race and its relationship with Europe has generally been credited to orientalist and philologist Sir William Jones (1746–1794). In an address for the Third Anniversary Discourse to the Asiatic Society of 2 February 1786, Jones put forward his theory of a linguistic and therefore historic relationship between the ancient Indian Sanskrit and European languages:

> The Sanskrit language, whatever be its antiquity, is of a wonderful structure; more perfect than the Greek, more copious than the Latin, and more exquisitely refined than either, yet bearing to both of them a stronger affinity, both in the roots of verbs and in the forms of grammar, than could possibly have been produced by accident; so strong indeed, that no philologer could examine them all three, without believing them to have sprung from some common source, which, perhaps, no longer exists: there is a similar reason, though not quite so forcible, for supposing that both the Gothic and the Celtic, though blended with a very different idiom, had the same origin with the Sanskrit.[17]

In this speech, Jones expressed his belief in a common source of European languages being the language of the once highly civilised ancient Aryan people. This seminal speech had a significant impact on the debate concerning the origins and subsequent dispersal of Adam's offspring. Although Jones initially made only a somewhat slender connection between the Aryan and the Northern European peoples, he had, nonetheless, opened up a debate that was to be incorporated, during the nineteenth century, into the nationalist agendas of a number of European states. From this, Nordicism evolved as a claim of Northern European supremacy notably in Germany and the USA.

In his authoritative work, *Race and the Third Reich* (2005), Christopher M. Hutton examines the origins and development of the racial dynamics of Nazism and Nordicism and their relationship with modernity. In his analysis, he discusses the significance of Jones' application of the biblical paradigm of Noah's descendants and the Tower of Babel:

> Applying the biblical model, Jones in identifying a linguistic connection between European languages and Sanskrit, had also suggested a historical affinity between the speakers of those languages. This statement, canonized in the context of a rising comparative and historical science of language, posed a profound set of questions for European intellectuals, concerning the nature of linguistic affinity and the original homeland of the Aryan people. The debate about the Aryans became a debate about the original locus and essence of the Europeans, and their relation to other peoples and territories.[18]

According to the narrative of *Genesis*, Noah's descendants who all spoke a common tongue were given different languages by God as a punishment for their attempt to reach heaven with a tower and subsequently dispersed to live in different lands. Japheth and his descendants were sent to 'the isles of the Gentiles divided in their lands; every one after his tongue, after their families, in their nations'.[19] According to the interpretation of Catholic scholars, Japheth's group travelled and settled in prehistoric Asia and Europe founding both an early form of Indo-European language and what became defined by academics, such as Jones, as the Aryan race. In this academic context, Japhet became the original Aryan, and the term 'Japhetic' was used during the late eighteenth and early nineteenth centuries to describe languages belonging to the Indo-European linguistic group as it came to be defined.[20]

The emerging field of philology attempted to resolve the question of race through the process of comparative linguistics associating the concept of race with language. This causal link was, however, progressively contested by the field of racial anthropology, which posited physical and behavioural characteristics as indicators of race. This engendered an enduring debate amongst scholars of the period as to the most appropriate indicator of race. In his work, Hutton discusses this debate, concluding that despite scholars accepting the distinction between racial and linguistic identities, 'the assumption was generally made that, at the point of origin, racial and linguistic identity had been congruent'.[21]

A founding figure of the emerging field of comparative philology was Jacob Grimm whose influential works *Deutsche Grammatik* (1819) and *Deutsche Mythologie* (1835) had a significant impact on the question of language and race. Grimm proposed that, through the study of rural Germanic folklore, commonalities between Northern European texts and classical Latin and Greek could be historically linked, at their source, to the Eastern language of the once noble Aryan. This theory was fundamental to later scholars who argued, for both political and cultural reasons, that the original dispersal point of Aryan civilisation in Europe was Northern Germany. Grimm, whose mission was arguably as political as it was scholarly, put forward the hypothesis that the field of philology provided scientific proof of the once-prominent role of Germanic culture in a pagan Europe predating the spread of the foreign belief system of Christianity.

In *A Revolution Reconsidered: Mythography and Mythology*, Tom Shippey compares the impact of Grimm's work on the humanities with that of Charles Darwin in the life sciences. He notes that both researchers based their theories on a mass of recorded observations and provided theoretical models (comparative and evolutionary), which were hugely influential in their fields, and whose work was later appropriated by subsequent scholars into the field of racial science. He also observes how both theories challenged the established biblical paradigm of creation and human dispersal, which no longer provided a scientifically plausible response. In his analysis, Shippey concludes:

> With Darwin, why were animal species different? And what did the fossils of strange creatures prove? To this the only answer before him had been the story of Noah's ark. With Grimm, the questions were, why did people speak

different languages, and why did languages change? To which the answer, equally unsatisfactory, was the story of the tower of Babel [...].[22]

The development of what came to be termed 'Grimm's law', mapping fundamental phonetic changes in the transition from Sanskrit to Germanic word formation, was fundamental in providing a methodology with which to analyse and discover the ancient origins of the German language and therefore the lost prehistoric national roots of the Germanic *Volk*. This principle became fundamental to later thinkers seeking to centre the dispersal point of Aryan culture in Germany and therefore claim the historic primacy of the Germanic people.

A notable synthesis of the competing fields of racial enquiry was attempted by French aristocrat, writer and racial theorist Joseph Arthur Comte de Gobineau (1816–1882). His *Essai sur l'inégalité des races humaines* (Essay on the Inequality of the Human Races), published between 1853 and 1855, had a significant impact, both in academic and popular circles, on the interpretation of the term Aryan and the study of the perceived physical, intellectual and moral differences between races. Writing in the historical context of the revolution of 1848 and his defence of the *Ancien Régime* against republican beliefs and drawing on the fields of religion, history, anthropology and linguistics, Gobineau developed his own thesis. In his work, he argued that racial differences were permanent stating that: 'Adam is the ancestor of the white race. The scriptures are evidently meant to be so understood, for the generations deriving from him are certainly white'.[23] From this racial interpretation of the biblical paradigm, Gobineau argued that the question of racial differences was a fundamental component of the dynamics of history. Dividing humanity initially into three major groupings of white, yellow and black, Gobineau placed the ancient Aryan race at the apex of the superior white race arguing that 'there is no true civilisation, among the European peoples, where the Aryan branch is not predominant'.[24]

MISCEGENATION: THE RACIAL CRISIS OF ARYANISM

Central to Gobineau's thesis of the decline of civilisations was the concept of interbreeding or miscegenation between the races, described in the original language of his work as *dégénération* (the loss or corruption of the genus), a process that had eroded the superior qualities of Northern Europe's social and biological elite. In his *Essai sur l'inégalité des races humaines,* Gobineau described this process whereby the noble, heroic attributes of superior races were being diluted by interbreeding:

> The word degenerate, when applied to a people (as it ought to mean) that the people have no longer the same blood in its veins, continual adulterations having gradually affected the quality of that blood. In other words, though the nation bears the name given by its founders, the name no longer connotes the same race; in fact, the man of a decadent time, the degenerate man properly so called, is a different being, from the racial point of view, from the heroes of the great ages.[25]

Gobineau perceived the nineteenth century, and particularly the renewed period of social upheaval following the 1848 revolution, as a decadent time during which the pure Aryan race was becoming adulterated beyond the point of recognition and comparison with its pure-blooded founders, the sons of Noah. In this context Gobineau further argued that although interbreeding improved certain races, it was always to the detriment of the superior people:

> It would be unjust to assert that every mixture is bad and harmful. If the three great types had remained strictly separate, the supremacy would no doubt have always been in the hands of the finest of the white races, and the yellow and black varieties would have crawled for ever at the feet of the lowest of the whites.[26]

Within his thesis of white European supremacy in which he presented his theories on the historic dispersal of the Aryan race, Gobineau established a significant link between the Aryan and Germanic people that was to have an impact on the later development of Nordicism. In his work, Gobineau described how ancient Germanic tribes had progressively regenerated vital elements of the Aryan race to create a superior European civilisation. Concluding that where 'the Germanic element has never penetrated, our special kind of civilisation does not exist', Gobineau had sown the seeds of what later thinkers were to consider the scientific legitimation for their claims of Pan-Germanic racial superiority.[27] Following its publication in France between 1853 and 1855, Gobineau's work was translated into English by Henry Hotze in 1856 as *The Moral and Intellectual Diversity of Races* and into German as *Versuch über die Ungleichheit der Menschenrassen* by racial theorist Ludwig Schemann in 1897. Through these publications, Gobineau's work arguably had a considerable influence on a number of contemporary and later racial theorists in Europe and America who built on his theories.

In his analysis of the development and impact of Gobineau's life and works in *Father of Racist Ideology* (1970), Michael D. Biddiss describes Gobineau as part of a number of extremist Northern European thinkers who felt increasingly alienated from the European civilisation that they considered to be in irreversible decline:

> In common with many extremist thinkers, Gobineau reveals the symptoms of alienation and cultural despair frequently encountered among those whose status is devalued by social and economic change [...] Gobineau strove, in a society that progressively refused recognition to himself and his caste, for self-legitimation by stressing that it was not he but the bulk of his contemporaries who were de-based.[28]

Gobineau viewed the French Revolutions as the destruction of the ruling aristocratic, Aryan elite by inferior social and racial classes. In his view, the revolutionary slogan of *Liberté, Égalité, Fraternité* represented the social, spiritual and biological overthrow of the *Ancien Régime* that had ordered society, providing it with its sense of hierarchical structure and meaning. This growing sense of social crisis, alienation and *anomie*, prompted thinkers, such as Gobineau, to look back nostalgically to the past in order to reconstruct and legitimise a mythologised 'Golden Age' of the Northern European race's once-noble origins that were becoming eroded and diluted. Although Gobineau did not propose any eugenics programme, his work was arguably influential on later racial thought and theories of racial cleansing. In his assessment of the impact of Gobineau's work, Biddiss concludes that 'the implications of depersonalisation and dehumanisation, eventually actualised in the concentration camps' were already present in the social and racial observations and theories of Gobineau.[29]

Locating the Homeland of the Aryan in the North

The myth of the Aryan race had considerable resonance across a Northern European intelligentsia that reacted to the 'seismic' events of the French Revolution and its subsequent 'after-shocks' across Europe. These thinkers fused the emerging cultural and political movement of National Romanticism with the developing field of racial science, to establish evidence to support the myth of a prehistoric racial Utopia of the Aryan. Within the active debates surrounding the concept of the Aryan race, which flourished during the late nineteenth century, emerged the important question of the original prehistoric homeland of the Aryan tribe. This point became actively contested between academics who proposed a range of different points of origin for the Aryan race according to the evidence emerging from their respective fields of linguistics, anthropology and archaeology and notably their own nationalist agendas. The impact of this debate was to become, in later years, central to the association of the Aryan and the Nordic and hence to the subsequent emergence of Nordicism as a cultural, political and scientific phenomenon.

Between 1859 and 1863, Swiss linguist Adolphe Pictet (1799–1875), published his major work *Les Origines Indo-Européenes ou les Aryans primitifs: Essai de paléontologie lingistique*, in which he drew on aspects of comparative linguistics to establish historical cultural links, a method he termed 'linguistic palaeontology'.[30] Through this method, he attempted to establish proof for his belief that the homeland of the Aryan was to be found on the Asian continent.[31] Although Pictet's thesis aligned broadly with current thought, many of his conclusions remained contested as a plethora of alternative sites were proposed by the increasing number of academics who became drawn into this contentious question.

In 1878, German American anthropologist and author Theodor Pösche (1824–1899) proposed a Northern European homeland that provoked further debate. Drawing on evidence from the fields of history and physical anthropology, he published in 1878, *Die Arier, ein Beitrag zur historischen Anthropologie* (The Aryans, a Contribution to Historical Anthropology), in which he argued the case for supremacy of a blond, fair-skinned, blue-eyed race centred in the Baltic region.[32] Pösche argued that, throughout history, there was evidence of cultural domination by an Aryan race, whose current physical characteristics were most densely clustered in this region. From this area, the peoples later migrated south towards more temperate climates in Southern Europe.[33] This theory constituted a significant shift in the perceived homeland of the original Aryan tribe and provoked a debate that would continue until the end of the Second World War.

Engaging with this debate, the contribution of Austrian philologist and anthropologist Karl Penka (1847–1912) was to have a considerable impact on the later conceptual fusion of the Aryan, the Germanic and the Nordic. In his publications *Origenes Aricae* (Origins of the Aryans) of 1883 and

Die Herkunft der Arier (The Descent of the Aryans) of 1886, Penka drew on the field of linguistics, archaeology and anthropology to posit the theory that Pösche had inaccurately centred the blond Aryan race in the Baltic. Penka claimed that the true centre of the distribution of the blond race lay in Scandinavia.

Penka's theories met with a mixed reaction, such as that of philologist Max Müller (1823–1900) who argued that Aryan was a linguistic term and should not be applied to race and linguistic palaeontologist Henri d'Arbois de Jubainville (1827–1910) who rejected his evidence and maintained that Asia should be considered the original Aryan homeland. Another critic of the conclusions of both Pösche and Penka was English philologist, toponymist and Anglican canon of York Isaac Taylor (1828–1901). In his work, *The Origin of the Aryans* (1890), he examined the on-going debate concerning the original homeland of the Aryans and suggested that the terrain of Scandinavia made it an unlikely homeland of the Aryan tribe, which he suggested had originated in the Russian continent:

> Penka has undoubtedly weakened his argument by the unnecessary contention that Scandinavia was the cradle of the whole Aryan race. It is difficult to believe that such a sufficiently extensive area for the growth of such a numerous people can be found in the forest-clad valleys of Norway and Sweden, which moreover are unadapted for the habitation of a nomad pastoral people, such as the primitive Aryans must have been.[34]

Others enthusiastically supported Penka's theories such as Gerald H. Rendall, who promoted Penka's theories amongst a popular British and American readership. In his presentation of the Austrian's work in *Cradle of the Aryans*, published in 1889, he described the physical superiority of the Nordic race, stating that: 'Norwegians not only retain the old physical characteristics, but exhibit the highest average structure, the most prolific productiveness, the lowest rate of child mortality, the highest average longevity of any European race'.[35] In support of Penka's theories, Rendall commented that 'the theory of the Asiatic origin of Aryan speech is devoid of solid evidence' and that 'Penka has gone far towards establishing an association between Aryan speech and the race of blond whites, whose central and immemorial home is found in Scandinavia'.[36]

From Aryanism to Nordicism

In *Race and the Third Reich,* Christopher M. Hutton discusses the significance of Penka's work describing him as a 'transitional figure between Aryanism and Nordicism' adding that 'Northern Europe offered an ideologically propitious site of origin' and 'the mountainous terrain of Northern Europe, in the Romantic imaginings, could be seen as a pure realm, an abode of Gods'.[37] This analysis identifies Penka's work as a significant point of convergence whereby the development of racial science became fused with the romanticised 'imperfect history' of the Nordic Revival that had been progressively appropriated by nationalist thinkers in Germany and the USA to support their theories of Nordic supremacy.

British-born author and later son-in-law of the German composer Richard Wagner, Houston Stewart Chamberlain (1855–1927), could be also considered a key figure in the transition between Aryanism and Nordicism. His works had a considerable influence on Pan-Germanic, *völkisch* and Nazi thought in Germany and the USA. Born in Hampshire, England, Chamberlain's education with a Prussian tutor drew him towards Germanic culture and the eventual rejection of his British homeland in favour of his adopted German fatherland. During the First World War, Chamberlain wrote numerous articles against Britain and became a German citizen in 1916. Chamberlain was very much a product of the fusion of the literary and artistic romanticisation of the Nordic and Germanic people and racial science, which had created both the myth of Northern European predominance and a theoretical scientific framework to support it. Having attended the première and the following five performances of Richard Wagner's *Parsifal* in Bayreuth during July 1882, Chamberlain became absorbed by the Germanic Romanticism of Wagner and his creative process. He later became part of the inner circle of Wagner's admirers by marrying the composer's daughter Eva von Bülow-Wagner in 1908.

Chamberlain discussed the works of Wagner in a number of critical and biographical works and articles such as *Das Drama Richard Wagner's— Eine Anregung* (Vienna, May 1892) and *Richard Wagner* (Munich, 1896). He was also influenced by the work of racial thinkers, such as Gobineau, whose theory of miscegenation reflected his own beliefs in the deterioration of the Nordic/Germanic race through interbreeding. In this context, Chamberlain was part of a generation of academics, intellectuals and cultural pessimists who considered modernity as more than just a socio-economic or political phenomenon but a biological struggle against the weakening of the human race through interbreeding. This perceived erosion of the established *nomos*, as previously established solid foundations of society were broken down by modernity, is highlighted by Hutton who describes the breakdown in previously existing geographical and social boundaries that was leading to the emergence of a new multicultural modernity which threatened the biological future of once noble races:

> Races, peoples, social groups, languages, cultures that had been clearly distinct and identifiable, held separate by geography or the operation of social or 'caste' boundaries, were now merging and blurring into one another. The pre-modern 'ecology' or 'natural order', in which different racial and cultural variants had their own 'place', was breaking down. The pure essences of the past were being lost, and a bastardized, mongrel and degraded humanity was emerging from the cities and ports of modern civilization.[38]

In *Historicizing Race* (2018), Marius Turda and Maria Sophia Quine consider the influence on Chamberlain's racial theories of Emmanuel Kant (1724–1804) and the theories of race and white supremacy that he proposed in *Von den verschieden Racen den Menschen*, first published in 1775. In their discussion of Chamberlain's work, they argue that his appropriation of Kant's theories went beyond seeking to academically 'underpin' his own; it aimed to provide evidence that civilisation and culture had been created by the Teutonic race.[39] For Chamberlain, the concept of race went beyond the objective reality of thinkers such as Gobineau to become an expression of biological unity and spiritual transcendence. Turda and Quine propose that:

> For him, race was a subjective and higher entity, internal to the human mind and within people, which shaped their impressions and actions [...] Race for him was immaterial but real. It comprised those higher intuitions and experiences, propelled individuals to greatness, and elevated human beings to transcendental heights, close to the Gods of any religion. Chamberlain's race was the soul of the people.[40]

Turda and Quine argue that this metaphysical interpretation of race was characteristic of a *fin-de-siècle* modernist idealisation of the Northern European race. This modernist reaction fused National Romanticism and scientific method to create a myth of the potential transcendental elevation and biological supremacy of the Teutonic race.

In 1899, on the cusp of the new millennium which, from the perspective of many racial theorists of the time, was to be an era dominated by the eroding forces of modernity, Chamberlain published his major work on the history of the Germanic people, *Die Grundlagen des neunzehnten Jahrhunderts* (The Foundations of the Nineteenth Century). In this work, he proposed the historic pre-eminence of what he defined as the Teutonic Race, its relationship to the Aryan people and its fall from greatness. In his analysis of the development of Chamberlain's racial thought and the impact of his work in *Evangelist of Race* (1981), Geoffrey G. Field proposes that Chamberlain's aim in writing this work was to substantiate two fundamental convictions. Firstly, that humanity could be divided into races that differed in their physical structure and their mental and moral capabilities and, secondly, that the struggle and interaction of these races was a main force behind the evolution of history and fundamental to understanding cultural, political and social development. Field concludes, however, that his work was 'designed to show that the Germanic or Teutonic race as the main architect of modern European civilization'.[41] In Chamberlain's own words:

> It was Teutonic blood and Teutonic blood alone (in the wide sense in which I take the word, that is to say, embracing the Celtic, Teutonic and Slavonic, or North European races) that formed the impelling force and the informing power. It is impossible to estimate aright the genius and development of our North-European culture, if we obstinately shut our eyes to the fact that it is a definite species of mankind, which constitutes its physical and moral basis. We see that clearly today: for the less Teutonic a land is, the more uncivilized it is.[42]

The wide sense of Chamberlain's use of the term 'Teutonic' embraced a number of Pan-Germanic European identities including, amongst others, Scandinavian, and through his application of the cephalic index, developed by Anders Retzius, Chamberlain defined and proposed the Teutonic or Germanic as the noblest and most civilised of the European and even world races. In his work, Chamberlain also linked the much-debated concept of the Aryan with the Teutonic asserting the superior nature of the Aryan people over other non-Aryan races:

> Certain anthropologists would fain teach us that all races are equally gifted; we point to history and answer: that is a lie! The races of mankind are markedly different in the nature and also in the extent of their gifts, and the Germanic races belong to the most highly gifted group, the group usually termed Aryan ... Physically and mentally the Aryans are pre-eminent among all peoples; for that reason they are by right ... the lords of the world.[43]

Chamberlain perceived the concept of the Aryan in his own terms, rejecting the theories of a nomadic tribe that had migrated from the East as impossible to determine as he rejected language as a reliable indicator of race. In a footnote to his work, he defined his interpretation of the concept of the Aryan as an innate sense of belonging, comparable with his own personal rejection of his Britishness and spiritual sense of belonging to the Germanic people:

> When I use the word Aryan in this book, I take it in the sense of the original Sanscrit "ârya," which means "belonging to the friends," without binding myself to any hypothesis. The relationship in thought and feeling signifies in any case a homogeneousness.[44]

Chamberlain's definition of the Aryan drew on a romanticised sense of spiritual belonging rather than taking a position amongst the plethora of contemporary debates concerning the meaning and application of the term 'race' and the unreliability of both philological and anthropological methods to establish a clear identity and point of origin of the Aryan people in the East. In proposing his location of the original Aryans, Chamberlain was attracted to the strand of thought established by thinkers such as Penka who, by analysing physical characteristics, had situated the dispersal point of the Aryan people in Northern Europe.[45] In his discussion of Chamberlin's work, Geoffrey G. Field comments that 'at the time Chamberlain began the *Foundations,* one of the hottest issues in academic debates concerned the exact location of the ancestral home of the Germanic or Aryan peoples'.[46] Field further argues that after 1850, a growing number of academics supported the theory of a Northern European centre of dispersal of the Aryan race and that, by the twentieth century, the term Nordic was progressively replacing the term Aryan in racial thought.[47]

Supporting current theories of miscegenation and the need for selective breeding, Chamberlain highlighted the need to protect the Teutonic branch of the Aryan race from destruction through interbreeding with genetically inferior peoples whose increase had been precipitated by the process of modernity's erosion of traditional communities and socio-racial boundaries. Chamberlain described this in terms of a struggle for life and death, a concept that was to form the core of Nazi ideology:

> No arguing about "humanity" can alter the fact that this means a struggle. Where the struggle is not waged with cannon-balls, it goes on silently in the heart of society by marriages, by the annihilation of distances which furthers intercourse, by the varying powers of resistance in the different types of mankind, by the shifting of wealth, by the birth of new influences and the disappearance of others, and by many other motive powers. But this struggle, silent though it be, is above all others a struggle for life and death.[48]

Chamberlain's depiction of the potential destruction of the Aryan race, by the progress of modernity, as a silent on-going biological battle for racial survival was to form the core of Nordicist thought and later Nazi ideology, which sought to protect and regenerate the purity of the Nordic/Germanic type against the non-Aryan. Chamberlain did not share, however, the pessimistic view of many of his contemporaries that the process of miscegenation was irrevocable. He believed that a noble race such as the Aryan could be re-established in favourable conditions, a futural vision of an alternate modernity, which became the regenerative nucleus of Nordicism. Chamberlain argued that:

> A noble race does not fall from Heaven, it becomes noble gradually, just like fruit-trees, and this gradual process can begin anew at any moment, as soon as accident of geography and history or a fixed plan (as in the case of the Jews) creates the conditions.[49]

In his discussion of the battle against extinction of the Aryan people, Chamberlain identified the Jew as the racial enemy of the Germanic race. In their analysis of his anti-Semitism, Turda and Quine propose that it combined aspects of both biological and cultural racism. The former identified them according to their physical characteristics, and the latter relied on a Christian view of their 'negative mentality' that could be seen in their cultural, moral and spiritual inferiority.[50] Turda and Quine propose that Chamberlain considered Christianity a moral revolt against decadence and degeneration. He viewed modern Germans as the means of creating a new

world order who would be the saviours of European culture and the creators of the modern mind.[51] In his analysis of this perceived battle for
racial survival, Field describes it as a 'fundamentally Manichaean' conflict,
explaining the world 'in terms of a relentless combat between the forces of
Good and Evil'. Field further argues that the existence of the Aryan, as
synonymous with Good in the world, necessitated the presence of a
destructive force of Evil and that this concept of a malignant, destructive
force of Evil became increasingly associated with nationalist circles as
the Jew.[52]

Although Chamberlain's work received a mixed reaction in academic
circles, it was a clear success in terms of its sales. In *The Rise and Fall of the
Third Reich*, William L. Shirer describes the publication of this work as
'something of a sensation', especially amongst the influential upper classes
of German society.[53] Shirer also notes that one of its most enthusiastic
readers was Kaiser Wilhelm II, who is reported as having written in a letter
to Chamberlain that 'It was God who sent your book to the German
people, and you personally to me'.[54] In January 1900, all 2500 copies of
its first edition in Germany had sold out, and, by March of 1904, further
editions brought sales to 20,000 copies. In 1906, a popular edition
(*Volksausgabe*) of the *Grundlagen* was published and 10,000 copies were
sold within one week. By 1914, it had sold 80,000 copies and been translated into a number of European languages.[55] It could therefore be considered a significant and influential element of the fusion of Romantic
Nationalism and racial science that led to the emergence of Nordicism as
an ideological movement. Assessing the impact of Chamberlain's work,
Turda and Quine conclude that Chamberlain succeeded in popularising a
synthesis of Aryanism, Social Darwinism, eugenics, anthropo-sociology,
anti-Semitism and German nationalism and provided an academic foundation on which many Nazi ideologues built their concept of Germanic/
Nordic supremacism.[56]

Another influential work that contributed, although somewhat indi-
rectly, to the case of those who argued in favour of the Germanic states'
predominance was published by American economist, sociologist and
racial theorist William Z. Ripley (1867–1941) in the same year as
Chamberlain's work. *The Races of Europe: A Sociological Study* was an
influential work in the field of racial taxonomy in which Ripley proposed a
tripartite system and designed maps based on racial characteristics that
were later used by Madison Grant in his racial works. Ripley divided
Europeans into three racial groups: Teutonic (Northern European),

Mediterranean (Southern) and Alpine (Central), basing his conclusions on a combination of geographical, environmental and anthropometric measurements and cultural factors. Ripley's work shows, however, that many thinkers of the period were beginning to view Aryanism with increasing scepticism. Ripley rejected any reliable correlation between the field of physical anthropology and philology, describing the results as 'havoc'.[57] Ripley proposed that culture and religious tradition also had a significant role in merging the myth of tall blond Europeans with the Nordic/ Germanic race, which became associated with light-skinned, high-caste 'Aryan' inhabitants of Asia. Ripley argued that:

> The first of these is that the 'Aryan race' was somehow blond, long-headed, and tall in other words that the ancestors of the modern Teutonic type were the original civilizers of Europe. For civilization and Aryanism were indissolubly considered as one and the same; all plausible enough, to be sure, until you look the matter squarely in the face. It is easy to see how this gratuitous assumption of a tall, blond 'Aryan race' originated. The sacred books of the East suggested that the chosen people were 'white men'.[58]

Ripley was also critical of the theories of Karl Penka that situated the original dispersal point of the Aryan race in Scandinavia, arguing that archaeological evidence indicated that Scandinavia, Denmark and the Baltic plain of Germany throughout the prehistoric period were 'characterised by backwardness of culture' compared with the rest of Europe.[59] Ripley argued that any migration of tall, blond social groups came from the centre of Europe where the climate was more suited to human development rather than what he described as the poor environmental conditions of Scandinavia:

> What can Penka say to this in his positive affirmation that the original Aryans got up into Scandinavia, having followed the reindeer from central Europe to the north after the retreat of the ice sheet? The fact is, archaeologically speaking from the evidence furnished by the kitchen middens, that if they ever did this they left a fine country, where deer were plenty, to subsist upon shellfish on the foggy coasts of Denmark.[60]

Differentiating between the Aryan and Teutonic races, Ripley established his definition of the Teutonic race as tall, with a long face and narrow nose, blond hair and blue eyes, which he categorised as being synonymous, in contemporary terminology, with the 'Delicholepto,

Reihengräber, Germanic, Kymric, Nordic and Homo Europaeus'.[61] Defining his perception of the Teutonic race and the established superiority of the tall, blond race that dominated prehistoric Europe, Ripley suggested a combined process of climate and what he termed 'artificial selection', whereby tall, blond, blue-eyed European people became associated with nobility and supremacy and had become a preferred characteristic for breeding.[62]

A notable contemporary critic of Ripley and Nordicist beliefs was French anthropologist, racial theorist and cartographer Joseph Deniker (1852–1918). Following a number of publications in French entitled *Les Races de l'Europe*, in which he catalogued and mapped the diversity of physical characteristics of the European peoples, Deniker broadened his racial scope in his 1900 publication, *Les Races et les Peuples de la Terre*, translated the same year into English as *The Races of Man*. In his work, Deniker disagreed with Ripley's tripartite system, suggesting six primary European racial types: 'the Nordic, centred in Scandinavia, Northern Germany, Frisia, the British Isles and the Baltic; the Littoral, from the Pyrenees and parts of Spain, western and southern France and north-western Italy; the Oriental, from Belarus, Ukraine and eastern Poland; the Adriatic, from France, Austria, Ukraine and Ciscaucasia; the Ibero-Insular from the Iberian Peninsula, Western France, Southern Italy and the Mediterranean islands; and the Occidental, a race comprising the Palaeolithic inhabitants of Europe'.[63] Although he differed from Ripley in his analysis of European racial composition, Deniker is comparable with Ripley through his scepticism concerning the concept of the Aryan race as the founders of the Germanic/Nordic race. Deniker rejected the theories of philologists such as Jacob Grimm who had posited the theory, based on linguistic grounds, of the existence of an Aryan race that had migrated from Asia but was equally critical of the racial theories of anthropologists, such as Pösche and Penka, maintaining that their evidence was equally questionable.[64]

Within the field of archaeology, German linguist and professor of archaeology, Gustav Kossinna (1858–1931), contributed to this debate with his Pan-Germanist theories of national identity based on the ethnic categorisation of ancient material culture. In his work, Kossinna defined *Kultur* as the material evidence designating the distinctive way of life of a particular people or race whose territory and central diffusion point could be identified by the distribution of associated artefacts. Kossinna applied this principle to his research into the migration and settlement of Germanic,

Celtic and Slavic tribes, which he identified as the descendants of the Aryan race. Associating the Linear Pottery culture (5500 BC–4500 BC) of Central and Northern Europe with an ancient ruling Nordic/Germanic tribe, Kossinna formulated his influential theory that supported later Pan-Germanic claims for Germanic predominance and justification for territorial expansion. This theory was presented in his 1914 publication, *Die deutsche Vorgeschichte—eine hervorragend nationale Wissenschaft* (German Prehistory: a Pre-eminently National Discipline), in which Kossinna posited the theory of a branch of the Aryan race superior to all peoples, the *Germani*, whose material culture was evidence of prehistoric Germanic domination of Europe. Kossinna's nationalist agenda of promoting the regeneration of an expanded Pan-Germanic, Nordic race, which had considerable influence on later Nordicists, was clearly set out in his dedication to this work which reads 'To the German people, as a building block in the reconstruction of the externally as well as internally disintegrated fatherland'.[65] During the course of the 1920s, Kossinna's 'building blocks' were to become the basis for later archaeologists, such as those tasked by Heinrich Himmler's *Ahnenerbe*, who applied ultra-nationalist principles to their own archaeological research aimed at scientifically supporting the Nordic creation myth of those directing their work.

Out of this 'melting pot' of often-conflicting and evolving cultural, nationalist and scientific theories, the school of Nordicist thought emerged as a distinct form of modernist ideology, initially concerned with the historical primacy of the Nordic race and its deterioration through contact with the various migrant populations which history and modernity had brought together. By the late nineteenth century, Nordicism proposed a programmatic account of the root causes of the alleged degeneracy of contemporary society, or at least implicitly how it could be overcome, by reversing the degenerative process of miscegenation and racial decline. It later emerged as a strand within the eugenics movement that sought to develop the cultural and nationalist framework of Nordicist beliefs into a practical political and scientific project of racial regeneration. This modernist project was a reaction against the prevailing state of modernity, through which industrialisation and urbanisation had eroded traditional values and communities, proposing an alternative future modernity based on resynthesised collective memories of national and ethnic predominance. In his analysis of the development of Nordicism from the Aryan hypothesis in *Race and the Third Reich*, Hutton identifies the shift from Aryanism to Nordicism as 'a shift from linguistic to racial indices of identity and in the location of the ancestral homeland from the east to Europe'.[66] He suggests that Nordicism provided a more home-grown and accessible mythology of Northern European superiority than that of Aryanism, which, by the turn of the century, had become both a semantic and conceptual point of contention amongst many scholars. This debate was to continue into the twentieth century as later Nazi ideologists and politicians struggled to reconcile theories of Aryanism and Nordicism with their concept of the Germanic *Volk*. Hutton also describes how, by locating the site of original physical and mental perfection in Northern Europe, followers of the 'Nordic ideal' provided evidence for their view that the Nordic race were responsible for the achievements of known civilisations.[67]

Hutton also links the concept of Aryanism with the enduring remnants of the biblical paradigm of eighteenth-century monogenists who had posited a linguistic link between European languages and the original proto-Aryan language form of Japhet, whose people had migrated to the West following their banishment from Babel. Hutton suggests that, as the field of racial anthropology overtook the field of linguistics in the debate over racial identity and categorisation, Nordicism emerged as the programme for establishing an alternative, healthy modernity. This modernist project, whilst initially sharing many features of Aryanism, began to replace it as a more viable ideological movement with its own nostalgic dynamics. In Hutton's words:

> Both Aryanism and Nordicism were oriented towards a lost perfection and implied an ill-defined hope of the restoration of that unity within modernity. These were nostalgic formations, looking back to lost essences, and lamenting the fall of superior peoples or races into racial hybridity. Under the impact of racial anthropology, the notion of a superior Nordic race became in part a substitute for the historically over-complex and confused notion of the Aryan.[68]

This distinction of Nordicism as an overlapping but discreet strand of racial ideology, governed primarily by racial anthropology, is fundamental to our understanding of Nordicism as a cultural and later political and scientific movement with its own dynamic, that of preserving and propagating the 'Nordic gene' against miscegenation with inferior races. Its synonymous use with the terms Germanic and Teutonic that led and still can lead to considerable confusion in its analysis are also indicative of its overlap and later appropriation by Pan-Germanist thinkers who sought to establish a new Germania. Their aim was to restore once again the blood-line of the ancient Northern tribes who, according to their romanticised hypothesis, were once the source of European greatness.

REGENERATION: FROM THEORY TO PRACTICE

The potential for the biological protection and regeneration of an increasingly pure-blooded future Nordic race, turning the racial theory and romanticised ideals of the nineteenth century into practice, was made possible through the development of the scientific field of eugenics. The emergence and subsequent development of eugenics in most modern nations, during the late nineteenth century, had a particular relevance to those who perceived the Nordic/Germanic people to be descendants of a once noble and superior race. The potential to control, select and manipulate the gene pool of the Northern European race with the aim of purifying and thereby enhancing it, to the exclusion of other 'less worthy' racial groups, was the vital element required to transform Nordicism from a theoretical school of cultural and nationalist thought into a practical cultural, scientific and political reality.

Although the concept of improving the physical condition of man can be traced back throughout history to ancient times, the emergence of modern eugenics is generally credited to the work of Sir Francis Galton (1822–1911), a prolific Victorian polymath who was the half-cousin of Charles Darwin. Darwin's theory of natural selection, together with renewed research into Mendelian inheritance theory, had considerable influence on Galton's research into his theory that, by controlling heredity, science could potentially enhance mankind as a species. Galton's opposition to the established Christian creation myth took the form of a consuming belief in the possibility of controlling evolution to create a physically and intellectually stronger human type. This would be achievable through the selective social and biological process that he introduced as 'eugenics' in his 1883 publication, *Inquiries into Human Faculty and Its Development*. In this work, Galton argued that:

> Whenever a low race is preserved under conditions of life that exact a high level of efficiency, it must be subjected to rigorous selection. The few best specimens of that race can alone be allowed to become parents, and not many of their descendants can be allowed to live. On the other hand; if a

higher race be substituted for the low one, all this terrible misery disappears. The most merciful form of what I ventured to call "eugenics" would consist in watching for the indications of superior strains or races, and in so favouring them that their progeny shall outnumber and gradually replace that of the old one.[69]

Galton's rationale for controlling and manipulating the genetic pool of future generations to favour the stronger, 'higher race' was based on the intention of eliminating the human suffering of the 'low race' in its struggle for survival. In this context, man could become the new master of the process of natural selection or as it had come to be termed, by a growing school of social Darwinists, 'the survival of the fittest'. This became such a biological mission for Galton that he described in religious terms as a potential new form of faith. Darwin's theory of natural selection had liberated him from what he described in his memoirs as the 'ancient authorities' and 'a multitude of dogmatic barriers'.[70] Eugenics offered Galton an alternative belief system based on science, in which man became the creative and guiding force of human destiny and future fulfilment through continuous physical and intellectual improvement. Like Nietzsche's Zarathustra, descending into the market place to announce the death of God, declaring the Superman to be the new 'meaning of the earth',[71] Galton presented his work to the Sociological Society in London, on 16 May 1904. In his paper, Galton professed his belief in eugenics as a potential new form of religious faith that would empower mankind with the control of its own destiny replacing the concept and worship of God with the secular belief of eugenic science and the obligation to fulfil humanity's potential as a race. Galton announced that:

> It must be introduced into the national conscience, like a new religion. It has, indeed, strong claims to become an orthodox religious, tenet of the future, for eugenics co-operates with the workings of nature by securing that humanity shall be represented by the fittest races. What nature does blindly, slowly, and ruthlessly, man may do providently, quickly, and kindly. As it lies within his power, so it becomes his duty to work in that direction. (...) I see no impossibility in eugenics becoming a religious dogma among mankind, but its details must first be worked out sedulously in the study.[72]

In this address, Galton shifted the task of improving humanity from God and nature to mankind and the laboratory. Equipped with the tool of scientific knowledge, mankind could become the most powerful agent of human development. In this context, eugenics became a modernist project, replacing established religious tradition and dogma with a new secular myth of human progress through science.

The potential of this progressive branch of scientific endeavour had considerable resonance amongst the turn of the century pessimists, disillusioned with the state of modernity and what they perceived to be a decline in the physical and psychological health of modernised nations. Galton's theories had, at their core, the concept of national regeneration, which he frequently expressed in terms of the preservation and enhancement of the nation's race. At a meeting of the Sociological Society on 16 May 1904, Galton referred to 'raising the average quality of our nation' and argued for the 'national importance of eugenics'.[73] In a published letter to *The Times*, dated 16 June 1909, Galton engaged in a debate raised at the Royal Societies Club concerning the supposed deterioration of the British race by arguing that:

> [...] the bulk of the community is deteriorating, which it is, judging from results of inquiries into the teeth, hearing, eyesight, and malformations of children in Board schools, and from the apparently continuous increase of insanity and feeble-mindedness.[74]

Most notable amongst the early European followers of Galton, who applied his eugenics theories to the question of preserving and regenerating the Northern European descendants of the ancient Aryan people, were Karl Pearson (1857–1936), Alfred Ploetz (1860–1940), Herman Bernhard Lundborg (1868–1943) and Count Georges Vacher de Lapouge (1854–1936). Central to the work of these eugenicists was the mission of classifying the nation into healthy and unhealthy racial characteristics and the eventual perfection of the physical beauty of the Nordic race. In *Modernism and Eugenics* (2010), Marius Turda discusses these eugenicists' use of the concept of race and racial imagery as a means of regenerating and promoting a sense of national awakening and unity in a time of political and social upheaval:

> The identity of any given race was delineated by the boundaries that separated those who belonged to the community from foreigners and outsiders who remained aliens or potential enemies. Prompted by the need to regenerate a powerful sense of cohesion and shared identity amongst its adherents in the wake of perceivably profound and structural social changes, eugenicists

appealed to racial imagery in order to justify their biologisation of national belonging.[75]

These eugenicists defined race both in a broad pan-national sense, as peoples whose physical characteristics were comparable but also as noble biological and cultural characteristics that had developed within the boundaries of their respective political states. The racial descriptors that they developed, based on the measurements of physical features, were also a means of identifying 'others' in a national community whose racial characteristics were deemed inferior.

In his work, *National Life from the Standpoint of Science* (1900), Karl Pearson expressed his view that the rise of a great race such as the Aryans came from a vital combination of climate and the elimination of the weaker race through conflict and domination, a struggle that had defined the course of history:

> History shows me one way, and one way only, in which a high state of civilization has been produced, namely, the struggle of race with race, and the survival of the physically and mentally fitter race. If you want to know whether the lower races of man can evolve a higher type, I fear the only course is to leave them to fight it out among themselves (…).[76]

Responding to what he considered to be the breakdown in European and notably in French society following what he considered the 'stunning failure' of the French Revolution, Vacher de Lapouge published *L'Aryen: son rôle social* in 1899.[77] In this work he also described what he perceived to be a modern emergence of racial conflict that had defined and which would continue to define the course of history. Vacher de Lapouge defined the superior European racial type as the Aryan, dochilo-blond or *Homo Europaeus*, which he contrasted with the inferior central and southern races of the *Homo alpinus* and *Homo mediterraneus*. In his analysis of the modern descendants of the Aryan, Lapouge expressed his belief in the superior social role of the Aryan as the leader and innovator of a European civilisation emanating from the plains of Northern Europe to form the highest echelons of modern society:

> The social superiority of the Aryan is becoming more marked in any case. In Europe, he lives on the plains, leaving the high ground to the Alpinus. He flocks into towns and in centres of activity where decisiveness and energy are

needed. The higher the social group, the more he can be found in great numbers. He dominates the arts, industry, business, science and letters. He is the great proponent of progress.[78]

Vacher de Lapouge had a significant influence on a growing number of Northern European eugenicists, who viewed their field as the practical solution to correcting faults in the process of natural selection by controlling human procreation in favour of the superior or, in Lapouge's analysis, the Aryan or Nordic races. Lapouge described what he termed 'selectionism' as a practical means of 'correcting the undesirable consequences of natural selection' and increasing types that were 'recognised as the best and most beautiful'.[79] He also built on a centuries-old tradition of European anti-Semitism to identify the Jew as the most threatening race to the Aryan. In his seminal work, he proposed that 'the only dangerous competitor of the Aryan, at present is the Jew',[80] describing a racial struggle for dominance and survival which was later to become a fundamental element of the Nordicist dimension of Nazi racial ideology.

Swedish physician and professor at the University of Uppsala, Herman Lundborg, also had a significant impact on the development of eugenics both in his country and in the growing international forum of eugenicists. In 1921, together with a group of like-minded Swedish contributors, he published *The Swedish Nation in Word and Picture* in which he traced the history of the Nordic race back to a Northern migration of a Teutonic race at the end of the glacial period, into what had become Scandinavia. Lundborg described the superiority of the Teutons as 'a race who has inscribed its name on many pages of the history of civilisation'.[81] He argued that miscegenation was detrimental to the potential of the Nordic race and that the noble racial qualities of any people could only continue to exist 'as long as the race in question keeps itself pure and unmixed'.[82] In this work, Lundborg and his contributors provided a detailed written and photographic description of the Swedish race, in its pure and variant forms, analysing its racial composition and purity and praising its physical and psychological virtues.

In 1895, Alfred Ploetz, who later became an advisor on Nazi racial legislation and eugenics policies and member of the Nazi Party in 1937, published *Grundlinein einer Rassen-Hygiene, Die Tuechtigkeit Unserer Rasse und der Schutz der Schwachen* (The Competence of our Race and the Preservation of the Weak). In this work, he promoted his concept of *Rassenhygiene* (racial hygiene) as a means of preserving both the physical superiority and the favourable Aryan characteristics of the German collective. To develop and diffuse his theories on racial hygiene, Plötz founded, in 1904, the periodical *Archiv für Rassen-und Gesellschaftsbiologie* (Archive for Racial and Social Biology), and in 1905 he established the Gesellschaft für Rassenhygiene (Society for Racial Hygiene).

The field of eugenics, which at an early conceptual stage had become merged with the developing field of racial science, quickly blossomed to become an established academic discipline at many universities across Europe, notably in France, Germany, Britain, Scandinavia and the USA. These institutions received considerable state and private funding to develop research into what was considered to be the solution to the decline in civilisation. To promote and support the international development and application of the eugenics movement, organisations such as the Eugenics Education Society (est.1907), the American Eugenics Society (est. 1921) and the Kaiser Wilhelm Institute of Anthropology, Eugenics and Human Heredity (est. 1927) were founded, and three International Eugenics Conferences were organised in 1912, 1921 and 1932 to bring together the expertise of specialists in the field.

Subsequently, many governments established research institutes and implemented eugenics policies designed to improve the gene pool of their individual nations. Such programmes often comprised both 'positive' measures, such as encouraging individuals deemed particularly fit to reproduce, and 'negative' measures such as marriage prohibitions and the forced sterilisation of people deemed unfit for reproduction. Individuals considered unfit to reproduce often included people with mental or physical disabilities, people who scored in the lower ranges of IQ tests, criminals, sexual deviants, alcoholics and members of minority groups who were judged to be against the nation's interests. Now that Darwinism had shifted mankind's position in the cosmos from the apex of God's creations, fixed in his own image, to that of a species within the evolving animal kingdom, eugenicists and their proponents began to view man as a form of domesticated breeding stock. This view was expressed in a private letter, dated 1913, from American President Theodore Roosevelt (1858–1919) to leading state eugenicist Charles Davenport (1866–1944) in which he wrote:

> I agree with you if you mean, as I suppose you do, that society has no business to permit degenerates to produce their kind. It is really extraordinary that our people refuse to apply to human beings such elementary knowledge

as every successful farmer is obliged to apply to his own stock breeding. Any group of farmers who permitted their best stock not to breed, and let all the increase come from the worst stock, would be treated as fit inmates for an asylum.[83]

Through the development of eugenics, mankind had progressively become a potential breeding stock that could be perfected through the application of science. Nordicist thinkers in the USA and Northern Europe, who considered themselves the hereditary gene bearers of the Old Norse people, saw in this emerging field more than just the possibility of improving the nation's health but the potential to rekindle a mythical, lost 'Golden Age' of Nordic racial purity and superiority.

Eugenics as a Form of Programmatic Modernism

Seeking fresh perspectives in his work, *Modernism and Eugenics* (2010), Marius Turda draws inspiration from recent scholarship, including the theories of Roger Griffin, on the impact of modernity in a range of historical and contemporary contexts. In his analysis of eugenics as a regenerative movement, he argues that:

> It is only recently that scholars have begun to approach eugenics as a cluster of diverse biological, cultural and religious ideas and practices that interacted with a variety of social, cultural and national contexts.[84]

Through the perspective of this new approach, Turda examines how the eugenics movement interacted with and influenced nineteenth- and early twentieth-century nationalist thinkers. This group formed what could be termed a 'consensus of pessimism' and sought to realise their forward-looking visions of ethnic regeneration in the form of political ideologies and potential models of racial and social engineering. Turda discusses how many thinkers, at the turn of the century, considered society to be in a state of social crisis, reacting against the contemporary state of European modernity and seeking, in eugenics, the potential to create a new beginning inspired by the vision of an alternative future modernity aligned with their nationalist and racial agendas:

> By "being able to begin history anew," when troubled by the prospect of racial dissolution and national defeat, the individual and the community

found in eugenics a persuasive strategy of how to protect the past from a dissatisfying present, and how to guide it into a redeeming future.[85]

Turda further suggests that by the turn of the century, nationalist and Romantic thought, together with the emergence of racial science, had progressively transformed the concept of the nation, from a mere geographical and political body into an organic entity focussed on the collective identity rather than the individual. A nation so-constructed was in need of scientific intervention to maintain its physical and mental well-being. This was particularly evident in Germany's developing concept of the Aryan/Nordic people as a collective entity in need of protection and regeneration. In his discussion of the way in which societies were evolving into living national organisms, Turda proposes that:

> By the end of the nineteenth century, nations were increasingly being portrayed as living organisms, functioning according to biological laws, and embodying great genetic qualities symbolising innate racial virtues transmitted from generation to generation. After 1900, especially, this shifting relationship between the individual and the racial community to which he or she belonged contributed significantly to the emergence of a eugenic ontology of the nation.[86]

This process, defined by Turda as the 'biologisation of national belonging' and the emergence of a national 'eugenic ontology', had a considerable impact on the development of eugenics and particularly on its application to the protection of the Nordic race, notably in Germany and the USA during the period of social crisis following the First World War.[87]

In his work, Turda argues that previous historical interpretations of nationalist eugenics have failed to reach what he considers to be the essential core of the matter; that of the impact of nineteenth-century pessimism towards what was perceived to be the failing project of modernity. Building on Peter J. Bowler's definition of eugenics as 'the original political expression of the ideology of genetic determinism' and Michael Burleigh's view that eugenics 'had evolved from primitive utopianism into a secular religion with scientific pretentions', Turda suggests that we have reached an academic point where we need to take these interpretations further.[88] Turda proposes that eugenics should be viewed in the context of the history of European modernism, shedding new light on the dynamics of eugenics projects in Nazi Germany and other totalitarian regimes. In the context of Nazism, Turda describes the application of eugenics as 'the creation of a new man purged of degenerative characteristics and decadent tendencies'.[89] He also underlines how the turn of the century pessimism had stimulated, amongst Nazi eugenicists, the need to regenerate society by creating a racially pure and even enhanced Germanic/Northern European type based on what National Romanticism and racial science had progressively determined to be the ideal Nordic phenotype both in physical and psychological terms.

CONCLUSION: NORDICISM AS A SOLUTION TO RACIAL AND CULTURAL DEGENERATION

By the end of the nineteenth century, Nordicism had arguably become a conceptual entity in its own right, emerging as an interwoven cultural, political and scientific reaction to what was perceived to be a society in moral, physical and intellectual decline. This ideological and biological crisis was founded on the perceived destructive effects of miscegenation as modernity transformed the social and economic landscape, stimulated international economic migration and eroded the bonds that had maintained traditional communities. Disenchanted with the negative spiritual, social and biological by-products of European and North American modernisation, many pessimistic thinkers became attracted to the concept of regeneration, rooted in visions of a mythical past created by National Romanticism. The rapidly emerging scientific field of eugenics provided Nordicist theorists with the practical means of fulfilling their project of creating an alternative modernity, rooted in Old Norse culture and the most desirable biological features of the Scandinavian type. Nineteenth-century scientific progress, notably Darwinism, had de-centred God as the determining force of the future of man, a role later assumed by Galton's eugenics movement. For these scientists, the true meaning of life on earth, the new religion, now lay in man's secular mission to surpass his current state of social decline to evolve into a higher form of physical and spiritual humanity, or as Nietzsche proposed, man became conceived as 'a rope stretched between the animal and the Superman'.[90] Through this process, Nordicism evolved from National Romantic idealism into a practical cultural, political and scientific reality. Having established the practical means, through eugenics, to reconstruct human society as a resynthesised, mythical ancestral homeland, Nordicist ideologists attempted to create their own means of reaching their final *telos* of racial perfection and world dominance.

The next chapters will analyse how, under intense social conditions of rapidly evolving modernity and deeper socio-economic crisis in both Nazi Germany and the USA, Nordicism became radicalised into a significant element of state legislation. It will further examine how, in Germany, it became transformed into an agenda of 'programmatic modernism' which led to the eventual genocide of millions to protect the Nordic health of the nation from those who were deemed inferior and to regenerate a mythical state of racial purity.

NOTES

1. The term 'Superman' is translated from the Nietzsche's original German, *Übermensch*. Other translations of this have been 'Beyond-man' (Tille, 1896), 'Superman' (G.B. Shaw, 1903) and 'Overman' (Kaufmann, 1954) and more recently the 'higher self' Miner, Robert (2011) *Nietzsche's Fourfold Conception of the Self.* An Interdisciplinary Journal of Philosophy 54, 4: pp. 337–360.
2. Nietzsche, Friedrich *Thus Spoke Zarathustra.* (Trans. Thomas Common, 1917) *Thus Spoke Zarathustra.* The Modern Library, New York p 7.
3. Nietzsche, Friedrich. *Thus Spoke Zarathustra.* p 6.
4. Montriou, J.A.L. (1786–7) *Elements of Universal History.* Fry and Couchman, London. Chapter 4 Noah. No page numbers shown. https://books.google.co.uk/books (Accessed 28/02/15).
5. Linnaeus, Carl (1740) *Systema Naturae* (2nd edition) Stockholm p 67 Google Books (Accessed 25/02/16).
6. *Carl Linnaeus* ucmp.berkeley.edu. http://www.ucmp.berkeley.edu/history/linnaeus.html   (Accessed 15/03/15).
7. These five taxa were: *Europæus albus* (white European), *Americanus rubescens* (red American), *Asiaticus fuscus* (brown Asian) and *Africanus Niger* (black African). Linnaeus later added *monstrosus* for wild and deformed humans and other unclassified groups.
8. Linnaeus, Carl. (1758) *Systema Naturae* (10th edition) Stockholm. pp. 20–21 https://www.biodiversitylibrary.org/item/10277#page/26/mode/1up (Accessed 10/07/18)

9. Ibid. 5 p 3.
10. Kyllingstad, Jon Røyne (2014) *Measuring the Master Race: Physical Anthropology in Norway 1890–1945.* Open Book Publishers, Cambridge p 11.
11. *Jean-Baptiste Lamarck* ucmp.berkeley.udu. http://www.ucmp.berkeley.edu/history/lamarck.html (Accessed 31/03/15).
12. *Letter from Darwin to Hooker.* University of Cambridge Digital Library. http://cudl.lib.cam.ac.uk/view/MS-DAR-00114-00003/4(Accessed 01/04/15).
13. Darwin, Charles *The Descent of Man.* (2004) Barnes and Noble, New York p 151.
14. Although Darwin used this phrase, it was in fact coined by Herbert Spencer (1820–1903) English philosopher, biologist, anthropologist and sociologist, who first used the phase in his work, *Principles of Biology*, published in 1864. *Herbert Spencer.* Encyclopedia Britannica Online http://www.britannica.com/EBchecked/topic/559249/Herbert-Spencer#ref145509 (Accessed 03/04/15).
15. Ruse, Michael (2009) *The Darwinian revolution: Rethinking its meaning and significance.* PNAS 106 (Supplement 1): 10040–10047.
16. Morris, Charles (1900) *Man and his Ancestor - A Study in Evolution.* MacMillan, London p 2.
17. Jones, William *Address for the Third Anniversary Discourse to the Asiatic Society of 2nd February 1786.* http://www.utexas.edu/cola/centers/lrc/books/read01.html (Accessed 02/04/15).
18. Hutton, Christopher M. (2005) *Race and the Third Reich.* Polity Press, Cambridge p 84.
19. *The Holy Bible.* (2012) King James Version. Cambridge University Press, Cambridge. Genesis 10.5.
20. Ibid. 18 p 84.
21. Ibid. 18 p 85.
22. Shippey, Tom A. (2005) *A Revolution Reconsidered: Mythography and Mythology in the Nineteenth Century. The Shadow-Walkers: Jacob Grimm's Mythology of the Monstrous.* Medieval and Renaissance Texts and Studies Volume 291. Arizona Center for Medieval and Renaissance Studies, Tempe p 6.
23. Compte de Gobineau, Joseph Arthur (Trans. A. Collins 1915) *Essay on the Inequality of the Human Races.* William Heinemann, London p 117.

24. Compte de Gobineau, Joseph Arthur. *Essay on the Inequality of the Human Races.* p 211.
25. Ibid. 23 p 24.
26. Ibid. 23 p 207.
27. Ibid. 23 p 92.
28. Biddiss, Michael (1970) *Father of Racist Ideology - The Social and Political Thought of Count Gobineau.* Weidenfeld and Nicolson, London p 266.
29. Ibid. 28 p 267.
30. Pictet, Adolphe (1859) *Les Origines Indo-Européenes ou les Aryans primitifs: Essai de paléontologie lingistique.* Cherbulier, Paris pp. V-VIII https://books.google.co.uk/books?id=3Twog10Wmm4C& pg=PA27&source=gbs_toc_r&cad=3#v=onepage&q&f=false (Accessed 14/07/18).
31. Ibid. 30 p 33.
32. Arvidsson, Stefan (2006) *Aryan Idols - Indo-European Mythology as Ideology and Science.* University of Chicago Press, Chicago p 143.
33. Ibid. 32.
34. Taylor, Isaac (1890) *The Origin of the Aryans.* Scribner and Welford, New York pp. 46–47 Google Books (Accessed 18/06/15).
35. Rendell, Gerald H. (1889) *The Cradle of the Aryan.* Macmillan and Co., London pp. 54–55. https://archive.org/stream/cradleofaryans00rend#page/n1/mode/2up (Accessed 14/06/15)
36. Rendell. Gerald H. *The Cradle of the Aryan.* pp. 62–63.
37. Ibid. 18.
38. Ibid. 18.
39. Turda, Marius, Quine, Sophia Maria (2018) *Historicizing Race,* Bloomsbury, London p 44.
40. Ibid. 39 p 44.
41. Field, Geoffrey G. (1981) *Evangelist of Race - The Germanic* Vision of Houston Stewart Chamberlain. Columbia University Press, New York p 180.
42. Chamberlain H.S. (Trans. Lees, John 1910) *The Foundations of the Nineteenth Century.* The Bodley Head, London p 188.
43. Chamberlain H.S. *The Foundations of the Nineteenth Century.* p 542.
44. Ibid. 42 p 266.
45. Ibid. 42 p 264.
46. Ibid. 41 p 210.

47. Ibid. 41 p 210.
48. Ibid. 42 p 577.
49. Ibid. 42 p 264.
50. Ibid. 39 p 82.
51. Ibid. 39 p 83.
52. Ibid. 41 p 210.
53. Shirer, William L. (1964) *The Rise and Fall of the Third Reich*. Pan Books, London p 141.
54. Shirer, William L. *The Rise and Fall of the Third Reich*. p 141.
55. *Publication Statistics of H.S. Chamberlain*. http://www.hschamberlain.net/timeline/timeline.html (Accessed 21/08/2015).
56. Ibid. 39 p 46.
57. Ripley, William Z. (1900) *The Races of Europe - A Sociological Study*. Kegen Paul, Trench and Trübner and Co. London p 456.
58. Ripley, William Z. *The Races of Europe*. p 454.
59. Ibid. 57 p 507.
60. Ibid. 57 p 511.
61. Ibid. 57 p 121.
62. Ibid. 57 p 469.
63. Deniker, Joseph (1900) *The Races of Man - An Outline of Anthropology and Ethnography*. Walter Scott Ltd. London p 318.
64. Deniker, Joseph *The Races of Man*. p 318.
65. Gustav Kossina quoted by Arnold, Bettina (1990) *The past as propaganda: totalitarian archaeology in Nazi Germany*. Antiquity 64: pp. 464–478.http://karant.pilsnerpubs.net/files/Propaganda.pdf (Accessed 14/11/15).
66. Ibid. 18 p 106.
67. Ibid. 18 p 106.
68. Ibid. 18 p 107.
69. Galton, Francis (1883) *Inquiries into Human Faculty and Its Development*. Macmillan, London p 199 http://www.galton.org. (Accessed 14/08/15).
70. Galton, Francis (1908) *Memories of my Life*. Methuen and Co. London pp. 287–88. http://www.galton.org (Accessed (14/08/15).
71. Nietzsche, Friedrich. *Thus Spoke Zarathustra*. p 157.
72. Galton, Francis (1904) *Eugenics: Its definition, scope, and aims*. The American Journal of Sociology 10 (1): 1–25. http://galton.org/essays/1900-1911/galton-1904-am-journ-soc-eugenics-scope-aims.htm (Accessed 15/08/15).

73. Ibid. 72.
74. Galton, Francis (1909) *Letter to the Editor of The Times.* www.galton.org (Accessed 07/11/15).
75. Turda, Marius (2010) *Modernism and Eugenics.* Palgrave Macmillan, Hampshire p 96.
76. Pearson, Karl (1901) *National Life from the Standpoint of Science.* Adam & Charles Black, London pp. 19–20.
77. Vacher de Lapouge, G. (1899) *La faillite de la Révolution est éclatante.* (My translation) *L'Aryen: son rôle social.* Thorin et fils, Paris. Preface. https://archive.org/stream/LaryenSonRoleSocial/ LAryenSonRoleSocial_Lapouge_594pgs51393937_djvu.txt (Accessed 14/06/15).
78. Ibid. 77 p 399.
79. Ibid. 77 p 544.
80. Ibid. 77 p 561.
81. Lundborg, Herman (1921) *The Swedish Nation in Word and Picture.* Hasse W. Tullberg, Stockholm p 11.
82. Ibid. 81 p 24.
83. *Letter from President T. Roosevelt to C. Davenport dated January 3rd 1913.* Facsimile from the American Philosophical Society Library. https://www.dnalc.org/view/11219-T-Roosevelt-letter-to-C-Davenport-about-degenerates-reproducing-.html (Accessed 11/11/15).
84. Ibid. 75 p 2.
85. Ibid. 75 p 7.
86. Ibid. 75 p 6.
87. Ibid. 75 p 6.
88. Ibid. 75 p 15.
89. Ibid. 80 p 93.
90. Ibid. 2 p 7.

BIBLIOGRAPHY

PRINTED WORKS

Arvidsson, S. (2006). *Aryan Idols – Indo-European Mythology as Ideology and Science.* Chicago: University of Chicago Press.

Biddiss, M. (1970). *Father of Racist Ideology – The Social and Political Thought of Count Gobineau*. London: Weidenfeld and Nicolson.

Chamberlain, H. S. (1910). (Trans. Lees, John) *The Foundations of the Nineteenth Century*. London: The Bodley Head.

Compte de Gobineau, J. A. (1915). (Trans. A. Collins) *Essay on the Inequality of the Human Races*. London: William Heinemann.

Darwin, C. (2004). *The Descent of Man*. New York: Barnes and Noble.

Deniker, J. (1900). *The Races of Man - An Outline of Anthropology and Ethnography*. London: Walter Scott Ltd.

Field, G. G. (1981). *Evangelist of Race - The Germanic Vision of Houston Stewart Chamberlain*. New York: Columbia University Press.

Hutton, C. M. (2005). *Race and the Third Reich*. Cambridge: Polity Press.

Kyllingstad, J. R. (2014). *Measuring the Master Race: Physical Anthropology in Norway 1890–1945*. Cambridge: Open Book Publishers.

Lundborg, H. (1921). *The Swedish Nation in Word and Picture*. Stockholm: Hasse W. Tullberg.

Marks, J. (1993). Historiography of Eugenics. *American Journal of Human Genetics, 53*(6), 1367–1368.

Miner, R. (2001). Nietzsche's Fourfold Conception of the Self. An Interdisciplinary. *Journal of Philosophy, 54*(4), 337–360.

Morris, C. (1900). *Man and His Ancestor – A Study in Evolution*. London: Macmillan.

Nietzsche, F. (1917). (Trans. Thomas Common) *Thus Spoke Zarathustra*. New York: The Modern Library.

Pascal, B. (1995). *Pensées*. London: Penguin.

Pearson, K. (1901). *National Life from the Standpoint of Science*. London: Adam & Charles Black.

Ripley, W. Z. (1900). *The Races of Europe - A Sociological Study*. London: Kegen Paul, Trench and Trübner and Co.

Ruse, M. (2009). The Darwinian Revolution: Rethinking Its Meaning and Significance. *PNAS, 106*(Suppl. 1), 10040–10047.

Shippey, T. A. (2005). *A Revolution Reconsidered: Mythography and Mythology in the Nineteenth Century. The Shadow-Walkers: Jacob Grimm's Mythology of the Monstrous. Medieval and Renaissance Texts and Studies* (Vol. 291). Tempe: Arizona Center for Medieval and Renaissance Studies.

Shirer, W. L. (1964). *The Rise and Fall of the Third Reich*. London: Pan Books.

Turda, M. (2010). *Modernism and Eugenics*. Hampshire: Palgrave Macmillan.

Turda, M., & Quine, S. M. (2018). *Historicizing Race*. London: Bloomsbury.

WEBSITES AND DIGITAL PUBLICATIONS (WITH DATE ACCESSED)

Linnaeus, C. (1758). *Systema Naturae* (10th edition). Stockholm. Accessed 10/07/18, from https://www.biodiversitylibrary.org/item/10277#page/26/mode/1up

Carl Linnaeus. ucmp.berkeley.edu. Accessed 15/03/15, from http://www.ucmp.berkeley.edu/history/linnaeus.html

Galton, F. (1904). Eugenics: Its Definition, Scope, and Aims. *The American Journal of Sociology, 10* (1), 1–25. Accessed 15/08/15, from http://galton.org/essays/1900-1911/galton-1904-am-journ-soc-eugenics-scope-aims.htm

Galton, F. (1883). *Inquiries into Human Faculty and Its Development.* London: Macmillan. Accessed 14/08/15, from http://www.galton.org

Galton, F. (1908). *Memories of My Life.* London: Methuen and Co. Accessed 14/08/15, from http://www.galton.org

Galton, F. (1909). *Letter to the Editor of The Times of 18th June.* Accessed 07/11/15, from www.galton.org

Hehn, V. (1885). *Cultivated Plants and Domesticated Animals in Their Migration from Asia to Europe.* Google Books. Accessed 14/06/15.

Herbert Spencer. *Encyclopedia Britannica Online.* Accessed 03/04/15, from http://www.britannica.com/EBchecked/topic/559249/Herbert-Spencer#ref145509

Index of Chamberlain's Publications on Wagner in the French and German Press. Accessed 21/08/2015, from http://www.hschamberlain.net/bibliography/bibliography.html

Jean-Baptiste Lamarck. ucmp.berkeley.udu. Accessed 31/03/15, from http://www.ucmp.berkeley.edu/history/lamarck.html

Letter from Darwin to Hooker. University of Cambridge Digital Library. Accessed 01/04/15, from http://cudl.lib.cam.ac.uk/view/MS-DAR-00114-00003/4

Letter from President T. Roosevelt to C. Davenport dated January 3rd 1913. American Philosophical Society Library. Accessed 11/11/15, from https://www.dnalc.org/view/11219-T-Roosevelt-letter-to-C-Davenport-about-degenerates-reproducing-.html

Montriou, J. A. L. (1786–7). *Elements of Universal History.* London: Fry and Couchman. Accessed 28/02/15, from https://books.google.co.uk/books

Pictet, A. (1859) *Les Origines Indo-Européenes ou Les Aryans Primitifs: Essai de Paléontologie Linguistique.* Paris: Cherbulier. Accessed 14/07/18, from https://books.google.co.uk/books?id=3Twog10Wmm4C&pg=PA27&source=gbs_toc_r&cad=3#v=onepage&q&f=false

Publication Statistics of H.S. Chamberlain. Accessed 21/08/2015, from http://www.hschamberlain.net/timeline/timeline.html

Rendell, G. H. (1889). *The Cradle of the Aryan*. London: Macmillan and Co. Accessed 14/06/15, from https://archive.org/stream/cradleofaryans00 rend#page/n1/mode/2up

Jones, W. *Address for the Third Anniversary Discourse to the Asiatic Society of 2nd February 1786*. Accessed 02/04/15, from http://www.utexas.edu/cola/centers/lrc/books/read01.html

Taylor, I. (1890) *The Origin of the Aryans*. New York: Scribner and Welford. Google Books. Accessed 18/06/15.

The Past as Propaganda: Totalitarian Archaeology in Nazi Germany. *Antiquity, 64*, 464–478. Accessed 14/11/15, from http://karant.pilsnerpubs.net/files/Propaganda.pdf

Vacher de Lapouge, G. (1899) *L'Aryen: Son Rôle Social*. Paris: Thorin et Fils. Accessed 14/06/15, from https://archive.org/stream/LaryenSonRoleSocial/LAryenSonRoleSocial_Lapouge_594pgs51393937_djvu.txt

CHAPTER 4

Towards Ragnarǫk

Nordicism as a Cultural, Political and Scientific Reality in Germany and the USA

In Norse mythology, the apocalyptic events of *Ragnarǫk*, foretold to *Oðinn* (Odin) by a seeress, prophesised the end of a mythical and temporal cycle, the demise of *Oðinn's* pantheon, the fall of *Asgarðr* and the destruction of life on earth as fire and raging seas consumed *Miðgarðr*, the realm of mankind. *Bifrǫst*, the Rainbow Bridge linking Earth with the realm of the Gods, shattered as the Sons of *Múspell*, led by *Surtr*, rode across it to join the final battle between the *Æsir* and their enemies, concluding this eschatological cycle of the Norse cosmos. Out of this devastation, a new earthly and spiritual era was foretold as the few remaining gods, *Viðarr*, *Váli*, *Móði* and *Magni* gathered together at the mythical plain of *Iðavǫllr* where they were reunited with *Hǫðr* and *Baldr*, who had returned from their death in *Hel*, to reflect on the past and the future that lay ahead. On earth, from the destruction of *Miðgarðr*, two surviving humans, *Líf* and *Lífthrasir*, emerged from their shelter into a green, replenished world where humanity could start anew.[1]

The events of *Ragnarǫk* vividly described a total social and spiritual collapse and renewal in Old Norse society. The prophecy foretold that, prior to the battles of the Gods, three continuous winters of hardship, called *Fimbulvetr*, would strike during which violent battles would break out across *Miðgarðr* and social ties would collapse as human society fell into

© The Author(s) 2020

G. E. Forssling, *Nordicism and Modernity*,
https://doi.org/10.1007/978-3-030-61210-8_4

ruin. Third Reich historians have frequently referenced Richard Wagner's interpretation of *Ragnarǫk* in *Götterdämmerung* (Twilight of the Gods) in their descriptions of the dramatic intensity of the suicide of Hitler and the collapse of Nazism as Soviet troops encircled the *Führerbunker* in Berlin during April and May of 1945.[2] In the context of this work, *Ragnarǫk* and the breaking of *Bifrǫst* also represent the downfall of Nordicism as a means of regenerating a lost connection with a mythological Golden Age of Nordic supremacy.

This chapter will examine the emergence of Nordicism as the basis of cultural politics and pseudoscientific social engineering: firstly in the USA, through its immigration and eugenics policies of the 1920s and 30s, and then in Northern Europe and in particular Nazi Germany, where Nordicism became an influential ideological driving force behind the Third Reich's racial and eugenics laws. This project of racial regeneration eventually led to the genocide of the death camps and the final collapse of Nazism in the ruins of the Reich's Chancellery in Berlin.

MODERNITY AND PRESERVING THE NORDIC AMERICAN

From the earliest days of pilgrim migration in the seventeenth century, America had been a nation of immigrants who, for a range of political, religious and economic reasons, had left their homelands, during the seventeenth and eighteenth centuries, in search of a new life in the 'land of opportunity'. During the nineteenth and early twentieth centuries, the USA experienced waves of increased immigration which produced growing social and economic unrest amongst the existing population, notably those of British, German and Scandinavian origin who considered that these new immigrants threatened the Northern European culture and prosperity that they, and their ancestors, had established. A significant wave of immigration occurred from around 1815 to 1865, and the majority of these new arrivals came from Northern and Western Europe. Amongst these newcomers, approximately one-third came from Ireland as a result of crop failures and famine, and in the 1840s almost half of America's immigrants were of Irish origin.[3] This influx included tens of thousands of immigrants from Latin America, Australia and Asia who were attracted to the West Coast by the California Gold Rush of 1848–1855.

Between 1880 and 1920, rapid industrialisation, which demanded an increased workforce, and urbanisation, attracted more than 20 million immigrants to the USA. Between 1890 and 1900, the majority of these arrivals were from Central, Eastern and Southern Europe including some 600,000 Italians, and, by 1920, more than 4 million had entered the USA. In addition, Jews from Eastern Europe fleeing religious persecution also arrived in large numbers, and between 1880 and 1920, it has been estimated that 2 million entered the USA.[4] A significant peak in immigration figures occurred in 1907 when over 1 million people entered the country in a single year.[5] During this year an estimated 1.25 million immigrants were processed through the Ellis Island Immigration Inspection Station in New York Bay, the nation's busiest immigration gateway. In the face of such surges in immigration, many existing Americans became critical of the government's 'open door' policy that was allowing uncontrolled influxes of immigrants who were poor, illiterate and in many cases unskilled. Many newcomers were also Catholic and Jewish and therefore from different socio-cultural and political backgrounds to the descendants of the original settlers whose Northern European origins were rooted in Protestantism, anti-Semitism and white supremacy.

In the context of this surge in immigration, Native White Americans, as they considered themselves, began to feel increasingly threatened by the intense waves of immigration into the USA by races that they considered biologically and socially inferior. In this context, Nordicism emerged as a reaction to the fast-paced change of nineteenth-century modernity as a distinct strand, within a spectrum of conservative thought in the USA that sought to maintain Northern European primacy against the flood of immigrants pouring into the country. These newcomers were creating a multi-cultural melting pot of national, religious and social thought which threatened the existing *nomos* of those who considered themselves to be a community under attack from the rapidly changing forces of modernity that were transforming the established national identity of the USA.

Against this background of increasing social and cultural turmoil, America was becoming a leading nation of the modernist project of eugenics. The centre for this research in America was the Cold Spring Harbor Laboratory on Long Island, New York. Between 1910 and 1939, this laboratory was the base of the Eugenics Record Office of biologist Charles B. Davenport (1866–1944) and his assistant Harry H. Laughlin (1880–1943), two prominent American eugenicists of the period. Their research into the racial hygiene of the nation studied, however, not only the most appropriate means of reducing heredity illness, insanity, criminality and sexual deviance but also the most effective means of managing what they perceived to be the growing threat to America through immigration.

MADISON GRANT: NORDICISM IN THE USA

Prominent amongst these thinkers was Madison Grant (1865–1937), a lawyer, writer, eugenicist and conservationist, who emerged as a significant figure in the Nordicist movement both in the USA and in Germany. Born in New York City, Grant could trace his maternal line back to Jessé de Forest, a Walloon Huguenot who, in 1623, recruited the first group of colonists to settle on the East Coast in New Netherland. On his paternal side, he could trace his American lineage back to Richard Treat, Dean of Pitminster Church in England, who became one of the first Puritan settlers in 1630. Grant's family line included Robert Treat, a colonial governor of New Jersey; Robert Treat Paine, a co-signatory of the Declaration of Independence, and Grant's father, Dr. Gabriel Grant, a prominent physician and health commissioner of Newark, New Jersey, who was awarded the Medal of Honour during the American Civil War of 1861–1865. In his comprehensive analysis of Grant's life and works, *Defending the Master Race* (2009), Jonathan Peter Spiro describes how Northern European descendants such as Grant considered themselves to be the upper echelons of American society:

> For centuries his antecedents had been accustomed to wealth, power and deference, and in a country without a titled nobility they could lay as good a claim as any to being true American aristocrats.[6]

Grant was therefore part of the influential Northern European elite of American society who claimed racial and social primacy over the waves of immigrants arriving on American shores who, in their view, were destroying the established social, cultural and biological fabric of their American society. In this context, Grant can be aligned with the cultural and biological pessimists of the preceding century such as Gobineau, Chamberlain and Guido von List who described the degeneration of society and its nobility through the dilution of the Nordic gene pool with those of inferior racial types. Grant, like these previous thinkers, sought to apply the developing field of eugenics to reconstruct a mythologised 'Golden Age' of the Northern European race's once noble origins, a 'mazeway resynthesis' of myth and science which fused National Romanticism's nostalgia for the past with forward-looking modern scientific progress.[7]

Educated at Yale University and Columbia Law School, Grant practiced law for a number of years before engaging himself fully in his many zoological conservationist projects and 'behind the scenes' political activities. These brought him into contact with many influential eugenicists and racial theorists in America such as Theodore Lothrop Stoddard (1883–1950), Charles Davenport (1866–1944) and Harry H. Laughlin (1866–1944), all of whom were significant in promoting white and particularly Nordic supremacy in the USA and Europe. Grant was also associated with notable politicians, who were sympathetic with his cause, such as New York mayor William Lafayette Strong (1827–1900) and Presidents Theodore Roosevelt (dates of office, 1901–1909) and Herbert Hoover (dates of office, 1929–1933). One of Grant's most notorious projects, in association with William Hornaday, director of the Bronx Zoo, was the exhibition in 1906, of a Congolese African Pygmy from the *Ituri* Rainforest, Ota Benga (c. 1883–1916), in the zoo's grounds and monkey house.

In 1916, Madison Grant published his major work *The Passing of the Great Race; or, The Basis of European History*, which brought him to the public forefront as a supporter of the protection of the Nordic race against the erosion of multi-culturalism and miscegenation. The first edition of this work was published in blue cloth with a gold seal of the heroic Viking leader, Rollo the Great, the first Duke of Normandy. In this work, Grant traced the prehistoric roots of the Nordic people whose superior racial characteristics were increasingly threatened by the uncontrolled immigration and population growth of those they considered racially inferior. Its first edition sold 16,000 copies, making it a best seller with revised editions published in 1918, 1920 and 1921; translations were also made into German, French and Norwegian bringing Grant's thesis into the international arena of eugenics and racial science.[8] In his assessment of Grant's work, historian Jonathan Spiro concludes that its greatest impact was in popularising the Nordicist theories that he proposed through his articulate synthesis of the principles of racial science that had emerged during the nineteenth century:

> [...] no one had brought them all together in one place and presented the whole with such esprit, audacity, and clarity. As a result, what had been the province of a few obscure academics was now made accessible to the general

reader. After *The Passing of the Great Race*, the biological threat posed by inferior races was no longer a speculative theory held by a few but a palpable danger feared by all.[9]

In *The Passing of the Great Race*, Grant called on the American descendants of Northern Europeans to be conscious of their current plight and support practical eugenic and legislative measures to halt the erosion of the northern blood of the 'founder Americans' from dilution with blacks and inferior European and Asian races. Grant described the Europeans as a superior world race within which three distinct subdivisions could be determined: the Nordic, the Alpine and the Mediterranean. Within this tripartite structure, the Nordic Race, emanating from the Scandinavian region, was biologically determined to be the 'alpha race' of world civilisation. Grant described the American descendants of these Northern Europeans as 'a native American aristocracy resting upon layer upon layer of immigrants of lower races' and claimed that the Nordic race had 'up to this time, supplied the leaders of thought, the control of capital, education and of the religious ideals and altruistic bias of the community'.[10] Grant also argued that the established ruling elite of Northern Europeans was under threat from a liberal democratic process that was progressively marginalising them politically and biologically, depriving them of the privileged place in society that he considered their birth right (Fig. 4.1).

Like Gobineau and many other racial theorists of this time, Grant argued that interbreeding between races led to a degradation of the superior gene pool in favour of inferior genetic characteristics. In the USA, he considered this process almost irreversible without immediate eugenics measures to restrict immigration and segregate racial communities. Grant dismissed the argument of American liberals that immigrants could better themselves within a supportive and progressive society attacking those who argued that environment could alter heredity in contrast with his determinist view that social characteristics were inherent and fixed. Grant argued that:

> Thus, the view that the negro slave was an unfortunate cousin of the white man, deeply tanned by the tropical sun, and denied the blessings of Christianity and civilization, played no small part with sentimentalists of the Civil War period, and it has taken us fifty years to learn that speaking English, wearing good clothes, and going to school and church, does not transform a negro into a white man.[11]

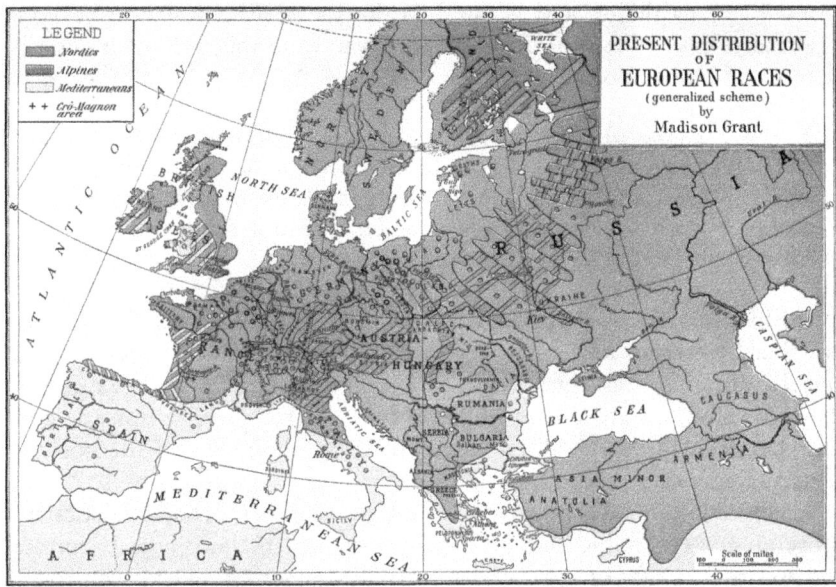

Fig. 4.1 The distribution of the European races divided into Nordics (red), Alpines (green) and Mediterraneans (yellow) according to Madison Grant placing the centre of dispersal in Scandinavia. Image from copy held at the British Library of Grant, Madison (1916) *The Passing of The Great Race*. New York: C. Scribner's Sons

In his elaboration of this argument about the fixity of racial characteristics, Grant also expressed his anti-Semitic sentiment towards Jewish immigrants from Poland by suggesting that their biological and social characteristics were equally immutable. Grant argued that America would have 'a similar experience with the Polish Jew, whose dwarf stature, peculiar mentality and ruthless concentration on self-interest are being engrafted onto the nation'.[12] This identification of the Jew as a significant biological and social threat to the racial health of the nation aligned him with many European and notably German thinkers who shared this view of the Jew as the racial 'other' of the Nordic.

In developing his thesis of the Nordic, Grant drew on the research of many nineteenth-century racial theorists such as Gobineau (miscegenation), Gregor Mendel (the laws of inheritance), Anders Retzius (the cephalic index) and Karl Penka (Scandinavia as the dispersal point of the blond race) to define and geographically locate his ideal Nordic type. Grant also linked the Nordic with the Aryan as in this following description of the Nordic race:

> This race is long-skulled, very tall, fair-skinned, with blond or brown hair and light colored eyes. The Nordics inhabit the countries around the North and Baltic Seas, and include not only the great Scandinavian and Teutonic groups, but also other early peoples who first appear in southern Europe as representatives of Aryan language and culture.[13]

In his analysis, Grant identified the English, Flemish, Dutch and Northern Germans as descendants of the pure Scandinavian Nordic race and the dominant class in Europe. He observed that 'no one can question the race value of stature who observes on the streets of London the contrast between the Piccadilly gentleman of Nordic race and the cockney costermonger of the old Neolithic type'.[14]

Much of Grant's work focused on the development, characteristics and subsequent geographic and biological dispersal of the physical, cultural and spiritual beauty of the Nordic race. His depiction owed much to the idealised type of the Nordic created by the fusion of racial science and the school of nineteenth-century National Romantic thought in Europe and America at this time:

> The Nordics are, all over the world, a race of soldiers, sailors, adventurers, and explorers, but above all, of rulers, organizers, and aristocrats in sharp contrast to the essentially peasant character of the Alpines. Chivalry and knighthood, and their still surviving but greatly impaired counterparts, are peculiarly Nordic traits, and feudalism, class distinctions, and race pride among Europeans are traceable for the most part to the North.[15]

Grant considered the Nordic people as the founders of civilisation whose genetic virtues had spread throughout Europe and could be found in pockets around the world. Grant even suggested that Jesus Christ had genetic characteristics of the Nordic Race as he argues in his analysis of traditional, artistic representations of the scenes from the Bible:

> In church pictures today all angels are blonds, while the denizens of the lower regions revel in deep brunetness. [...] and in depicting the crucifixion no artist hesitates to make the two thieves brunet in contrast to the blond Saviour. The latter is something more than a convention, as such

quasi-authentic traditions as we have of our Lord indicate his Nordic, possibly Greek, physical and moral attributes.[16]

This appropriation of Jesus as a Nordic figure by Grant was a noticeable feature of later attempts to align Christianity with Nazism through the theory of 'Positive Christianity', proposed by thinkers such as the official Nazi ideologist Alfred Rosenberg (1893–1946). There was even a failed attempt to create a state-sanctioned church, based on a fusion of Nazi and Christian belief, by Ludwig Müller (1883–1945) who led the *Deutsche Evangelische Kirche* (*German Evangelical Church*).

Grant positioned the Nordic race at the apex of human society and promoted its protection from further erosion by liberal multi-culturalism and miscegenation, proposing the application of eugenics measures aimed at the preservation and regeneration of the Nordic race. To improve the American people overall, Grant suggested a system of progressively eliminating, through sterilisation, social undesirables who he referred to as those 'who crowd our jails, hospitals and insane asylums'.[17] In his explanation of this process, however, Grant also made it clear that this project of human improvement could be eventually extended to the issue of race:

> This is a practical, merciful and inevitable solution of the whole problem, and can be applied to an ever-widening circle of social discards, beginning with the criminal, the diseased, and the insane, and extending gradually to types which may be called weaklings rather than defectives, and perhaps ultimately to worthless racial types.[18]

Grant concluded that mankind had two means of racial improvement: firstly, the selective breeding of the elite Nordic race or, secondly, the elimination of the 'other' through segregation and sterilisation, a Janus face of modern eugenics. He concluded, however, that in modern society, under a democratic government, it would be difficult to obtain a consensus as to what constituted the elite class and legally difficult to implement measures against those eventually deemed suitable for elimination.

Within the structure of democratic government that Grant clearly viewed as an impediment to the radical measures that he proposed, he was an active campaigner for government action to control immigration to preserve the racial hygiene of the nation. From 1922 until his death in 1937, he served as the vice president of the Immigration Restriction League, a group of conservatives who worked to raise public awareness of

immigration issues and lobby politicians to support protectionist legislation. He was also president of the Eugenics Research Association and, in
1918, founded the Galton Society with American eugenicist and biologist
Charles B. Davenport. Grant was also instrumental in putting his program
of Nordic protection and regeneration into effect by supporting and providing data for the *Immigration Act of 1924.*

THE IMMIGRATION ACT OF 1924: NORDICISM AS POLITICAL AND LEGISLATIVE REALITY IN THE USA

The Immigration Act of 1924 consolidated and extended previous legislation and was introduced in the House of Representatives by Congressman
Albert Johnson (1869–1957) who served for a number of years as chairman of the Committee on Immigration and Naturalisation and was head
of the Eugenics Research Association. Republican David Reed
(1880–1953) later introduced it in the Senate. This legislation limited the
number of immigrants allowed entry into the USA through a national
origin's quota. This quota was originally calculated on the basis of 2% of
the total number of people of each nationality in the USA as recorded in
the 1910 national census. The greatest wave of immigrants from Eastern
Europe arrived, however, during the thirty-year period prior to the start of
the First World War in 1914. Thus, the basis for the immigration quota
was changed from the census of 1910 to that of 1890, when far fewer
southern and eastern Europeans resided in the USA. The immediate
impact of this legislation impact in terms of immigration figures can be
seen in Table 4.1. Although this summarised table does not show the full
time span covered in the original document, it does show the immediate
impact of the 1924 legislation, and it can be seen that, in 1925, immigration to the USA was reduced overall by 58%. The greatest impact, however, is shown in the percentage decrease of the countries classified as part
of Eastern and Southern Europe. It is clear that the legislation favoured
the nationalities of the Native White Americans from Northern Europe
and notably the German population who suffered only a 39% decrease in
comparison with the Eastern and Southern European states whose
decrease exceeded 80%. The act also consolidated previous legislation by
excluding all Asian immigration.

This legislation favoured the national groups classified by Grant as
Nordic and is evidence of the emergence of Nordicism as a political and

Table 4.1 US immigration figures 1924–1925

US immigration statistics 1924–1925 immigrants by country of origin

Year	1924	1925	Difference	% Change
Country of origin				
All countries	706,896	294,314	-412,582	-58.37
Europe total	364,339	148,336	-216,003	-59.29
Northwestern Europe				
Great Britain	59,490	27,172	-32,318	-54.33
Scandinavia	35,000	16,810	-18,190	-51.97
Others	16,077	8548	-7529	-46.83
Central Europe				
Germany	75,091	46,068	-29,023	-38.65
Poland	28,806	5341	-23,465	-81.46
Others	32,700	4701	-27,999	-85.62
Eastern Europe				
USSR and Baltic States	20,918	3121	-17,797	-85.08
Other Eastern	13,173	1566	-11,607	-88.11
Southern Europe				
Italy	56,246	6203	-50,043	-88.97
Others	9105	2186	-6919	-75.99

Adapted from figures published 1949 by the US Department of Commerce

Source: https://www2.census.gov/prod2/statcomp/documents/HistoricalStatisticsoftheUnited States1789–1945.pdf (Accessed 13/02/18)

biological reality in the USA. These statistics demonstrate the immediate effects of this protectionist policy towards the Nordic race and the intended exclusion of those deemed racially undesirable. Hence, Grant and his fellow legislators succeeded in implementing a pro-Nordic immigration policy that was to remain largely unchanged until it was replaced by the *Immigration and Nationality Act of 1952*.

Grant was also an active supporter and advisor for the drafting of legislation for state laws preventing miscegenation, notably the *Racial Integrity Act of 1924* that was passed in the state of Virginia. Aimed primarily at miscegenation between whites and blacks, this legislation required that a racial description be established and recorded at birth either as 'white' or 'coloured'. A process that had come to be known as the 'one-drop' rule determined this classification. This rule stated that any person with even one ancestor of African descent was to be classified as 'coloured'. This legislation expanded and defined the scope of existing bans in some states on interracial marriage by criminalising all marriages between white and non-white persons. The application of this 'one-drop rule' was adopted by a number of fellow states, notably in the South and remained in place, in Virginia and a number of other states, until the US Supreme Court over-turned it in 1956. Through this legislation, Grant and his supporters suc-ceeded, on a limited scale, to control interbreeding between Nordics and inferior races to prevent further miscegenation and protect the remaining Nordic bloodline.

NORDICISM AS A MODERNIST BELIEF SYSTEM IN AMERICA

In his analysis of the influence of *The Passing of the Great Race* on American thought in the 1920s, Spiro describes the supporters of Grant who cited and disseminated his work. Amongst these were Seth K. Humphrey, *The Racial Prospect* (1920); Albert E. Wiggam, *The New Decalogue of Science* (1922); William Sadler, *Race Decadence, The Truth about Heredity* (1930); and one of Grant's closest friends and associates, the influential racial the-orist, Lothrop Stoddard (1883–1950). These writers became part of a substantial movement of followers in the 1920s who believed passionately in Grant's theories and who Spiro describes as 'evangelists' and 'disciples', believing passionately in Grant's theories and promoting them with a quasi-religious fervour. This description echoes the words of Francis Galton's paper to the Sociological Society in London, on 16 May 1904 in which he announced that eugenics 'must be introduced into the national conscience, like a new religion'.[19] For many, the superiority of the Nordic race and the necessity of regenerating it for mankind to reach its potential was more than just a bio-political agenda; it had also become a modernist belief system, a diagnosis and remedy to the growing problems of a degen-erating society, rooted in a mythical racial past. In his description of Grant's followers Spiro describes how:

> In scores of books, hundreds of articles, and thousands of speeches delivered to women's clubs, businessmen's luncheons, fraternal organizations, and reform groups, Grant's disciples spread the good word of scientific racism throughout the land in the early 1920's. They preached that inequality was a biological fact, and that the Nordics were the superior race.[20]

This fervent belief in and dissemination of Grant's Nordicist ideology by his followers had a significant impact both in the USA and on a growing number of nationalist, Pan-Germanic thinkers in Northern Europe.

AMERICAN NORDICIST REALITY AS A BLUEPRINT FOR NAZI RACIAL POLICIES

Outside America, Grant's publications, speeches at international conferences and practical application of Nordicist theories through legislation, had considerable resonance with right-wing German thinkers who were seeking to establish their own sense of Pan-Germanic identity rooted in the superiority of the Germanic and Nordic race. These thinkers looked to America as a world leader in eugenics legislation aimed at the protection and regeneration of the Northern European people and sought to apply it to their own national situation following the devastation of the First World War and impact of the Spanish flu pandemic to rebuild a sense of national strength, identity, unity and rootedness. Within this movement that considered American legislation as a potential model for the restoration of Germanic greatness was the aspiring ultra-nationalist politician Adolf Hitler who, in his second volume of *Mein Kampf* (1926), expressed his admiration of American eugenics and citizenship legislation:

> There is today one state in which at least weak beginnings towards a better conception are noticeable. Of course it is not our model German Republic, but the American Union, in which an effort is made to consult reason partially. By refusing immigration on principle to elements in poor health, by simply excluding certain races from Naturalisation, it professes in slow beginnings a view, which is peculiar to the folkish state concept.[21]

In *Hitler's Private Library* (2010), Timothy W. Ryback analyses a number of works recovered from the Berghof and other locations, which had belonged to Hitler's extensive library. Ryback discusses the impact of Madison Grant's work on Hitler's early political thinking, and in his analysis, he proposes that: 'few surviving books in Hitler's library had as clear or measurable an impact on Hitler's thinking'.[22] He also provides an anecdote from 1934 of Leon Whitey of the American Eugenics Society who described how Madison Grant showed him a letter from Hitler describing the book as 'his Bible'.[23]

Although the original copy to which Ryback had access had no margi-
nalia indicating Hitler's actual thoughts and areas of interest, as did other
works in his collection, Ryback establishes a convincing argument for the
influence of Grant through comparisons with sections of *Mein Kampf* and
other early writings and speeches of Hitler from the 1920s. Ryback also
points out that Hitler's knowledge of Grant could also have come from
secondary sources, such as writers like German race researcher and eugenicist Hans F.K. Günther (1891–1968), who referenced Grant in his own
writings. There is, nonetheless, a valid argument that Grant's *The Passing
of the Great Race* had a formative influence on Hitler's racial thinking.
Ryback suggests that Grant's selective synthesis of current strands of political and racial thought corresponded exactly with the scientific rationale
and legislative framework that Hitler sought as a blueprint for his project
of reawakening and regenerating the German nation. Ryback concludes
that Grant's selective and generalised synthesis of racial theory into 'an
emphatic, single-minded, merciless and unapologetically racist message'
was the 'sort of intellectual posture that appealed to Hitler'.[24]

Ryback's research sheds interesting light on the possible influence of
Madison Grant's theories on the racial eugenics program that Hitler envisaged for the protection and regeneration of the Aryan race. Hitler developed and discussed these theories in *Mein Kampf* and other early writings
and was later able to transform them into a practical reality when he took
power in 1933, as Ryback concludes, 'Hitler was to transform Grant's
treatise from Holy Scripture to state policy'.[25] In *Mein Kampf* the fusion
of Nordicism with Aryanism, so typical of Grant and so central to the Nazi
racial myth, found expression in Hitler's fears of the corruption of Aryan-
Nordic bloodline and assertion that the Aryans were the original 'founders
and creators of culture' (*Kulturbegründer und Kulturschöpfer*). In Hitler's
words, the noble Aryan was the 'Prometheus of Mankind', from whose
'bright forehead the divine spark of genius has sprung at all times'.[26]

Eugenics legislation aimed at racial hygiene and particularly the preservation of the Nordic bloodline, promoted by notable figures such as
Madison Grant, was always restricted by the fundamental basis of American
constitutional democracy: the importance of establishing a national consensus. In an increasingly multi-cultural society, an elitist group of
Nordicist thinkers was too marginal to implement legislation far-reaching
enough to fulfil the Nordicist manifesto that Grant set out in *The Passing
of the Great Race*. In *The Pure Society* (2001), André Pichot comments on

how democracy in Britain, where the field of eugenics was rapidly developing, also prevented the passing of laws relating to racial hygiene:

> The propaganda and lobbying of associations and biologists came up against the English democratic tradition, and the political authorities opposed the demands of these scientists. Several bills for sterilization were rejected by the House of Commons, particularly in 1931 and 1934, the time when eugenic legislation crossed the Atlantic from the United states, where it had been pioneered.[27]

As discussed previously, the development of Nordicism in Britain into anything beyond a cultural phenomenon and the aims of a few isolated groups were very limited as the nation's democratic parliamentary system prevented the emergence of racial eugenics in any legislative form. It was only under the totalitarian regime of Nazism that ultranationalism, eugenics and Nordicism were able to flourish and become intertwined without any ethical or legal boundaries.

MODERNITY AND REGENERATING THE NORDIC RACE IN INTER-WAR GERMANY

The years following Germany's defeat in the Great War of 1914–1918 were marked by an intense period of radicalisation as the damaged nation sought to recover from defeat and reinvent itself following the devastation of the First World War. For many nationalist thinkers, the defeat of Germany was a sign of the nation's racial weakness and that a project of national renewal and re-awakening should be based on a biological process of the purification of the Germanic race. Within this emerging radical movement, the emerging school of Nordicist thinking gained ground as a means of turning nineteenth-century theories of regenerating a lost racial primacy into a political and biological reality. Nordicism became radicalised in post-war Germany into a significant element of Nazi state legislation and thereby into an agenda of programmatic modernism to protect the Nordic biological health of the nation from what were deemed weaker, inferior races and regenerate its mythical racial purity.

At the conclusion of the war, it was estimated that Germany had lost an estimated 1.78 million men and the nation's sense of catastrophic defeat was compounded by the punitive conditions of the *Treaty of Versailles* forced on Germany by the allied victors. The treaty obliged Germany to

accept total blame for the war, disarm, make substantial territorial conces-
sions and make reparation payments for damage caused during the conflict. In 1921 the total cost of these reparations was assessed at 132 billion
marks (then $31.4 billion or £6.6 billion, roughly equivalent to $442
billion or £284 billion in 2017),[28] an immense financial burden which was
only settled in 2010.[29] The impact of the Great War on Germany cannot,
however, just be assessed in demographic, economic and territorial terms.
The social impact of the violent deaths of so many young soldiers in apocalyptic conditions confronted the surviving population with the experience
of mass killing as modern technology was applied to the destruction of
human beings on an unprecedented scale. The modernity of nineteenth-
century industrialisation had replaced the concept of the individual with
that of the urban industrial and commercial collective, and through the
process of the technologisation of warfare, death had become an anonymous, random, unpredictable and brutal dimension of modernity. This
apocalyptic mood was reflected in the brutality of warfare depicted in
Erich Maria Remarque's (1898–1970) *Im Westen nichts Neues* (All Quiet
on the Western Front), published in 1929, and the stark, nightmarish
Expressionist images of artist Otto Dix (1891–1969).

Within these immense social pressures, the perception and representation of the Jew as the cultural and biological 'other' became increasingly
crystallised, in nationalist circles, into the essence of a myth based on a
conflict, rooted in the past, between the once-noble and pure Northern
European race and the biologically inferior Jew. Within the cultural context of the 'imperfect histories' of the nineteenth century, which sought to
re-establish and legitimise the cultural roots of Germanic identity and primacy and the emerging strand of biological Nordicism in the field of
eugenics, the Jew became perceived as a malignant force within German
modernity. This aspect of anti-Semitism, emerging as a reaction to modernity, is examined by Zygmunt Bauman in *Modernity and the Holocaust*
(1989), in which he describes how traditional German anti-Semitism
became radicalised by the social transformations brought about by early
twentieth-century modernity that were eroding and transforming the
established social landscape of German society. In this work, Bauman
describes how urban modernity brought a number of Jewish intellectuals
and businessman into positions of power and influence in German society.
He further describes how, in the aftermath of the Great War, this added to
the anxieties of those who saw the established social status quo rapidly col-
lapsing and led to the emergence of a cultural and biological anti-Semitism

that had arguably existed as undercurrents for centuries both in Germany and across Europe. In his description of this process, Bauman uses the image of established 'solids' melting and of those trapped in an *anomic* state seeking the refuge of a 'mazeway resynthesis' of anti-Semitism:

> Truly, the fate of the Jews epitomized the awesome scope of social upheaval and served as a vivid, obtrusive reminder of the erosion of old certainties, of melting and evaporating of everything once deemed solid and lasting. Whoever felt thrown out of balance, threatened or displaced, could easily— and rationally—make sense of his own anxiety through articulating the experienced turbulence as the imprint of Jewish subversive incongruity.[30]

This perception of the Jew, amongst German conservatives and nationalists, as a destructive force within modernity is also reflected in Christopher M. Hutton's analysis of the anti-Semitic dimensions of Nazi ideology, in which he describes the emerging world-view of the nationalist *Kriegsgeneration* who cast the Jew as the cultural and biological 'other' of a progressively weakening Germanic race.[31] In his discussion of anti-Semitism and modernity, Hutton argues that:

> Anti-Semitism was fundamental to the world-view of almost all ultra-nationalist (*völkisch*) ideologues and, increasingly in the post-war era, of race theorists. Jews were the essence of modernity, in that they thrived in cities and in modern consumer capitalism. They represented materialism, liberalism, internationalism, Marxism; they embodied the promiscuity of modernity, in that they were citizens of all countries, spoke many languages and lacked any organic relationship to territory and landscape [...] The fact that Jews thrived in modernity gave them unique power and influence over the distressed German Volk.[32]

This perception of the Jew as a malevolent, parasitic aspect of modernity, eroding and destroying the social, economic and cultural fabric of the post-war German nation, radicalised nationalist thought into the elaboration of futural projects of national, cultural and biological regeneration that racial science and eugenics had now made a potential reality. Within this strand of radical right-wing thinkers, the biological agenda of Nordicism had considerable resonance in both the fields of ultra-nationalist politics and the eugenics movement emerging as what could be termed a 'revitalisation movement' founded on an idealised image of the past.

In his analysis of the religious dynamics of Nazism, in *National Socialism and the Religion of Nature* (1986), Robert Pois discusses the extent to which the idealisation of Germany's past was built on the mythical foundations of a romanticised rural society that had existed prior to industrialisation. Pois points out that a number of studies have established that the collective memory of close-knit large pre-industrial families and communities was based more on Romantic musings that reality:

> All in all, the notion of the pre-industrial family, at least in Germany, being a warm-hearted collectivity in which individuals could attain fulfilment is seen to be an absurdity [...] Thus that worshipping of presumed vanished solidarities of the past—a shared tendency, albeit for different respective reasons, of the left as well as the right—must be seen as romanticism, in the worst possible sense.[33]

Drawing on theories published by Mircea Eliade in *The Myth of the Eternal Return* (1949), Pois proposes that this idealisation of the past stemmed from what Eliade terms 'a terror of history'. In this context, Pois defines history as a process of change in which human beings are constantly recreating themselves to keep up with the increasingly relentless pace of changes brought about by modernity. Pois proposes that, in comparison with earlier primitive societies in which archetypes played an important role, modern society, faced with constantly destabilising change, could be considered as 'being virtually paralysed by the terror of history'.[34] As a reaction to this terror, Pois suggests that both the individual and society attempt to annul the past and recreate their own history through a process that he describes in Eliade's own words as the 'periodic abolition of time and collective regeneration'.[35] This aligns with the concept of the 'mazeway resynthesis' of Anthony F.C. Wallace who also describes this process of creating new adapted belief systems, allowing society to maintain a viable sense of rootedness and transcendence against a changing social landscape. Pois also describes Eliade's division of the 'time of history' into 'profane' and 'sacred'. According to this theory, 'profane' time signifies the chronological time in which we lead our daily lives, whereas 'sacred' time is a timeless space in which totems and archetypes, which give meaning to our lives, are rooted. In this context, Pois proposes that religious belief and 'sacred time' functions as a means by which 'harassed moderns, deprived of comforting archetypes and repetitions, can escape, or at least minimise the terrors of temporal life'.[36] Pois applies this theory to the Nazi project of national regeneration and the creation of a unified, timeless *Volksgemeinschaft* to reveal what he considers an attempt to abolish the 'terror of history' during the inter-war years in Germany. He also points out that an essential element of this sense of community was the depiction of the Jew as 'a deracinated element that threatened the whole panoply of archetypes central to a mythological past'.[37] In his discussion of the 'terror of history' and the Nazi regime, Pois argues that:

> It is obvious, though, that in the National Socialist religious revolution, we can see an effort to escape from the 'terror of history' by essentially abolishing it. The very real terror necessitated by such an action was not of crucial significance since it would be directed against those who stood in opposition to the emergence of 'sacred' time within that 'profane' time over which it must inevitably triumph.[38]

The physical manifestation of this need to create 'sacred' time and space can be seen in impressive national monuments such as the *Walhalla* monument in Bavaria (1842) and the *Kyffhäuser* monument in Thuringia (1896). It is also apparent in the Nazi regime's later creation of national monuments to Nazi ideology such as the *Feldherrnhalle* in Munich and ceremonies such as the annual ritual of the *Blutfahne* (Blood Flag) at the Nuremberg rallies whose pseudo-religious qualities created a sense of transcendence and national mythology. These ritual ceremonies took the nation far away from the everyday concerns and struggles of life in Germany following the defeat of the First World War. Pois' theory of collective regeneration as a reaction to the terror of history aligns with Roger Griffin's theory of modernism and revitalisation movements that emerged during the twentieth century, and when applied to the phenomenon of Nordicism, these social and political theories reveal its nature as one of a cluster of reactions to modernity that emerged during this period.

NORDICISM AS A TWENTIETH-CENTURY REVITALISATION MOVEMENT

In his discussion of revitalisation movements in *Modernism and Fascism* (2007), Roger Griffin draws, in part, on the theories of British cultural anthropologist Victor Turner. In his work, Turner discusses how, during the post-war years, a growing number of conservative and nationalist thinkers found themselves in a liminoid state, a state of separation and extreme social stress, as the established identity and traditions, the *nomos* of their established society, was being rapidly eroded by the seemingly unstoppable forces of change brought about by post-war modernity. In reaction to this perceived threat, many fascist thinkers sought the creation of a new 'sacred canopy' of belief. Griffin describes the social need to create an alternative modernity as crucial to the historical evolution of human culture:

> 'Liminoidality' and adaptive, innovative, *revolutionary* social reactions to it which create a *new* order and a 'new world', have certainly been as constitutive of human history as the evolving but conservative liminal processes that maintain and regenerate the status quo.[39]

The liminoid state of complete separation from a social *nomos*, which has been destroyed or damaged beyond repair, is the condition in which revitalisation movements emerge with visions of an alternative modernity deemed essential to the survival of a society in ruins. Situating this social theory within the context of twentieth-century fascism Griffin quotes Victor Turner's description of how a new society enters into and emerges from a liminoid state:

> People who are similar in one important characteristic [...] withdraw symbolically, even actually, from the whole system, from which they may in various degrees feel themselves 'alienated' to seek the glow of *communitas* among those with whom they share some cultural and biological feature they take to be their most signal mark of identity Through the route of 'social category' they escape the alienating structure of a 'social system' into 'communitas' or social anti-structure.[40]

This model of a liminoid state of alienation, by a social group who seek the *communitas* of those with which they share common features, views and experiences, reflects the sense of alienation from modernity felt by the ultra-nationalists of the *Kriegsgeneration*. Their common experience and aspirations had become so misaligned with modernity that it caused many to break away and seek an alternative modernity, acting as a social 'anti-structure' within a Weimar society that they rejected as being uninhabitable and doomed to eventual destruction.

Griffin links this development of Turner's 'social anti-structure' with the concept of revitalisation movements analysed by Anthony Wallace and Kenneth Tollefson as a 'mazeway resynthesis'. This creation of an adapted world-view or socio-cultural model to take the place of a society perceived as defunct is the means by which the liminoid state is converted into the futural vision of an alternative modernity. This takes place as a reaction to the alienating force of a structure that they exclude themselves from, as it is incompatible with their established world-view. In his explanation, Griffin quotes Tollefson's description of cultural revitalisation as an 'adaptive social response whereby the past and present values, customs, and beliefs—which produce dissonance arising from the distortions that exist between them—are analysed and recombined into a new synthesis, a new mazeway, or a new *Gestalt*'.[41] By applying Griffin's model of fascism, as a revitalisation movement, to Nordicism as a specific generic strand within this broader school of thought, then its function as a modernist project of protecting and promoting the Nordic race in both the USA and Germany becomes more apparent. Nordicism in both countries combined nostalgia, through its quest for rootedness in Old Norse traditions, folklore and mythology with forward-looking modern scientific advances in the field of racial science and eugenics. These eclectically chosen foundations of their historical legitimacy and controversial scientific methods were fused into a pseudo-scientific rationale that became the radicalised world-view of a Pan-Nordic/Germanic *communitas* spanning both sides of the Atlantic. This world-view subsequently became the basis of a futural vision based on a re-synthesised past. Griffin describes how:

> They project the new vision, the new temporality contrived deep inside their inner world onto 'history', planning utopian ways in which society can be harmonized and synchronized with it [...].[42]

During the late nineteenth century, Nordicists emerging from the National Romantic period had projected their new vision of racial primacy onto the history of the Germanic *Volk* who they claimed to be the descendants of a once great Aryan tribe that had settled and dispersed from the racially formative environment of the Nordic lands. With the development of racial science and eugenics, they were able to hypothesise a future new order to harmonise their racial world-view with the futural society that they envisaged. Griffin describes this duality by describing the scene in *Harry Potter and the Philosopher's Stone*, when the young wizard is confronted with the sight of his schoolmaster Quirrell who appears as a single head with two faces, one facing forward, the other backwards.[43] Through this Janus image, Griffin explains what he perceives as a contradictory but symbiotic and vital relationship between the nostalgic and the futuristic in fascist revitalisation movements. In Nordicism, this seemingly contradictory duality was bound together by the belief that it would be possible to scientifically reconstruct a lost past from the surviving pure Nordic bloodstock, a scientifically reconstructed future of a mythical past.

From this synthesis, this alienated Nordicist 'anti-structure' elaborated a conceptual map or 'mazeway' for a future society in which the primacy of Nordic blood was restored to its former greatness. The prophets of this movement, in the fields of science and ultra-nationalist politics, excluded their followers from the current state of modernity, which they perceived as being rapidly eroded by the forces of multi-culturalism and miscegenation. In response to this threat to their established *nomos* of racial superiority, Nordicism became transformed, in radical circles, into a secular belief system of the primacy of the Nordic race comparable with Francis Galton's call for eugenics to be introduced into the national conscience 'like a new religion'.[44] The final stage of its 'mazeway resynthesis', its transformation from theory into a political and scientific reality, was however still in flux. In the USA, the democratic process resting on the consensus of a broad public limited its full development. In Germany, however, this process had been weakened by the failings of the Weimar Republic and the socially turbulent post-war years. In this *anomic* socio-political context, the practical application of Nordic thought continued to develop on both sides of the Atlantic as Nordicist eugenicists collaborated to establish a scientific blueprint for the preservation and restoration of the Nordic race. It was, however, only under the totalitarian regime of Nazism, established in 1933, that this process could be unleashed to its full destructive effect.

THE INTER-WAR NORDICIST SCIENTIFIC *COMMUNITAS* IN SCANDINAVIA, GERMANY AND THE USA

Although the aftermath of the First World War was characterised by continuing international tensions, with Germany remaining a political outsider in international affairs, the pre-war collaboration previously established between leading racial eugenicists such as Madison Grant, Theodore Lothrop Stoddard and Charles Davenport in the USA and

Erwin Baur, Eugen Fischer and Fritz Lenz in Germany soon resumed. They formed what could be termed a Nordicist scientific *communitas*, which Stefan Kühl studies, in *The Nazi Connection—Eugenics, American racism and German National Socialism* (1994). In this work, Kühl frames his analysis of the Nazi period within a critique of aspects of the eugenics research of the right-wing British anthropologist and businessman Roger Pearson (1927–) and the financial backing of the Pioneer Fund with which he is associated. Kühl discusses the significant interaction that took place during the inter-war period between American and German scientists. He claims that in the USA, the role of American scientists in promoting and supporting Nazi eugenics legislation and action has been largely sidelined as 'a silent presence in works about eugenics, even when not mentioned specifically'.[45]

From his archive research in the USA, Germany, Great Britain and France, Kühl highlights the relationship between Nazi and American racial eugenicists and the extent to which their interaction was vital to the development of Nazism's political and scientific racial programmes. Kühl claims that Charles B. Davenport played a central role in reintegrating German scientists back into the international eugenics community and promoting their status within it and that by 1924, German and American eugenicists were again in full collaboration.[46] He also argues that the American Rockefeller Foundation played a significant role in the establishment and sponsorship of major eugenics institutions in Germany such as the Kaiser Wilhelm Institute for Anthropology, Eugenics and Human Heredity, founded in Berlin in 1927. This research centre soon became closely associated with Nazi theories of eugenics and racial hygiene through the direction of its leading theorists Fritz Lenz (1887–1976), Eugen Fischer (1874–1967), Otmar von Verschuer (1896–1969) and Ernst Rüdin (1874–1962). Between 1921 and 1940, *Menschliche Erblichkeitslehre* (*Principles of Human Heredity and Race Hygiene*) by Erwin Baur (1875–1933), Eugen Fischer and Fritz Lenz was republished in five editions and became a key work on eugenics, published on both sides of the Atlantic. This work influenced many other Nordicist thinkers such as H.F.K. Günther who built on their work by applying it to the future rebuilding of the Nordic race and popularised it for a general public readership.

Within this transatlantic collaboration into a range of research areas within the developing science of eugenics, the field of racial hygiene had a significant role. In his work, Kühl points out that the Committee on Race

Crossing (linked to the International Federation of Eugenics Organizations, IFEO) was jointly led by Fisher and Davenport. He also refers to the collaboration in the late 1920s between the Eugenics Record Office, the Station for Experimental Evolution in Cold Spring Harbor and the Kaiser Wilhelm Institute who co-authored a questionnaire distributed to 1000 physicians, missionaries and consulates to collect information on miscegenation.[47] Kühl also describes how, at a conference of the IFEO in 1928, Fritz Lenz, chairman of the Committee for Race Crossing, urged the Foundation to be more engaged in supporting their work on race mixing.[48] This Pan-Nordic *communitas*, a scientific 'anti-structure' within the American and German Eugenics movement, sought to promote and develop their own racial agenda of Nordic racial hygiene beyond national boundaries as part of a Pan-Nordic revitalisation movement.

In Scandinavia, the concept of racial hygiene and the need to protect and improve the health of the Nordic race also gained ground during this period. In Sweden, Herman Lundborg (1868–1943) became a prominent eugenicist both in Sweden and internationally. In 1918, he toured Sweden with an exhibition of *folktypsutställning* (folk types) exhibiting models of Swedish racial types and also helped to organise a beauty contest to find the perfect Swedish-Germanic racial type. He also established the State Institute for Racial Biology in 1922.[49] In Norway Jon Alfred Mjøen (1860–1939), who had been a personal friend of Alfred Ploetz since the 1880s, and who held a German doctoral degree in organic chemistry, also rose to national and international note as a prominent figure in the eugenics movement.[50] Mjøen argued that Norway, like the other Scandinavian states, had to fight for the protection of their Nordic racial heritage. According to his assessment of the contemporary situation, Mjøen argued that Norwegians had a responsibility towards both their own nation and the world to protect their racial purity and quality. Like many cultural and biological pessimists of the time he believed that modern civilisation had disrupted the process of natural selection and that mass migration from Norway to America was also draining the country of its superior racial types.[51] To counter this trend, Mjøen proposed a range of positive eugenics measures such as racial education, a return to rural life and health checks before allowing marriages, to protect and promote the reproduction of racially superior individuals and negative measures such as forced segregation and sterilisation. In his work *Measuring the Master Race: Physical Anthropology in Norway 1890–1945* (2015), Norwegian historian Jon Røyne Kyllingstad points out that the application of the theories of

Nordicist eugenicists, such as Lundborg and Mjøen, was limited in Scandinavia by the disapproval of many other thinkers who opposed their theories in a liberal democracy. According to Kyllingstad, Mjøen and Lundborg were, nonetheless, part of an influential group within the IFEO who sought to create a 'Blond International' to purify and propagate the Nordic Race:[52]

> The Nordicist element within the Scandinavian eugenics movement was therefore marginalized within their own countries both by scientific opposition the liberal democracies which prevented the passing of racist eugenics measures without a broad public consensus. They were, however, well received within a growing German academic community of Nordicists who sought to develop relations with their Scandinavian counterparts with the aim of furthering their research into the protection and purification of the Nordic race.[53]

Notable in this academic collaboration between Scandinavian and German racial theorists was the Norwegian physician and physical anthropologist Halfdan Bryn (1864–1933). Like many of his contemporaries, Bryn reacted to the modernity of the time by blaming the poor working and living conditions of the cities' working classes where hygiene and health was becoming a major concern. He maintained, however, that it was not just industrialisation and urbanisation that was to blame, but the degenerating racial composition of the population that was taking place through poor social selection. Bryn argued that, at an individual level, racial mixing could lead to 'genetic chaos', individuals who were ugly and unfit for intellectual development, whereas at a societal level, mixing led to alienation.[54] Bryn perceived that the Norwegian race was being threatened by migrants from eastern regions of Europe and, in Northern Norway, through miscegenation with Lapps. He argued that this problem was comparable with that of the 'Negro problem' in the USA, which was being controlled through a range of racial legislation to prevent interbreeding between blacks and the white population.[55]

During 1923 and 1924, Halfdan Bryn met with German anthropologist and writer H.F.K. Günther (1891–1968), and the two collaborated closely on a number of research and publication projects. According to Kyllingstad, Günther saw Bryn as a key collaborator in his mission to spread his concept of the Nordic race throughout Scandinavia. In 1926, Bryn joined the German Nordic association, the *Nordische Ring*, through which he connected with an extensive network of like-minded thinkers.[56] This growing association with German Nordicists, who were influential members of the rapidly expanding Nazi Party, increasingly marginalised Bryn within the Norwegian eugenics community, and he remained academically isolated until his death in 1933. According to Kyllingstad, the death of Bryn ended any further anthropological interest in scientific Nordicism in Norway amid growing public criticism of his ideas and his association with the brutal racial doctrine of Nazism.

THE NORDICIST *COMMUNITAS* WITHIN NAZISM

Alongside this scientific 'anti-structure' or *communitas* in the field of eugenics, German Nordicist thinkers in the fields of politics, history, geography, religion and anthropology built on the earlier work of pre-war racial theorists who had centred the origins of the Germanic tribes in ancient Nordic tribes who had migrated south from Scandinavia. Through their work, Nordicism became more clearly distinguished from nineteenth-century Aryanism as a purely racial indicator, a racial category where the body became the focus of human identity. Within the emerging National Socialist movement of aspiring ultranationalist politicians such as Adolf Hitler, Nordic ideologues were a strongly represented and influential strand of the Party's *völkisch* world-view and developing racial policies.

Notable amongst these thinkers was anthropologist Hans Friedrich Karl Günther (1891–1968) who became a prominent and influential Nordicist writer in the inter-war period and taught at the universities of Jena, Berlin and Freiburg, publishing numerous books and essays on racial theory. A former student of eugenicist Eugen Fischer, Günther drew on the work of many contemporary eugenicists and racial theorists to formulate his concepts of *Nordische Gedanke* (Nordic thought), *Entnordung* (denordification), *Wiedervernordung* (renordification) and *Aufnordung* (nordification). These racial theories had a considerable resonance amongst leading members of the Nazi Party, and Günther saw this movement as the ideal means of bringing about his project of regenerating the Nordic gene pool. He joined the Nazi Party in 1932, and he was awarded a number of prestigious honours during his career.

Part of the *Kriegsgeneration* who grew up during the Great War, Günther began his academic and writing career with the support of the Munich publisher of medical and nationalist literature Julius Friedrich Lehmann (1864–1935). Lehmann was an influential figure among early

Nazi members through his involvement in the Munich Beer Hall Putsch of 1923 and his participation in the Thule Society, a group that attracted many influential early party members. The *Thule-Gesellschaft* (*Thule Society*) was a German occultist and *völkisch* group in Munich, established after the First World War, named after a mythical northern country from a Greek legend. The Society sponsored the early *Deutsche Arbeiterpartei* (*DAP*). Through these connections and the popularity of his publications, Günther soon became a leading figure in establishing the foundations of later Nazi eugenics policies.

Günther's numerous publications included racial works such as *Rassenkunde des deutschen Volkes* (*Racial Characteristics of the German People*, 1922), *Rassenkunde Europas* (*The Racial Elements of European History*, 1924), *Kleine Rassenkunde Europas* (*A Short Ethnology of the German People*, 1925), *Der Nordische Gedanke unter den Deutschen* (*Nordic Thought Among the German People*, 1925), *Adel und Rasse* (*Nobility and Race*, 1926), *Rasse und Stil* (*Race and Form*, 1926) and *Rassenkunde des jüdischen Volkes* (Racial Characteristics of the Jewish People, 1930). In these works, Günther built on the work of earlier racial anthropologists, rejecting the linguistic term Aryan to base his racial analysis on physical measurements using the cephalic index and his own general observations to discuss the physical and psychological attributes and deficiencies of different racial types.

In *Rassenkunde des deutschen Volkes* (1922), Günther defined five racial types that made up the German *Volk*: the Nordic, Mediterranean, Dinaric, Alpine and East Baltic and described their racial characteristics, placing the Nordic type at the apex of his racial hierarchy as a heroic, predominant race that possessed superior physical and mental attributes. He also described Scandinavia, Germany and North America as areas where there was still a strong strain of Nordic blood. In this work, Günther also discussed the process of *Entnordung*, the progressive depletion of the Nordic gene pool through a historic process of miscegenation with inferior races that had led to the social, cultural and political downfall of the Nordic people. To remedy this, Günther proposed a policy of *Wiedervernordung*, the regeneration of the Nordic gene pool through a range of eugenics measures aimed at protecting and regenerating the Nordic race such as selective breeding and the exclusion of inferior races.

For Günther, the Nordic was the model of human physical beauty and perfection that he described in Romantic terms in *Rassenkunde Europas* (1924):

The skin of the Nordic race is rosy and fair; it allows the blood to glimmer through, and so it looks alive, often quite lustrous, and always rather cool, or fresh, "like milk and blood." The veins shine through (at least in youth) and show "the blue blood." The hair is smooth and sleek or wavy in texture, in childhood it may be curly. Each hair is thin and soft and often "like silk". In colour it is fair, and, whether light or dark blond always shows a touch of gold, or a reddish undertone.[57]

Günther also praised their mental characteristics claiming that ambition, judgement, truthfulness and energy were key attributes of the Nordic mentality, which drove them onto great achievements:

He is distinguished by a highly developed sense of reality, which in combination with an energy that may rise to boldness, urges him onto far-reaching undertakings. Together with this he has a decided sense for competitive achievement, and develops a characteristic passion for the real [...] His inclinations are always towards prudence, reserve steadfastness, calm judgment.[58]

Günther imbued his depictions of the Nordic with admirable characteristics, a race of physically beautiful and noble leaders of mankind. Günther concluded his praise for the leadership qualities of the Nordic race by stating that the bloodline of the Nordic had produced important leading figures in both Northern Europe and America.[59]

Like many Nordicist thinkers in Germany at this time, Günther expressed his admiration for the Nordicist statesmen in the USA, such as Madison Grant, for putting into place legislation such as the Immigration Act of 1924, which favoured Northern Europeans with the aim of protecting the existing Nordic bloodstock from further miscegenation. Günther speculated that:

It may be presumed that the Immigration Laws as now passed are only the first step to still more definite laws dealing with race and eugenics. In North America, especially, where there is the opportunity to examine the races and racial mixtures of Europe from the point of view of their civic worth, the importance of the Nordic race could not stay hidden.[60]

Günther also expressed his lack of confidence in the Weimar Republic to maintain the Nordic race believing that only the unification of the Nordic people could protect the gene pool. In order for the Nordic race to flourish, he argued that the process of 'nordification' was not a national but racial issue and it was important to bring about the unification of Nordic types in the right economic conditions to allow the race to proliferate.[61]

The inability of Nordicism to flourish under the liberal democracy of the Weimar Republic, perceived as corrupted by Jewish influence by German nationalists, such as Günther, necessitated a radical change in the political system, the potential for which Günther must have seen in the growing popularity of the Nazi Party. In 1933, German-born American political philosopher Eric Voegelin (1901–1985), who fled Germany before the outbreak of war, suggested in his 1933 work, *Rasse und Staat* (Race and State), that the Nordicist theories posited by Günther would require a totalitarian regime, such as that created by National Socialism. This would enable his modernist project of 'Nordic thought' and 'renordification' to become a political, social and scientific reality. In his analysis, Voegelin argued that:

> Günther sees very clearly that the current political order of the European-American world of nations makes it impossible for the Nordic idea to prevail in the political struggle. A national policy of Aufnordung would have to be preceded by a radical internal change that eliminates all institutions of mass democracy.[62]

In *Der Nordische Gedanke unter den Deutschen* (1927), Günther outlined what he considered to be the principles of 'Nordic thought' amongst the German people. In this work, Günther called for the regeneration of the Nordic gene pool and described what he saw as the coming of a new age of racial consciousness and purification. Günther argued that, in order to achieve this, education should promote the idea that the future progress of humanity no longer lay in the nineteenth-century 'Age of Technology' but in the future 'Age of Biology' in which 'renordification' would bring about an increase in high-value hereditary traits and the eventual regeneration of Nordic supremacy. To achieve this enhancement of the human race, Günther proposed the practice of positive eugenics to increase the racially desirable and reduce the racially inferior:

> [...] the enhancement of mankind is only possible through an increase in the high-value hereditary traits, that is via a higher birth rate among the racially sound, and a check on the procreation of the less hereditarily-valuable.[63]

To support this call for racial awareness, which he described as a form of moral conscience, Günther quoted the Austrian philosopher Christian von Ehrenfels (1859–1932), who proposed that racial awareness should be a 'third person' in sexual relationships, acting as a moral guide to selecting a racially desirable sexual partner. Ehrenfels argued that:

> The idea is gaining ground that sexual intercourse, viewed morally, is not a duet but a trio—more exactly that the interests of the coming generation, and with those of the collective, often come more into consideration than those of the participants.[64]

In this work, Günther sought to present a scientific argument for a programme of positive eugenics and distanced his theory of 'Nordic thought' from the Ariosophy of esoteric, mystical Nordicists such as Guido von List. He described their works on Nordic/Teutonic mythology and runes as 'an attempt to reinvigorate faded German myths and extinct symbols' stating that 'the Nordic Movement must ruthlessly reject such aberrations'.[65] Günther rejected this form of cultural Nordicism, considering it to be a romanticisation of the Nordic ideal, rooted in an irrational, mythologised past. Günther sought to limit his project of 'renordification' to the field of science, defining it as a 'forward-looking will to self-improvement' not 'a reinvigoration of the past'.[66] Günther also distanced himself, in contradiction with his earlier idealisation of the blond Nordic in *Rassenkunde Europas* (1924), from Nordicists who saw the blond, blue-eyed Nordic as the physical ideal, a strand within the Nazi movement that effectively excluded many Germans, notably in southern regions who did not fit this Nordic type. This broader interpretation of the Nordic is noticeably more in line with Nazi racial policies that used the term Germanic or Aryan in preference to Nordic:

> No less important is the Nordic Movement's rejection of the image of the Nordic race as an exemplar of blondness. Those that are schooled in racial science know that some Nordic are dark-haired and dark-eyed, and some of the blond and blue-eyed are, especially, East-Balkans. That is, in itself, an objection to the infatuation with blondness. More importantly, however, that infatuation can disguise the true sense of the Nordic idea.[67]

In *Hitler's Private Library*, Timothy W. Ryback suggests that, from an early stage, Hitler was quite familiar with Günther's work and was

influenced by his Nordicist theories of miscegenation and racial revitalisation. Ryback describes how Hitler's library in Landsberg prison, where he
wrote *Mein Kampf* following the Beer Hall *Putsch* of 1923, contained a
'well-thumbed', 1923 edition of Günther's *Rassenkunde des deutschen
Volkes*, inscribed to Hitler by the work's publisher Julius Lehmann.[68] In
The Master Plan (2006), historian Heather Pringle comments on the public impact of Günther's works in promoting the concept of 'Nordic
thought' and 'nordification' as a scientific, racial solution to the growing
social crisis, brought about by modernity. Pringle notes that, by 1945,
Günther's *Rassenkunde des deutschen Volkes* (Racial Characteristics of the
German People), published in 1922, had sold 400,000 copies in
Germany.[69] This figure suggests a considerable public diffusion of
Günther's Nordicist racial theories. Pringle describes how:

> Günther's racial works became best sellers in Germany, flying off bookstore
> shelves. Under their powerful spell, German nationalists began to graft the
> physical characteristics of the imagined Nordic race onto the increasingly
> popular idea of the ancient Aryans.[70]

Another influential Nordicist thinker who emerged from the Thule
Society was Alfred Ernst Rosenberg (1893–1946), a Baltic German who
had left Estonia following the Russian Revolution of 1917 and arrived in
Germany as an anti-Semitic and anti-communist German pan-nationalist
who joined the early *Deutsche Arbeiterpartei* (*DAP*) in 1919. Rosenberg
made a significant contribution to the academic development of Nordicist
ideology within the early Nazi Party, becoming a regular contributor to,
and later editor of, the *Völkischer Beobachter* published by a founding
member of the Nazi Party, Dietrich Eckhart (1868–1923). This newspaper soon became the official newspaper of the Nazi Party. Rosenberg was
also placed in significant and influential posts where he could implement
his Nordicist theories, such as Leader of the Foreign Policy Office of the
NSDAP (1933–1945), Commissar for the Supervision of Intellectual and
Ideological Education (1934–1945) and Reich Minister for the Occupied
Eastern Territories (1941–1945). In 1933, he also took over control of
the *Nordische Gesellschaft* (Nordic Society), founded in 1921 to develop
German-Nordic cultural cooperation. Heinrich Himmler and Walther
Darré also became influential members of this Nordicist group. From
1934 to 1939, the society organised annual *Reichstagungen* (Reich
Meetings) to bring together experts in the field of 'Nordic thought' to

establish contacts in Scandinavia and spread their Nordicist ideology. In an address to the first conference in 1934, Rosenberg ended his speech with a call for Nordic unity and cooperation in Northern Europe:

> We also send our greetings far across the sea to all those men and women in other states who are honestly and similarly willing to accept the challenges of our time, to serve them and thus work together for peace in our ancient Europe, in the best interest of every single people in Scandinavia and around the Baltic; uniting the European destiny with the well-being of each nation.[71]

In 1930, the year that he was elected to the Reichstag as a deputy, Rosenberg published his major work on racial theory and Nordicism *Der Mythus des 20. Jahrhunderts* (The Myth of the Twentieth Century). Building on the works of Arthur de Gobineau, Madison Grant and Houston Stewart Chamberlain, Rosenberg reflected both their turn of the century pessimism and the post-war sense of social alienation of the *Kriegsgeneration*. In his work he described the loss of traditional values and beliefs in the devastation of the war:

> Once, such ultimate aim was the "Christianizing of the world" and its redemption through the second coming of Christ. Another goal was represented by the Humanist dream of "Mankind." Both ideals have been buried in the bloody chaos of the Great War, despite the fact that now one, and now the other, still find increasingly fanatical adherents and a venerable priesthood. These are processes of petrification and no longer of living tissue: A belief, which has died in the soul, cannot be raised from the dead.[72]

Rosenberg's pessimism and sense of alienation emerge in his description of the breakdown of the metanarratives of Christianity and the development of mankind, in the apocalyptic events of the war. Rosenberg viewed the *nomos* of society, the social elements or constructs creating meaning and purpose, as being broken beyond repair even by those who he described as 'fanatical adherents' of a lost belief system. For Rosenberg, the collapse of Germany in the devastation of the Great War marked the breakdown of the *nomos* that had shaped and maintained society, leaving Germany in an *anomic* state of political turbulence, economic strife and social degeneracy. In Rosenberg's words:

> All present-day struggles for power are outward effects of an inward collapse. All State systems of 1914 have already collapsed […] Collapsed also

have social, church and ideological creeds and values. No highest principle, no supreme idea governs undisputed the life of the *Volk*, group struggles against group, party against party, [...] life is uprooted.[73]

Rosenberg expressed his post-war sense of deracination as traditional social structures were rapidly eroded by a modernity from which Nordicist thinkers felt alienated as their established *nomos* of traditionalism was smashed by the catastrophic events of the war. Rosenberg described a fragmented society, in search of a higher, supreme, unifying ideal transcending the individual, an ideal that he situated in a romanticised 'sacred space' outside the fragmented contemporary world, in which the regeneration of the Nordic race offered a new path of national identity, cohesion and spirituality which was uniquely Germanic. Rosenberg described this as his 'new Myth—a new supreme value' which had to be presented to the masses as a new belief system, a 'mazeway resynthesis' founded on a mythical *Vorzeit* of racial supremacy which had been progressively eroded through miscegenation with inferior racial types. Rosenberg believed that this lost racial primacy could be biologically regenerated through positive eugenics and the founding of a culture based on Germanic cultural and religious traditions, a principle which he referred to as *Blut und Boden* (Blood and Soil). This ideology linked the ethnicity of a people to their bloodline and the land that they had historically occupied and cultivated and became a core strand of the Nazi ideology.

In *Der Mythus des 20. Jahrhunderts,* Rosenberg proposed a racial reinterpretation of history based on the supremacy of the Nordic race, carried in the blood of the Germanic people, in contrast with the eroding, corrupting influence of the Jews. Rosenberg described his concept of blood as the embodiment of the Nordic soul, a biological and spiritual synthesis that had been eroded through miscegenation. Rosenberg's thesis was based on the diffusion of the Nordic people from Scandinavia where the once nomadic Aryan tribe had settled. According to Rosenberg, the basis of Western culture had evolved through the leadership of those carrying the Nordic bloodline. In this context, Rosenberg perceived blood in a spiritual context, as a religion in itself, defining race as 'the image of the soul' and the history of this belief system as 'the great world story of the rise and fall of peoples, their heroes and thinkers, their inventors and artists'.[74] Rosenberg proposed a new mythology, a new Germanic belief system that fused ancient traditions with futural visions of racial regeneration through the concept of blood, a transcendence that merged past, present and future.

Rosenberg also argued that the Roman Catholic Church had historically aligned itself with Freemasons, Jesuits and the Jews to erode once-noble German spiritual values and its vital sense of *völkisch* community. Rosenberg rejected both the religious dogma of both the established Christian Catholic and Protestant churches and the image of Christ that they portrayed. He criticised the emphasis that Christianity placed on humanitarianism, which in his view had protected the weak and progressively eroded the Nordic concept of honour and the protection of the its gene pool. Rosenberg argued that:

> Thanks to the preaching of humanitarianism and the doctrine of human equality, every Jew, negro and mulatto can become a citizen of equal rights in a European state [...] thanks to humanity negroes and Jews can marry into the Nordic race, indeed even occupy important offices.[75]

Rosenberg criticised key aspects of Christian belief such as original sin, the Virgin birth and the resurrection, which he saw as 'the denial of natural life'.[76] He also attacked what he perceived to be a historical misrepresentation of Jesus by religious groups that had distorted the original historical figure of Christ to support and spread their own belief systems. Rosenberg claimed that:

> The great personality of Jesus Christ, whatever form it may have taken originally, was distorted and confused immediately after his death with all the rubbish of Jewish and African life.[77]

In his work, Rosenberg rejected the Jewish heritage of Jesus claiming that he was possibly of Aryan descent referring to H.S. Chamberlain, Friedrich Delitzsch and Dr. E. Jung whose research had established Jesus as being Syrian on his maternal side and Roman on his paternal side. Rosenberg described these as being two of the greatest ancient civilisations.[78] Rosenberg presented Jesus as a bold, heroic figure who had opposed both the might of Rome and Judaic tradition and whose image the early Christian Church had misappropriated as a symbol of love, sympathy and humanitarianism.

As part of his new mythology, Rosenberg called for the rejection of the Christian dogma, which had weakened the spirit of the German people and a return to the Nordic principles of honour and duty that had been eroded by centuries of Christian teaching:

> [...] It is evident that almost everything which has preserved the character of our race, our peoples and nations, has been in the first place the concept of honour and the idea of duty inseparably connected with it [...] but from the moment at which love and sympathy (or if one wishes: fellow feeling) become predominant, there also began the epochs of racial, national and cultural dissolution in the history of all once Nordically determined states.[79]

Rosenberg described how this concept of honour and its relationship with the soil could be found 'embodied in the lives of the Viking, the Teutonic Knight, the Prussian officer, the Baltic Hansa, the German soldier, and the German peasant'.[80] He argued that the foundation of a new German civilisation should be based on a shared sense of nobility, honour and eternal relationship with the soil of their Nordic ancestors.

In his discussion of Christianity, Rosenberg proposed the Nazi religious ideology of 'Positive Christianity' that attempted to align National Socialist political and religious ideology with the established Catholic and Protestant churches in Germany. In his work, Rosenberg discussed the historical conflict between what he terms 'Negative Christianity', based on 'abstract dogmas and hoary old customs' and 'Positive Christianity', which in his words 'calls upon the Nordic blood to awaken'[81] and which presented Jesus as a heroic Aryan figure. This state-sanctioned form of Christianity was one of many new religions of the period that attempted to fuse Aryanism and Nordicism with the tradition of the Bible to create a national belief system that promoted Northern European values and supremacy. Alongside and often in opposition to the Positive Christianity of the *Deutsche Evangelische Kirche* (*German Evangelical Church*) of Ludwig Müller, the *Deutsche Glaubensbewegung* (German Faith Movement) of Jakob Wilhelm Hauer (1881–1962) proposed what they considered a truly Germanic belief system. This centred on a return to ancient forms of Northern European pagan worship and the rejection of both Christianity and Judaism as foreign faiths.

Rosenberg's myth, his biological and spiritual vision of a future Pan-German society, was founded on the 'imperfect history' established by nineteenth-century nationalist writers and racial scientists who sought to establish the primacy of the Nordic/Germanic race. Rosenberg attempted to provide Nazism with its own Nordic creation myth based on the 'renordification' of Germany and the diffusion of its people into territories where the Nordic people could expand and re-establish their essential relationship with the soil. The impact of Rosenberg's *Mythus* has been the subject of some debate despite its circulation figures that exceeded 1 million copies by 1944. Rosenberg's work was allegedly rejected by Hitler who claimed that he had hardly read the book and who stated that Rosenberg's *Myth of the Twentieth Century* was not to be regarded as an expression of the official doctrine of the Party.[82] Its publication figures and the prominent positions held by Rosenberg in the Nazi regime suggest, however, that his Nordicist views had some influence with receptive thinkers at the time.

In her analysis of the development of *völkisch* new religions alongside Nazism in *New Religions and the Nazis* (2006), Karla Poewe discusses the influence of Rosenberg and the conflict between the emerging new forms of *völkisch* faith and the established forms of Catholicism and Protestantism during the inter-war period. Poewe's work focuses in particular on the *Deutsche Glaubensbewegung* (German Faith Movement) of Jakob Wilhelm Hauer whose rejection of Christianity as a foreign faith aligned him with the early Nazi movement and leaders of the SS. According to Poewe, Hauer joined Alfred Rosenberg's *Kampfbund für deutsche Kultur* (Battle-League for German Culture) in May 1933 and the *Hitlerjugend* (Hitler Youth) in December 1933. In 1934, he was persuaded by Reinhard Heydrich and Himmler to join the SS and SD, and in 1937 he joined the Nazi Party.[83] In 1933, from an amalgamation of like-minded *völkisch* religious groups, he founded what became officially known, in 1934, as the *Deutsche Glaubensbewegung*. This movement fused Germanic neo-paganism with Hauer's attraction to Hinduism and Buddhism to form a belief system, in touch with Germany's prehistoric Nordic roots and vehemently opposed to all forms of Christianity. In her work, Poewe states that, by 1934, 'Hauer equated religion with race' and attempted to convince his followers of a struggle between two *Glaubenswelten* (faith-worlds): the Indo-Germanic and the Near-Eastern Semitic.[84]

According to Poewe, two-thirds of the board members of the *Deutsche Glaubensbewegung* were Nazis and notable members including H.F.K. Gunther and director of the *Ahnenerbe*, Herman Wirth.[85] Poewe finds, from a study of his correspondence, that Hauer shared many ideas with influential party members such as Deputy Führer Rudolf Hess (1894–1987); Minister of the Interior, Wilhelm Frick (1877–1946); and Alfred Rosenberg. She points out, however, that establishing any accurate membership of his movement is problematic because 'opportunism, secretiveness and deceit played into this numbers game'.[86] The movement was significant, however, in attempting to develop a faith movement compatible with Nazi Party doctrine. This movement appealed to many Nordicists within the Party as a return to early forms of Nordic pagan worship and was generally compatible with their anti-Semitic world-view and vision of an approaching final conflict between the Nordic and the Jew. In this context the *Deutsche Glaubensbewegung* of Hauer could be considered as a form of cultural Nordicism that overlapped with aspects of political and biological Nordicism providing a new adapted form of religion that appealed to many Nordicist thinkers during the 1930s.

Another significant figure in this Nazi Nordicist community who became an influential member of the Nordicist strand within the Nazi state was Richard Walther Darré (1895–1953). During the late 1920s and early 1930s, Darré became one of the leading theorists of the 'Blood and Soil' movement. He also served the Nazi regime as Reich Minister of Food and Agriculture from 1933 to 1942 and served Himmler in the *Rasse- und Siedlungshauptamt der SS* (*RuSHA*), (The SS Race and Settlement Main Office), the organisation responsible for safeguarding the racial purity of the SS.

As a young man in Germany, Darré developed a keen interest in agriculture and joined the *Artamanen-Gesellschaft* (Artaman League), a *völkisch* youth group committed to the 'back to the land' movement where he began to develop the idea of the linkage between the future of the Nordic race and the soil. This youth group was formally established in 1924 to restore core values of rural life and traditions. It also sought to expel Polish migrant workers from the countryside and establish a future land army or *Wehrbauern* to protect Germany's land from the political and biological threat from the communist and Slavic east.[87] Through this organisation, Darré met a number of like-minded Nordic thinkers, notably the young Heinrich Himmler, with whom he developed a close working relationship. Following a period in the *Freikorps*, he went to university to pursue his interest in agriculture and animal breeding, completing his doctorate in 1929. Darré was a keen writer and published fifty-six articles between 1925 and 1930 on agricultural methods and the essential link between the Nordic and the Soil.[88] He also published two notable works, *Das Bauerntum als Lebensquell der nordischen Rasse* (The Peasantry as Life Source of the Nordic Race, 1928) and *Neuadel aus Blut und Boden* (A New Nobility of Blood and Soil, 1930).

In his works, Darré expanded on H.F.K. Günther's concept of *Wiedervernordung* (renordification) defining the German peasantry as a homogenous racial group of Nordic antecedents, who formed the cultural and racial core of the German nation. He saw that a healthy rural youth would eventually provide a key source of population for urban growth. However, since the Nordic birth rate was lower than other races, the Nordic race was under a long-term threat of extinction.[89] He also asserted that if Germany wanted to grow strong once again, it had to return to its agricultural traditions as well as implementing measures to restore the purity of the Nordic race. Darré argued that selective breeding would eventually bring about a renordified Germanic people and included in his measures the extermination of the sick and impure. He also argued that inheritance laws, redrafted after the French Revolution that permitted landowners to divide their land between their heirs, had weakened the quality of the rural Nordic breeding stock by allowing weaker siblings to inherit land.[90]

Darré's strand of Nordicism was founded and interwoven with his theories on racial science, eugenics, animal breeding and Nordic supremacy. He was also anti-Christian and proposed a return to local folklore and the celebration of ancient pagan festivals. In her analysis of Darré in *Blood and Soil: Walther Darré and Hitler's Green Party* (1985), Anna Bramwell suggests that Darré's 'Blood and Soil' theories and intellectual skills brought a vital dimension to the Nordicist movement. Bramwell describes how:

> Darré brought a new element into the Nordic movement. His training in agriculture, his farming experience, his animal breeding, his liking for evidence and argument, and his capacity to inspire enthusiasm and activity all galvanised the movement.[91]

Through his 'Blood and Soil' ideology, Darré provided Nordicism with a scientifically based programme, based on contemporary issues of eugenics, population policy and rural development, for the 'renordification' of Germany. He also legitimised a national mythology of an essential synergy between Blood, which represented race and ancestry, and Soil that expressed the eternal bond between a people and the land that they had occupied and cultivated for generations. In this context, Darré's theories aligned with Nordicism's resynthesis of mythology with modern science to plan an alternative modernity of Nordic racial supremacy over inferior races.

Associated with Darré and later with Himmler, wartime artist Wolfgang Willrich (1897–1948) became famous for his widely published portraits of military heroes and for his representations of the noble Nordic characteristics of the rural community. Funded by the SS, Willrich travelled around the countryside sketching German peasants who he saw as representative of the concept of 'Blood and Soil' and evidence of the remaining Nordic gene pool in the rural population. In 1935, he published a collection of his work entitled *Bauerntum als Heger Deutschen Blutes* (The Peasantry as Guardians of the German Blood) which contained a foreword by Darré. Himmler himself wrote a foreword in 1935 to *Vom Lebesbaum Deutscher— Art Bilder und Gedanken zur Rassenfrage* (From the Tree of Life of German Art—Pictures and Thoughts on the Racial Question). Willrich also published a number of artistic works, photographic features and essays on race and art in the journals, *Velhagen und Klasings Monatshefte* and the *Odal*, founded by Darré to promote the concept of 'Blood and Soil'.[92] Many of Willrich's portraits of war heroes and the *Volk* were reproduced in a popular postcard format. Willrich became particularly well known for these widely published postcards that members of the *Hitlerjugend* would collect and often send to their war heroes for autographs. Through his prolific work and the patronage of figures such as Darré and Himmler, Willrich became one of Germany's most popular wartime artists, promoting Nordic thought throughout Germany and leading what could be termed a school of state-sanctioned Nordicist art (Fig. 4.2).

Although this Nordicist strand within Nazism was influential in creating and later executing Nazi racial policy, the concept of Nordicism remained nevertheless politically marginalised within mainstream Nazism. The political issue centred around the fact that the German population was by no means a homogenous Nordic ethnic group especially in the south where the population appeared more alpine and Southern European by the racial classifications of the time. According to Heather Pringle, Günther attempted to assess the Nordic population of Germany and published his results in 1925. According to his results, just 50–55% of the German population possessed a trace of Nordic blood, and only 6–8% were of pure Nordic descent.[93] Given this ethnic profile of the nation, Nordicist theorists associated with the NSDAP risked alienating a large section of the German public from Nazism. It is significant to note that the word Nordic was hardly used in Hitler's *Mein Kampf* and speeches in which he favoured the term Aryan to describe Germany's ethnic heritage. It is also noticeably absent from the twenty-five-point programme of the

Fig. 4.2 Wolfgang Willrich. Portrait of Ellen Luise Petersen née Feddersen Hoyer (1939). An idealised image of the natural beauty of the Nordic bloodline. From *Des Elden Ewiges Reich* (The Noble Eternal Empire). Verlag Grenze und Ausland, Berlin (1941). Scan kindly provided from the collection of Jens Peter Mortensen

NSDAP announced by Hitler on 24 February 1920 and the Nuremberg Race Laws which kept to the broader terms, used by mainstream Nazism of Aryan, Germanic, non-German and Jewish. As a unifying nationalist party, the NSDAP could not risk the internal divisions that may have appeared within the nation by publicly promoting the Nordic race as a social and biological ideal type. In her analysis of 'Nordic thought' in Germany, Anna Bramwell discusses this political issue of Nordicism that risked a division between the more Nordic northern Germans and their southern counterparts:

> The exclusive and tribal character of the Nordic movement meant that Hitler's National Socialism could never fully absorb it. The Nordic offered Northerness as the best, the most important part of the German Heritage, in doing so, they excluded the Catholic parts of Germany including the blonde blue eyed German Catholics of Austria and much of south Germany, also the Rhineland states.[94]

In *Race and the Third Reich* (2005), Christopher M. Hutton also discusses the politically sensitive issue that a policy of Nordic supremacy could not be fully aligned with the apparent racial diversity of the German *Volk*. Hutton points out that following a Nordicist biological policy would have eventually lead to certain groups within the *Volk* being considered racially inferior and progressively eliminated from the German population to ensure a growing purity of Nordic blood:

> The promotion of the Nordic Race raised the question of whether, say, the Dinaric or Mediterranean racial elements in the German Volk could be seen as racially inferior. This had implications for any understanding of the regional make up of the German Volk, and was highly sensitive in relation to the strong regional, cultural and confessional divisions in German society [...] If the Nordic race was identified with the superior element, then should not the same racially inferior elements be eradicated from the Volk in the same way as other foreign elements?[95]

In analysing the emerging strand of Nordicism within Nazism, Hutton points out that we should consider Nordicism as a spectrum of belief. This ranges from what he terms 'fundamentalist Nordicism' (those who believed in the absolute supremacy of the Nordic race), and those more moderate thinkers who argued that the German *Volk* had benefitted to various degrees from its 'hybrid quality' and that all variants of the Germanic *Volk* had its own qualities to contribute to the restoration of the German Nation.[96] In his examination of the issue of Nordic elitism, Hutton quotes the objections of public figures such as the Protestant theologian Helmuth Schreiner (1893–1962) who rejected the physical racial criteria of Nordicists such as Rosenberg and Günther who idealised the tall, blue-eyed blond as the ideal Nordic type. In a 1934 publication, he objected to the 'privileging of the Nordic race within the German people', stating that 'even the dark, heavy-set, round-headed Germans are predominantly of Nordic race'.[97] Hutton also quotes *völkisch* writer Martin Otto Johannes who, in a 1934 publication, criticised the way in which the Nordicist ideal had been promoted as the perfect German:

> Martin Otto Johannes argued that the Nordic question had to be approached with tact and objectivity. The dissemination of ideas about race had sometimes been badly handled, giving rise to uninformed discussion of race in educational contexts, which the Party was now rightly seeking to bring

under control. It had to be stressed that the Nordic component was the unifying bond between the racial elements of the German people [...].[98]

Johannes argued that Nordic identity had been mishandled politically and should be evaluated on the basis that Nordic blood could manifest itself both physically and psychologically and that physical appearance should not be a primary indicator of racial value. In his view, the most important factor was the 'Nordic spirit, Nordic soul and Nordic mind-set'.[99] Within Nazism there was a clear spectrum of thought within Nordicism from those who saw the Nordic bloodline in terms of the Nordic ideal physical type and those who took a more moderate, inclusive and arguably more politically expedient view of the German population. This view promoted the concept of the Nordic soul of Germans even if they actually looked far from Nordic in appearance. This differentiated view of a Nordicist spectrum is fundamental to a deeper understanding of Nordicism as being far from a homogeneous movement within Nazism. The Nordicist strand within Nazism can be seen to express a range of varying political, biological and religious strands, all reacting against the eroding forces of modernity. They were, however, all united by the core belief that the German people had originated from a Northern tribe of racially pure, strong and spiritually noble warriors whose gene pool had been weakened through centuries of miscegenation.

Nazism, as a political organisation, did therefore not publicly place such a potentially divisive policy as Nordic thought to the forefront of its political agenda, especially under the democratic Weimar Republic. Hitler allowed it, nonetheless, to develop as a significant strand of its political, social and religious agenda through the placing of prominent Nordicist thinkers in positions of power and influence. In the USA democracy placed considerable limitations on the ability of the relatively marginal Nordicist strand to implement its futural projects of regenerating the Nordic race. This was going to change, however, in 1933 when Hitler gained full power over the state and the German people. For the first time, Nordicism was able to flourish and become a political, social and religious reality and play its part in Germany's destructive path to the industrial-scale genocide of the holocaust.

NOTES

1. Anon (Trans Larrington, C. 2014) *The Poetic Edda*. Oxford Classics, Oxford p 12.
2. Notably Shirer, William L. (1959) *The Rise and Fall of the Third Reich*, Fest, Joachim C. (1973) *Hitler* and Speer, Albert (1970) *Inside the Third Reich.*
3. *US Immigration before 1965.* History.com. http://www.history.com/topics/u-s-immigration-before-1965 (Accessed 03/01/16).
4. Ibid. 3.
5. *US Immigration Statistics.* http://www.nps.gov/elis/learn/education/upload/statistics.pdf (Accessed 03/01/16). The actual figure shown is 1,004,756 based on annual reports from the Commissioner General of Immigration on immigration through the Ellis Island Immigration Station.
6. Spiro, Jonathan Peter (2009) *Defending the Master Race; Conservation, Eugenics, and the Legacy of Madison Grant.* University of Vermont Press, New England p 7.
7. Mazeway resynthesis—a term used by sociologists Anthony FC Wallace and Kenneth Tollefson; see Chap. 1.
   In *Revitalizations and Mazeways* (Nebraska: University of Nebraska Press, 2003), Wallace defines mazeways as 'mental maps that join personalities with cultures and thereby illustrate how individuals embrace their culture, conduct everyday life, and cope with illness and other forms of severe personal or cultural stress'.
8. *The Passing of the Great Race.* Publication figures shown in introduction. wolfweb.unr.edu. http://wolfweb.unr.edu/homepage/calabj/pdf/Great%20Race.pdf (Accessed 30.10.16).
9. Spiro, Jonathan Peter *Defending the Master Race,* pp. 157–158.
10. Grant, Madison (1916) *The Passing of The Great Race.* C. Scribner's Sons, New York p 5.
11. Ibid. 10 p 14.
12. Ibid. 10 p 14.
13. Ibid. 10 pp. 17–18.
14. Ibid. 10 p 26.
15. Ibid. 10 p 198.
16. Ibid. 10 p 199.
17. Ibid. 10 p 46.

18.   Ibid. 10 pp. 46–47.
19.   Galton, Francis. (1904) *Eugenics: Its definition, scope, and aims.* The American Journal of Sociology. 10 (1): 1–25. http://galton. org/essays/1900-1911/galton-1904-am-journ-soc-eugenics-scope-aims.htm (Accessed 15/08/15).
20.   Ibid. 6 p 170.
21.   Hitler, Adolf (Trans. Manheim, R. 1995) *Mein Kampf.* Pimlico, London p 400.
22.   Ryback, Timothy W. (2010) *Hitler's Private Library: The Books that shaped his Life.* Vintage, London p 94.
23.   Ryback, Timothy W. *Hitler's Private Library.* p 114.
24.   Ibid. 23 p 96.
25.   Ibid. 23 p 115.
26.   Ibid. 21 p 290.
       See also Chapoutot, Johann (2016) *Greeks, Romans, Germans: How the Nazis Usurped Europe's Classical Past.* University of California Press, Berkeley pp. 30–31.
27.   Pichot, André (Trans. D. Fernbach, 2009) *The Pure Society - From Darwin to Hitler.* Verso, London, New York p 148.
28.   *Treaty of Versailles - 1919.* ushmm.org. https://www.ushmm. org/wlc/en/article.php?ModuleId=10005425   (Accessed 25/03/17).
29.   Hall, Alan (2010) *Germany Ends World War One Reparations.* Daily Mail Online http://www.dailymail.co.uk/news/article-1315869/Germany-end-World-War-One-reparations-92-years-59m-final-payment.html (Accessed 21/05/17).
30.   Bauman, Zygmunt (1989) *Modernity and the Holocaust.* Polity Press, Cambridge p 45.
31.   Translates as the 'War Generation' and used in German to describe young men in the 1920s and 1930s who had survived the War or been children growing up during the conflict and the aftermath of the post-war years.
32.   Hutton, Christopher M. (2005) *Race and the Third Reich.* Polity Press, Cambridge p 12.
33.   Pois, Robert (1986) *National Socialism and the Religion of Nature.* Croom Helm, London and Sydney pp. 41–42.
34.   Ibid. 33 p 141.
35.   Ibid. 33 p 142.
36.   Ibid. 33 p 142.

37. Ibid. 33 p 142.
38. Ibid. 33 p 142.
39. Griffin, Roger (2007) *Modernism and Fascism – The Sense of a Beginning under Mussolini and Hitler.* Palgrave Macmillan, Basingstoke and New York p 110.
40. Ibid. 39 pp. 110–11.
41. Ibid. 42 p 111.
42. Ibid. 42 p 69.
43. Ibid. 42 p 105.
44. Ibid. 19.
45. Kühl, Stefan (1994) *The Nazi Connection - Eugenics, American Racism, and German National Socialism.* Oxford University Press, Oxford p 134.
46. Ibid. 45 p 19.
47. Ibid. 45 p 21.
48. Ibid. 45 p 21.
49. Kyllingstad, Jon Røyne (2015) *Measuring the Master Race: Physical Anthropology in Norway 1890–1945.* Open Book Publishers, Cambridge. Digital edition. p 2587.
50. Ibid. 49 p 2587.
51. Ibid. 49 p 2603.
52. Ibid. 49 p 2858.
53. Ibid. 49 p 2858.
54. Ibid. 49 p 3261.
55. Ibid. 49 p 4896.
56. Ibid. 49 p 4942.
57. Günther, Hans F.K. (Trans. Wheeler G.C. 1927) *The Racial Elements of European History.* Methuen and Co, London p 12.
58. Ibid. 57 p 32.
59. Ibid. 57 p 34.
60. Ibid. 57 p 197.
61. Ibid. 57 p 197.
62. Voegelin, Eric (1997) *The Collected works Volume 2 Race and State.* University of Missouri Press, Baton Rouge p 217.
63. Günther, H.F.K. (1927) *Der Nordische Gedanke unter den Deutschen.* Lehmanns Verlag, Munich p 13 Translation provided by Roger Moorhouse.
64. Ibid. 63 p 12.
65. Ibid. 63 p 66.

66. Ibid. 63 p 71.
67. Ibid. 63 p 67.
68. Ibid. 23 p 69.
69. Pringle, Heather (2006) *The Master Plan - Himmler's Scholars and the Holo*caust. Harper Perennial, London p 335.
70. Ibid. 69 p 36.
71. Rosenberg, Alfred quoted by Michael Müller-Wille in Roesdahl, Else and Sorensen, Preben Meulengracht (1996) *The Waking of Angantyr: The Scandinavian Past in European Culture.* Arhus University Press, Arhus p 159.
72. Rosenberg, Alfred (Trans. Bird V. 1993) *The Myth of the Twentieth Century.*
    Noontide Press, California p 3.
73. Rosenberg, Alfred *The Myth of the Twentieth Century.* p 5.
74. Ibid. 72 p 18.
75. Ibid. 72 p 139.
76. Ibid. 72 p 53.
77. Ibid. 72 p 51.
78. Ibid. 72 p 401.
79. Ibid. 72 p 100.
80. Ibid. 72 p 148.
81. Ibid. 72 p 54.
82. Hitler, Adolf (Trans. Trevor-Roper, H. 2000) *Adolf Hitler's Secret Conversations.* (3rd edition) Enigma Books, London p 400 Hitler's comments about Rosenberg's work were set down by Hitler's secretary Martin Bormann and later published.
83. Poewe, Karla (2007) *New Religions and the Nazis.* Routledge, New York and London p 97.
84. Ibid. 83 p 11.
85. Ibid. 83 p 97.
86. Ibid. 83 p 97.
87. Ibid. 69 p 39.
88. Ibid. 69 p 53.
89. Bramwell, Anna (1985) *Blood and Soil: Walther Darré and Hitler's Green Party.* Kensal Press, Buckinghamshire p 55.
90. Ibid. 89 p 40.
91. Ibid. 89 p 50.

92. *Óðal* ᛟ refers to the Elder Futhark rune signifying heritage and inheritance. This runic symbol became popular amongst followers of Blood and Soil theories.
93. Ibid. 69 p 41.
94. Ibid. 89 p 50.
95. Ibid. 32 p 111.
96. Ibid. 32 p 114.
97. Ibid. 32 p 131.
98. Ibid. 32 p 132.
99. Ibid. 32 p 132.

BIBLIOGRAPHY

PRINTED WORKS

Anon. (2014). (Trans. Larrington, C.) *The Poetic Edda*. Oxford: Oxford Classics.

Bauman, Z. (1989). *Modernity and the Holocaust*. Cambridge: Polity Press.

Bramwell, A. (1985). *Blood and Soil: Walther Darré and Hitler's Green Party*. Buckinghamshire: Kensal Press.

Grant, M. (1916). *The Passing of the Great Race*. New York: C. Scribner's Sons.

Griffin, R. (2007). *Modernism and Fascism – The Sense of a Beginning Under Mussolini and Hitler*. Basingstoke: Palgrave Macmillan.

Günther, H. F. K. (1927a). *Der Nordische Gedanke unter den Deutschen*. Munich: Lehmanns Verlag.

Günther, H. F. K. (1927b). (Trans. Wheeler G.C.) *The Racial Elements of European History*. London: Methuen and Co.

Hitler, A. (2000). (Trans. Trevor-Roper, H.) *Adolf Hitler's Secret Conversations*. (3rd edition) Enigma Books, London.

Hitler, A. (1995). (Trans. Manheim, R.) *Mein Kampf*. London: Pimlico.

Hutton, C. M. (2005). *Race and the Third Reich*. Cambridge: Polity Press.

Kühl, S. (1994). *The Nazi Connection - Eugenics, American Racism, and German National Socialism*. Oxford: Oxford University Press.

Kyllingstad, J. R. (2015). *Measuring the Master Race: Physical Anthropology in Norway 1890–1945*. Cambridge: Open Book Publishers.

Pichot, A. (2009). (Trans. Fernbach D.) *The Pure Society - From Darwin to Hitler*. London: Verso.

Poewe, K. (2007). *New Religions and the Nazis*. New York: Routledge.

Pringle, H. (2006). *The Master Plan – Himmler's Scholars and the Holocaust*. London: Harper Perennial.

Roesdahl, E., & Sorensen, P. M. (1996). *The Waking of Angantyr: The Scandinavian Past in European Culture*. Arhus: Arhus University Press.

Rosenberg, A. (1993) (Trans. Bird, V.). *The Myth of the Twentieth Century*. California: Noontide Press.

Ryback, T. W. (2010). *Hitler's Private Library: The Books that Shaped His Life*. London: Vintage.

Spiro, J. P. (2009). *Defending the Master Race; Conservation, Eugenics, and the Legacy of Madison Grant*. New England: University of Vermont Press.

Voegelin, E. (1997). *The Collected Works Volume 2 Race and State*. Baton Rouge: University of Missouri Press.

Wallace, A. F. C., & Tollefson, K. (2003). *Revitalizations and Mazeways*. Nebraska: University of Nebraska Press.

WEBSITES AND DIGITAL PUBLICATIONS (WITH DATE ACCESSED)

Galton, F. (1904) Eugenics: Its Definition, Scope, and Aims. *The American Journal of Sociology, 10* (1): 1–25. Accessed 15/08/15, from http://galton.org/essays/1900-1911/galton-1904-am-journ-soc-eugenics-scope-aims.htm

Hall, A. (2010). Germany Ends World War One Reparations. *Daily Mail Online*. Accessed 21/05/17, from http://www.dailymail.co.uk/news/article-1315869/Germany-end-World-War-One-reparations-92-years-59m-final-payment.html

The Passing of the Great Race. Publication Figures Shown in Introduction. wolfweb.unr.edu. Accessed 30.10.16, from http://wolfweb.unr.edu/homepage/calabj/pdf/Great%20Race.pdf

Treaty of Versailles - 1919. ushmm.org. Accessed 25/03/17, from https://www.ushmm.org/wlc/en/article.php?ModuleId=10005425

US Immigration Before 1965. History.com. Accessed 03/01/16, from http://www.history.com/topics/u-s-immigration-before-1965

US Immigration Statistics. Accessed 03/01/16, from http://www.nps.gov/elis/learn/education/upload/statistics.pdf

CHAPTER 5

Nordicism Unleashed

By 1933, the NSDAP had become the largest elected party in the *Reichstag* leading to Hitler's appointment as Chancellor on 30 January 1933. This, however, was to become a 'stepping stone' to totalitarianism. Following the *Reichstag* fire of 27 February 1933, used as evidence of a communist plot against the government, the Nazis declared a state of emergency. The following day, 28 February, President Paul von Hindenburg issued the *Reichstagsbrandverordnung* (The *Reichstag* Fire Decree), which permitted the Nazi-led regime to arrest and imprison political opponents without specific charge, dissolve political organisations, and to control publications. It also gave the central government the authority to overrule state and local laws and governments. This emergency legislation paved the way for the subsequent passing of the *Ermächtigungsgesetz* (The Enabling Act) of 24 March 1933. This further legislation gave Hitler plenary powers including the authority to enact laws without the involvement of the *Reichstag*, effectively putting an end to democracy in Germany creating a totalitarian regime under Hitler's absolute control. This gave the Nordicist stand within Nazism the unprecedented opportunity to engage the processes that they had hitherto only been able to hypothesise.

© The Author(s) 2020

G. E. Forssling, *Nordicism and Modernity*,

https://doi.org/10.1007/978-3-030-61210-8_5

THE RISE OF NAZISM IN THE USA DURING THE 1930s

The rise to power of Nazism in Germany and its renewed sense of national identity was reflected in the USA during the 1930s through the emergence, in 1933, of the *Bund der Freunde des Neuen Deutschland* (Friends of the New Germany). This group was established to promote German nationalism and in particular Nazism and was initially led by German immigrant American Heinz Spanknöbel (1893–1947). This organisation lasted until the mid-1930s and was formally dissolved in 1936, after the Department of State protested against the pro-Nazi activities of the group.[1] From the demise of the Friends of New Germany, the *Amerikadeutscher Bund* (The German American Federation) was established in New York under the leadership of Fritz Julius Kuhn (1896–1951). The *Bund* was active in promoting German American nationalism through publications such as its newspaper, the *Deutsche Weckruf und Beobachter* (The German Wake-up Call and Observer) and through uniformed parades and public gatherings. On 20 February 1939, the birthday of George Washington, a crowd of 20,000 supporters attended a rally in Madison Square Garden, New York, for the 'True Americanism' event led by Kuhn. Its poster and program cover showed a Nordic/Germanic warrior spearing a snake, a reference to *Þórr*'s battle with the *Miðgarðr* serpent. On his shield the American flag bore thirteen stars to represent the original founding states of Germanic/Nordic settlers in the Northeast. This mass-rally provoked violent clashes with an even greater number of anti-Nazi protesters.[2]

Despite widespread opposition, the *Bund* succeeded in establishing twenty training and youth camps across America, notably in the North Eastern States of Sussex County, New Jersey, New York and Wisconsin.[3] Its high-profile and growing public concern over Nazism in Germany marginalised the group, which attracted government investigations into its activities and membership as well as criticism of its loyalty to Hitler over America during a period of increasing international tension. During this time, even the Nazi government in Germany sought to distance itself from this party and on 1 March 1938, the German Foreign Office made an announcement that forbade German citizens from being members of the *Bund* that was finally formally dissolved when the USA declared war on Germany in 1941. Although this was a relatively marginal group, it was nonetheless significant as an indicator of the surge in German nationalism as many German/Nordic Americans saw Nazism as a means of regenerating both their national and racial predominance over an increasing immigrant population.

A LEGAL FRAMEWORK FOR NORDICISM IN GERMANY

1933 and the years that followed were marked by a proliferation of legislation aimed at eliminating Jews, gypsies, homosexuals, habitual criminals, those suffering from a range of hereditary conditions and others deemed threatening to the racial hygiene of the nation. The Nazi regime and its strand of influential Nordicist thinkers, many of whom worked as advisors to the State, were able to pass a plethora of legislative measures based on principles of positive and negative eugenics aimed at purifying the gene pool and revitalising the German nation.

Within this eugenics legislation, for the political reasons discussed, the term Nordic was rarely used, and the term Germanic or Aryan was generally favoured to describe the *Volk*. Many detailed discussions also took place to establish a legal definition of both a German and a Jew, which would be applicable in practice. In April 1933, the Nazi state began to issue the *Ariernachweis* (Aryan certificate). This proof of Aryan descent was divided into two main types. Firstly, the *Kleiner Ariernachweis* (short Aryan certificate), which required seven birth or baptism certificates (the applicant, parents and grandparents) and three marriage certificates (parents and grandparents). It also required an *Ahnenpass* (ancestry record) and a certified *Ahnentafel* (genealogical table). Secondly, the *Grosser Ariernachweis* (full Aryan certificate) required additional proof dating back to 1 January 1800 that no Jewish or Black African blood was in the family lineage.

One of the earliest pieces of legislation was announced on 7 April 1933, the *Gesetz zur Wiederherstellung des Berufsbeamtentums* (Law for the Restoration of the Professional Civil Service), excluding Jews from the civil service. Further laws that followed during that month restricted non-Aryans from practising law and medicine. Further anti-Semitic legislation up to 1939 succeeded in excluding Jews from public and national service, education, business and the press and placed close controls on the personal assets and property of Jewish families as well as their freedom of movement. It has been estimated that during the Nazi period, Jews felt the effects of more than 400 decrees and regulations that restricted all aspects of their public and private lives.[4] On 14 July 1933, the *Gesetz über den Widerruf von Einbürgerungen und die Aberkennung der deutschen*

Staatsangehörigkeit (denaturalisation law) allowed the state to revoke citizenship of Jews and other 'undesirables' who had settled in Germany after 19 November 1918. This was a significant law, which effectively removed German nationality and the rights of a citizen from 'non-Aryans', legally creating a stateless, racial group of *Untermensch* (sub-humans), who without the protection of the law could now be legally excluded and eliminated from German society. The concept of the *Untermensch* had developed within the field of Nordicism and racial science to signify a 'caste' of racially inferior beings that were deemed unworthy of life. In his *Mythus*, Rosenberg quoted the work of American racial theorist Theodore Lothrop Stoddard, *The Revolt Against Civilization: The Menace of the Under-man* (1922), as he described the racial mix of inferior races that drove the Russian Revolution of 1917 as 'a living reproach against the type of man whom Lothrop Stoddard rightly described as the underman'.[5] The denaturalisation law and the subsequent Nuremberg Laws of 1935 created a legal framework, which, through its application, created the reality of the *Untermensch* in Germany.

On 14 July 1933, Germany passed one of its fundamental eugenics laws the *Gesetz zur Verhütung erbkranken Nachwuchses* (Law for the Prevention of Hereditarily Diseased Offspring) that allowed doctors to carry out the forced sterilisation of all persons who suffered from diseases that were considered hereditary such as mental illnesses, delayed development and physical deformities. This was to be the foundation for the T4 racial hygiene programme, named after its Berlin address at *Tiergartenstrasse 4*. In October 1939, Hitler signed the 'Euthanasia Decree', which authorised the so-called *Gnadentod* (mercy death) of some 70,273 handicapped or incurably sick people in Germany and occupied territories, judged unworthy of life.[6] This programme developed methods of killing by the inhalation of toxic fumes and lethal injections that were later applied on a larger scale in the death camps of the occupied eastern territories.

To encourage and promote the recovery of the Germanic people (and the Nordic race within it), legislation was passed in July 1933 to promote marriage and childbirth by allowing all newly married German couples a government loan of 1000 marks. The birth of one child reduced the loan by 25%, the second child by 50%, and with four children, the loan was cancelled. This incentive to produce an increasing future population was later extended in 1939 to include the *Ehrenkreuz der Deutschen Mutter* (The Cross of Honour of the German Mother), issued from 1939 to

1945. The gold cross was awarded to women who had produced eight children, silver for six children and bronze for four children.

To implement his Nordicist 'Blood and Soil' theories, Walther Darré issued the *Reichserbhofgesetz* (Hereditary Farm Law) on 29 September 1933. This law stated that selected lands of between 7.5 and 125 hectares were declared an *Erbhof*. This status meant that the land had to be passed from father to eldest son and could only be owned by a person in possession of the *Grosser Ariernachweis* (full Aryan certificate); there were also restrictions in place regarding its sale or mortgage. This protected the Nordic breeding stock that Darré sought to regenerate in the German countryside by protecting their land from foreclosure or sale and re-establishing the Germanic rural tradition of the eldest, strongest son taking over his ancestors' land.

Two further key pieces of eugenics legislation were announced at the Party Rally of 1935 and became known collectively as the Nuremberg Race Laws. These clarified and extended previous legislation by further defining Aryan and Jewish racial identity and protecting the German blood from the erosion of miscegenation. These two laws were the *Reichsbürgergesetz* (Reich Citizenship Law) and the *Gesetz zum Schutze des deutschen Blutes und der deutschen Ehre* (Law for the Protection of German Blood and German Honour). The Reich Citizenship Law extended previous legislation from 1933 to remove German citizenship from those in Germany with at least three or more grandparents born into the Jewish religious community. This legislation also defined those considered to be of German ancestry and those who were given the status of *Mischling*, of mixed blood. The law for the protection of German Blood and Honour banned marriage and sexual relations between Jewish and non-Jewish Germans. These relationships were labelled as *Rassenschande* (race defilement) and made punishable by law. This law also forbade Jewish males to employ female German domestic staff under the age of 45, on the assumption that Jewish men might abuse their position of authority.

Through these laws and further legislation, the Nazi regime rapidly put in place a legal framework in which Nordicism was able to emerge as a number of racial programmes aimed at creating an alternative modernity in which the tall, blond, blue-eyed Nordic type would be protected and progressively restored to its former position of racial supremacy. Unleashed from the constraints of the Weimar republicanism and democracy, Nordicism could define its own legal and moral limitations in pursuing its ultimate aim of renordification and the expansion of the Nordic race as rulers of a new era in world history.

HIMMLER'S SS: THE IMPLEMENTATION OF NORDICISM

During Nazism's rise to power, Heinrich Himmler's *Schutzstaffel* (SS) expanded from being Hitler's personal protection squad to the driving force behind the implementation of Nazism's policies of racial protection and regeneration. Under his leadership, from 1929 onwards, the SS rapidly developed to become the most influential and extensive military, political, commercial and ideological infrastructure within the Nazi regime, answerable only to Hitler.

In his comprehensive biography, *Heinrich Himmler—A Life* (2012), Peter Longerich draws on personal correspondence, official documents and diary entries of Himmler to describe how he grew up as part of the *Kriegsgeneration* to become a leading figure in the Third Reich. As a young man, Himmler developed a passionate interest in the genetics of animal breeding and developed his racial theories from his readings of a wide range of historical, political, racial and cultural materials, which he synthesised into an eclectic 'world-view' of Aryan and Nordic prehistoric supremacy. From these sources, Himmler developed the belief that a struggle for existence was taking place between the Nordic people of Northern Europe and the Jewish threat from the East, brought about by the state of modernity and Germany's historic failure to protect its vital Nordic bloodstock.

In *The Master Plan—Himmler's Scholars and the Holocaust* (2006), Heather Pringle describes Himmler's early intentions to use the SS as a foundation for the 'renordification' and expansion of Germany. Pringle argues that Himmler intended to transform the SS into a racial showplace of the Nordic type and breed pure Aryans to establish a new generation of nobility in the Third Reich. Part of this project included searching through Germany's past to create a narrative of historical racial supremacy that could be taught to these future leaders.[7]

Through his readings and his growing circle of Nordic-minded advisors and collaborators, Himmler had developed a complex, eclectic belief system that included the Nordicist 'world-view' of a link between the Nordic blood, carried to various degrees within the German *Volk*, and the ancient Aryan tribe that had migrated from the East to Scandinavia. From Scandinavia they had spread into Northern Germany where they had lived as a high-caste racial elite forming the basis of a Teutonic Knighthood in the Middle Ages. Himmler saw this as a 'Golden Age' of Germanic honour and sought out new forms of Germanic faith to replace the foreign, eastern faith of Christianity that had eroded and destroyed the original pagan faiths of the Germanic *Volk*. In his view, these essential beliefs and traditions had bound them to their soil and the heritage of their ancestors for countless generations. Peter Longerich describes Himmler's view of Christianity as 'the Teutons' decisive original sin, preventing Germanic virtues from unfolding to their full extent in the medieval Empire.[8]

In his examination of Himmler's racial theories, Longerich draws on an early document from June 1931 recording a speech that Himmler gave to his SS leaders entitled *The Purposes and Aims of the SS, the Relationship between the SS, the SA, and the Political Formations*. To his assembled leaders, Himmler announced the future role of the SS in selecting and preserving the finest examples of the Nordic blood stock in Germany and creating a new Germanic mythology based on a community linked by the heritage of their Nordic blood and its relationship with the soil. In his speech, Himmler stated that: 'The SS must become a force that includes the best human material that we still possess in Germany. The SS must be held together by the shared community of blood'.[9] Later in this speech, Himmler also spoke of the role of the SS in 'renordifying' the nation and his futural vision of expanding the *Lebensraum* (living space) of an expanded Germanic peasantry overcoming the threat of Bolshevism from the East, a fight to the death between the Nordic and the *Untermensch*. In this speech Himmler also described his intentions of purifying and propagating the Nordic race in the conquered territories:

> Shall we, by filtering out the valuable blood through a process of selection, once again succeed in training and breeding a nation on a grand scale, a Nordic nation? Shall we once again succeed in settling this Nordic people in surrounding territory, turning them into peasants again and from this seedbed create a nation of 200 million? Then the earth will belong to us![10]

Longerich also refers to further speeches made by Himmler during this period such as an address to the Reich Peasants' Rally of 1935, a lecture to a *Wehrmacht* course on national politics in January 1937 and a speech made in 1938 to his *SS-Gruppenführer*. In these addresses, he underlined the SS mission of restoring the Nordic race and the essential conflict that was to take place between the Nordic and the *Untermensch*. Answerable only to Hitler, Himmler was able to develop the SS into an extensive organisation, freed from legal constraints and following its own code of ethics, whose mission was the elimination of the *Untermensch* and the 'renordification' and expansion of the Germanic *Volk*. To accomplish this, Himmler used his considerable talent for bureaucracy and organisation to develop the SS into the physical realisation of his Nordicist beliefs and aims. At the core of this expanding organisation, the *Rasse- und Siedlungshauptamt der SS* (RuSHA) (SS Race and Settlement Main Office) became the intellectual and organisational hub for Himmler's Nordicist ideology.

Organising and Applying Nordicism: The RuSHA

To realise his plans of renordification, Himmler founded the *Rasse- und Siedlungshauptamt der SS* (RuSHA) (SS Race and Settlement Main Office) in 1931 and placed it under the control of fellow former member of the *Artamanen-Gesellschaft*, Walther Darré, whose work on the Nordicist concept of 'Blood and Soil' had greatly impressed and influenced Himmler. In his biography, Peter Longerich points out that this was a key appointment, as Himmler's talents lay more in organisation than ideas and dissemination, but Darré, with his academic credentials and successful career within the NSDAP, was an ideal collaborator to lead Himmler's project of 'renordification':

> With Darré's appointment to the Racial Office Himmler exposed the SS to the blood-and-soil ideology and mythologizing of the 'Teutons'. Himmler, who owed his career in the Party not to original ideas but to his role as a functionary, would have had difficulty imposing these ideas on the SS as required beliefs. Darré, however, through his published works and his political success, was regarded as an authority [...][11]

Under the leadership of Darré and Himmler, the RuSHA, whose members wore the *Óðal* rune ᛟ (heritage/ancestral home) as their uniform insignia, developed rapidly into seven departments reflecting the main strands of their mission of putting 'renordification' into practice though a range of positive eugenics measures. The *Amt Organisation und Verwaltungsamt* dealt with organisation and administration, the *Amt Rassenamt* with race, the *Amt Schulungsamt* with education, the *Amt Sippen und Heiratsamt* with family and marriage, the *Amt Siedlungsamt* with settlement, the *Amt für Archiv und Zeitungswesen* with records and the press and the *Amt für Bevölkerungspolitik* with population policies. This initial structure, which administered specialist sub-sections such as the *Lebensborn* (Spring of Life) and *Ahnenerbe* (Ancestral Heritage), based in offices in Munich and Berlin, could in many ways be seen as a physical mind map of Himmler's project of 'renordification' and its subsequent restructuring as refinements of this undertaking.

The main task of the RuSHA was to protect and develop the Nordic gene pool within the SS. From 1931 until the outbreak of war, when the exigencies of conflict and the increasing expansion of the SS forced Himmler to lower his initial recruitment requirements, the RuSHA undertook the task of screening SS applicants on the basis of their Nordic traits. The RuSHA required candidates to provide photographs, submit to a medical examination and provide detailed proof of Aryan descent. In *The SS—A New History* (2010), Adrian Weale describes how, in 1932, Walther Darré recruited the services of anthropologist Dr Schulz and army veterinarian Dr Rechenbach to develop a five-point racial scale to determine the ratio of Nordic characteristics of each applicant and therefore their suitability to serve in the SS. These five groups were: 'pure Nordic, predominantly Nordic or Phalic; harmonious bastard with slight Alpine, Dinaric or Mediterranean characteristics; bastards of predominantly East Baltic or Alpine origin; and bastards of extra-European origin'.[12] According to these criteria, only those in the first three categories were eligible to join the SS. This illustrates that the SS were not just interesting in recruiting good Germans but the best Germans, the most Nordic, based on mainly physical criteria, accepting by preference those of pure Nordic appearance and tolerating only 'harmonious' and 'slight' traces of the other European races. Weale describes how:

> In the SS offices in Munich, the examiners pored over thee photographs, searching for supposed Nordic traits—long head, narrow face, flat forehead, narrow nose, angular chin, thin lips, tall slender body, blue eyes, fair hair. They rated the bodies of the applicants on a scale of one to nine, then graded them on a five-point scale from "pure Nordic" to "suspected non-European blood components" [...] A green card meant "SS suited"; red marked rejection.[13]

This rigorous selection process enabled Himmler to initiate his project of creating an SS organisation based on a strict racial selection, a Nordic community within the military and political structure of Nazi Germany, which he envisaged would become the Nordic nobility of the soon-to-be conquered eastern territories of a Greater Reich. On 18 January 1943 at a speech before the Leaders of the *WE-Lager* of the Hitler Youth, Himmler explained how the selection process of the RuSHA could be compared with the agricultural task of recovering and reinstating a once superior and established strain of plant that had been all but lost through hybridisation. In *The Order of the Death's Head: The Story of Hitler's SS* (2002), Heinz Höhne describes Himmler as:

> [...] a nursery gardener trying to reproduce a good old strain which has been adulterated and debased; we started from the principles of plant selection and then proceeded quite unashamedly to weed out the men whom we did not think we could use for the build-up of the SS.[14]

One of the earliest and most contentious eugenics policies of the RuSHA was to undertake the control of marriage within the SS with the aim of ensuring that the offspring of SS marriages would constitute a refinement of the Nordic race within this racial elite. On 31 December 1931, Himmler issued his *Heiratsbefehl* (Marriage Order), on the basis of which, the RuSHA would only issue a permit for a member of the SS to marry after detailed background enquiries. These assessed the racial fitness of both prospective parents and established evidence that both were of Aryan descent back to 1800. Himmler introduced this order with the statement: 'The SS is a band of German men of strictly Nordic descent chosen according to certain principles', underlining that the aim of this directive was 'to create a hereditarily healthy clan of a strictly Nordic German sort'.[15] Himmler's order also established the role of the RuSHA in establishing and maintaining the book of the *SS-Sippengemeinschaft* (Clan Book of the SS), in which the families of the SS would be entered after their marriage. Failure to comply would usually mean expulsion from the SS and Himmler obviously anticipated the resistance that he would meet in applying this measure of positive eugenics when he concluded his written order with the phrase: 'The SS believes that, with this command, it has taken a step of great significance. Derision, scorn and incomprehension do not move us; the future belongs to us!'[16] These closing comments, aimed at Himmler's critics in the SS, Wehrmacht and political circles, underline both his determination and intention to establish the SS as an expanding elitist caste within the nation that was destined to rise to dominance, despite the opposition of mainstream Nazis and nationalists who did not share his Nordicist belief system and sense of mission.

THE AHNENERBE: RESEARCHING THE NORDIC

Within the RuSHA structure, Himmler founded the *Studiengesellschaft für Geistesurgeschichte, Deutsches Ahnenerbe* (Study Society for Primordial Intellectual history, German Ancestral Heritage), later renamed in 1937 as *Forschungs- und Lehrgemeinschaft des Ahnenerbe* (Research and Teaching Community of the Ancestral Heritage). The main role of this new department was to discover new evidence of Germany's prehistoric Nordic and Aryan origins and to communicate the outcomes of this research to the public through publications, exhibitions and scientific conferences. Himmler devoted considerable time and energy to developing this section of his SS, housed in an exclusive Berlin villa, providing it with laboratories, libraries and museum workshops. By 1939, the *Ahnenerbe* employed 137 German scholars and scientists as well as 82 specialist support workers such as filmmakers, photographers, librarians and laboratory technicians.[17]

Himmler's original collaborators on this project were RuSHA organiser Walther Darré and controversial scholar and historian of German-Dutch origin, Herman Wirth (1885–1981). Having served for a brief period with the German army during the First World War without seeing combat, Wirth settled in Germany and became an early member of the NSDAP in 1925. In 1928, he published his first work, *Der Aufgang der Menschheit - Untersuchungen zur Geschichte der Religion, Symbolik and Schrift der Atlantisch- Nordischen Rasse* (The Accession of Mankind—A study of the history of religion, symbols and writings of the Atlantic-Nordic race). In this work, Wirth posited his theory of an advanced, Atlantean, female-led civilisation that had spread across Europe, Siberia and North America from a polar diffusion point. The traces of this migration were to be found in Nordic and Germanic prehistory and their ancient symbology. In 1933, Wirth edited the publication of *Die Ura Linda Chronik* (The Oera Linda Book), from a manuscript originally written in Old Frisian, discussing historical, mythological and religious themes in Northern European prehistory. Between 1931 and 1936, Wirth published his developing ideas in a number of volumes that he collectively titled *Die Heilige Urschrift der Menschheit* (The Sacred Prehistoric Writings of Mankind). In these works he studied the significance and relationship between ancient symbols that he found carved on rocks during field trips to Scandinavia.

The *Ahnenerbe* was the coordinating body for a number of diverse institutes founded to research aspects of Germany's cultural and material prehistory. These included *Indogermanisch-arische Sprach- und Kulturwissenschaft* (Indogermanic-Aryan Language and Cultural Studies), *Indogermanische Glaubensgeschichte* (Indogermanic Faith history), *Deutsche Volksforschung und Volkskunde* (German Ethnic Research and Folklore), *Volkserzählung, Märchen und Sagenkunde* (Folktales, Fairy Tales and Myths), *Runen, Schrift und Sinnbildkunde* (Runes, Alphabets, and Symbols), *Orientalistische Indologie* (Oriental Indology), *Urgeschichte* (Prehistory) and *Klassische Archäologie* (Classic Archaeology). Another branch of the *Ahnenerbe* was dedicated to the study of natural sciences applicable to the regeneration and healthy development of the Nordic race, which included the departments of *Gesamte Naturwissenschaft* (Natural Science), *Biologie* (Biology), *Astronomie* (Astronomy), *Pferdezucht* (Horse Breeding), *Pflanzengenetik* (Plant Genetics), *Tiergeographie und Tiergeschichte* (Zoogeography and Animal History) and *Volksmedizin* (Folk Medicine).

The research activities of the *Ahnenerbe* also included a number of archaeological surveys and excavations at prehistoric sites around Germany such as the *Externsteine*, in the Teutoburg forest, believed to be a site of ancient pagan worship and the Viking Age trading settlement at Hedeby, at the southern end of the Jutland peninsula. In June 1936, it organised a number of research expeditions to the Karelia region of Finland, to study and record songs and music related to pagan worship and in August 1936, it sent researchers to the Bohuslän region of Sweden to study, record and make plaster casts of petroglyphs (rock carvings). Further expeditions included a study of supposedly Nordic rock carvings in Italy in 1937 and the well-documented Tibet Expedition of 1938–1939, led by zoologist Ernst Schäfer (1910–1992). On these trips, his team collected thousands of artefacts and a significant number of plants and crops such as barley, wheat and oats and animals, including some live specimens, which were transported back to Germany for further research. Accompanying Schäfer on this expedition was racial anthropologist Bruno Beger (1911–2009), a former student of H.F.K. Günther, who measured and recorded the physical racial characteristics of the local tribes to research traits linking the Tibetan people with the ancient Aryan/Nordic race. In 1971, Beger was convicted by a German court as an accessory to eighty-six murders for his part in acquiring and preparing concentration camp victims for the Jewish skeleton collection at Auschwitz concentration camp.

The publishing role of the *Ahnenerbe* produced a diverse range of works supporting the Nordicist and racial theories of the Nazi regime. Notable works were the *Germanien* magazine issued to all SS officers and books such as *Axt und Kreuz bei den Nordgermanen* (*Axes and Crosses of the North Germanic Peoples*, 1939), *Die Hausmarke, das Symbol der germanischen Sippe* (*House Markings, Symbols of Germanic Heredity*, 1939) and *Indogermanisches Bekenntnis* (*The Indo-Germanic Faith*, 1943). In her analysis of the Ahnenerbe in *The Master Plan - Himmler's Scholars and the Holocaust* (2006), Heather Pringle describes the role of the *Ahnenerbe* as a 'think-tank' for German supremacy. Its task was to reconstruct a Germanic prehistory to underpin Nazi claims to racial predominance, providing a scientific and historical rationale for Nazi racial ideology and disseminating, through its exhibitions and publications, the Nazi myth of the 'Master Race'. Pringle argues that despite its claims to being a scientific organisation:

> In reality, however, the elite organization was in the business of myth-making. Its prominent researchers devoted themselves to distorting the truth and churning out carefully tailored evidence to support the racial ideas of Adolf Hitler. Some scholars twisted their findings consciously; others warped them without thought, unaware that their political views drastically shaped their research. But all proved adept at this manipulation, and for this reason, Himmler prized the institute.[18]

The mission of the *Ahnenerbe* was therefore, in many senses, to align modern scientific techniques of historical and scientific enquiry with the myth-making of the nineteenth century. As Pringle points out, this often required some manipulation to align fact with often-flawed theories. In her analysis, Pringle also underlines what she perceived as Himmler's ambition to use the research of the *Ahnenerbe* to rewrite the history and plan the future of a Nordic SS elite:

> From the very beginning, he had regarded the Ahnenerbe as the source of a glorious new history of the Aryan race, a history that could be used to teach SS men and their progeny to act and truly think like Aryans. Moreover, he had long hoped that such knowledge of the ancestors could be used to

convince SS men to return to the countryside to take up the simple life with their families on special SS farm colonies.[19]

For Himmler, the role of the *Ahnenerbe* was central to his search to establish a scientifically based foundation myth of 'Blood and Soil' on which he could build a society of Nordic SS warriors. This elite warrior caste would colonise the conquered eastern territories and fulfil his ambition to regenerate the Nordic gene pool and provide it with the *Lebensraum* that it would need to thrive. In this context, the *Ahnenerbe* was established to provide the academic, scientific scaffold for Nazi racial myth-making and Himmler's personal Nordicist 'mazeway resynthesis' through which he constructed his vision of a utopian Nordic society.

Lebensborn: Propagating the Nordic Gene Pool

On 12 December 1935, to boost the Nordic bloodline against a declining birth rate in Germany, Himmler ordered the RuSHA to establish the *Lebensborn* (Spring of Life) network. The following day he issued a communication to SS members outlining the role of the *Lebensborn* organisation and its responsibilities. These were assistance for racially valuable families, the accommodation of racially valuable mothers in appropriate homes and the care of the children of these families as well as the care of the mothers.[20] The initial purpose of this positive eugenics project was to establish a network of comfortable purpose-equipped homes for wives of SS officers for birthing and support with family matters. The first *Lebensborn* home was opened in 1936 in Steinhöring, a village near Munich. The *Lebensborn* centres also provided discreet surroundings for unmarried women who were either pregnant or had already given birth and were seeking support, provided that both the woman and the father of the child were classified as racially suitable. Parents of non-SS families had to pass a selection process that involved a physical examination of their Nordic characteristics and scrutiny of family genealogical and medical records. It was recorded that out of the total number of women who applied for the programme, only 40% were accepted and out of those selected until 1939, 57.6% were unmarried, a figure which had risen to around 70% by 1940.[21]

This initial welfare role evolved into a more pro-active project during the course of its existence to focus more directly on Himmler's project of regenerating the Nordic race and the network was rapidly expanded. To boost the number of Nordic-type children, many young, single girls in Germany and occupied northern European countries were encouraged to have children with suitable SS soldiers and officers, after which the child would be given to the SS organisation that took charge of the child's education and adoption by a suitable German family. SS officers in Germany and occupied countries were actively encouraged by Himmler to attend *Lebensborn* centres and have children outside wedlock with suitable partners to expand the Nordic gene pool. At its height, the *Lebensborn* project included ten homes and offices in Germany, nine in Norway, two in Austria, six in Poland and single homes in Belgium, Holland, France, Luxembourg and Denmark.

In a 1946 interview with journalist Louis Hagen, Hildegard Trutz, who was an aspirational eighteen-year-old leader of the *Bund Deutscher Mädel* (League of German Maidens) in 1936, describes her experiences in the *Lebensborn* project after her youth leader had encouraged her to attend a home and have a child to support the nation's blood stock. Trutz's account records how the woman in charge of the home instructed them about their duty and the privilege of their position as part of a racial elite:

> She said that Reich Leader SS Heinrich Himmler had been charged by the Führer with the task of coupling a small elite of German women (who had to be purely Nordic and over five foot five tall) with SS men of equally good racial stock in order to lay the foundation of a pure racial breed. To help in the Nordification of the nation was an honourable duty and each one of us should be proud of it.[22]

Trutz describes how the girls had to sign a legal agreement renouncing all maternal rights to the children who would be cared for by the state. Her account also describes how, during the following days, the girls were introduced socially to a group of SS men who she described as 'all very tall and strong with blue eyes and blond hair' from which the girls were expected to choose a suitable mating partner.[23] In her account she describes how:

> We were given about a week to pick the man we liked and we were told to see to it that his hair and eyes corresponded exactly to ours. We were not told the names of any of the men. When we had made our choice we had to wait till the tenth day after the beginning of the last period, when we were

again medically examined and given permission to receive the SS men in our rooms at night.[24]

Hildegard Trutz's frank account of this procedure and the birth of her child, who she handed over to the state, illustrates the role of the *Lebensborn* as more than just a welfare organisation but as a well-organised breeding centre for the Nordic race forming an integral part of Himmler's overall project of 'renordification'. It has been estimated that, in Germany alone, at least 7500 children were 'produced' in this way.[25]

One of the most successful projects of Nordic regeneration through the *Lebensborn* project took place in Norway where it has been estimated that some 10,000 children were born as a result of relations between the SS and *Wehrmacht* soldiers stationed in Norway and Norwegian women. Himmler, like many Nordicists, considered that the Scandinavian countries carried the purest Nordic bloodline and actively encouraged sexual relations between his SS elite and the local population. The *Lebensborn* project was initiated in March 1941 in Norway following a meeting in February between Himmler, Reichskommisar Josef Terboven (chief of the German civil administration in Norway), SS leader Wilhelm Rediess and Max Sollmann who administered the *Lebensborn* in Germany. Hotels and suitably sized villas were requisitioned, and by the winter of 1941, 730 babies were registered at *Lebensborn* centres in Norway. By the end of 1942, more than 2200 were registered, and by the end of the occupation in 1945, more than 8000 children were registered according to *Lebensborn* files recovered at the end of the war, covering the ten centres established across Norway.[26] Many of these children were taken away for relocation and adoption. Giving birth to the baby of a German soldier carried a significant social stigma, and many Norwegian girls in this situation were rejected by their family, friends and local community and had nowhere else to turn for help other than the *Lebensborn* centres. These centres offered to support the mother through childbirth as well as providing valuable practical and financial support. After the war, many of these *Lebensborn* children suffered considerably at the hands of a Norwegian society that rejected them and their mothers for collaborating with the enemy of occupation. Many women, accused of consorting with the enemy, were assaulted, and some had their hair cut off before being paraded through the streets in a wave of reprisals that took place against collaborators following Norway's liberation. In recent years, former *Lebensborn* children have brought a number of legal cases against the Norwegian government for its treatment of them as children and failure to protect them.

One of the most notorious actions of the RuSHA and the *Lebensborn* centres, during the course of the war, was their involvement in the selection, education and adoption of children from occupied eastern territories whose Nordic physical appearance and genealogical background justified their removal for *Eindeutschung* (Germanisation) and adoption by suitable German families. The invasion of Poland, which began in September 1939, presented Himmler with the opportunity to initiate his project of using the Nordic blood stock of occupied countries and the newly acquired agricultural land to realise his vision of SS settlements flourishing and populating their newly created *Lebensraum* with their Nordic offspring. This role of the RuSHA and the *Lebensborn* programme was a component part of the overall *Generalplan Ost*, the Nazi master plan for the east. This was a secret working document ordered by Hitler and elaborated by Himmler and his racial experts in various branches of the SS organisation into a detailed plan for the management and implementation of the Nazi policy of *Lebensraum* in the eastern territories. This plan entailed large-scale ethnic cleaning: the enslavement, expulsion and mass murder of Jewish and Slavic peoples and the selective removal of children who appeared to possess a sufficient range of Nordic characteristics. On 7 October 1939, Hitler appointed Himmler as *Reichskommissar für die Festigung deutschen Volkstums* (Reich Commissioner for the Strengthening of German Folkdom) with the role of planning the resettlement of the occupied territories with a German population. In this role, following Hitler's direct orders but also having considerable autonomy of action, Himmler was in an ideal position to implement his own Nordicist agenda through the actions of his increasingly expansive SS organisation that was becoming a self-governing power structure within Nazism itself.

In a letter, dated 18 June 1941, Himmler explained his plans to use his organisation for the recovery of Nordic-type children from the occupied territories in Poland for re-education and adoption by selected and carefully vetted childless families:

> I would consider it right if small children of Polish families who show especially good racial characteristics were apprehended and educated by us in special children's institutions and children's homes, which must not be too large. After half a year, the genealogical tree and documents of decent of those children who prove to be acceptable should be procured. After

altogether one year it should be considered to give such children as foster children to childless families of good race.[27]

In February 1942, SS-Gruppenführer Ulrich Greifelt, Chief of Staff of Himmler's office of the Reichskommissar für die Festigung deutschen Volkstums (Reich Commissioner for the Consolidation of German Nationhood), issued Directive 67/1 which ordered that suitable Polish children should be removed under the pretext that their health was at risk. Within this operation, which spanned a number of Himmler's SS departments and military units in the field, the RuSHA and *Lebensborn* played a significant advisory and practical role. In 1943, with the operation in full effect, Himmler addressed a group of *Gauleiters* in Posen in October 1943, describing the forced removal and separation of racially suitable children from their families in Poland, who unlike their parents could be 'Germanised'. For Himmler, this duty meant the protection of Nordic children from death if they could be used to expand the Nordic gene pool in the Fatherland:

> Obviously in such a mixture of peoples there will always be some racially good types. Therefore, I think that it is our duty to take their children with us, to remove them from their environment, if necessary by robbing or stealing them. Either we win over any good blood that we can use for ourselves, and give it a place in our people, or we destroy this blood.[28]

Although many records were destroyed towards the end of the war, it has been estimated that some 200,000 Polish children were removed by the Nazis between 1939 and 1944 and sent back to Germany to be 'Germanised'; many more would have been rejected and sent for deportation to concentration and death camps. A smaller but significant number were also removed from Czechoslovakia, Slovenia, Belorussia and the Ukraine.[29]

Children would be sent to holding camps at Lodz or Kalisz in Poland where they would be photographed and examined according to the criteria of sixty-two physical characteristics established and administered by the RuSHA.[30] This list included height, hair and eye colour, skin complexion and the shape and length of the head and nose and was designed to select not just the most suitable children but also the most Nordic. If the children were found to be suitable, those between the ages of two and six were processed by the *Lebensborn* homes that cared for the child and prepared them for adoption by a childless German family. This preparation included the creation of a new identity with false birth certificates bearing new German names and birthplaces to hide the child's provenance. Older children, who could not be adopted immediately, were usually sent to *Heimschulen*, SS-run boarding schools where they were made to forget their past, taught to speak German and educated in Nazi beliefs.

In her preparations for *Hitler's Forgotten Children: My life inside the Lebensborn* (2016), Ingrid Von Oelhafen examines the Nuremberg testimony of Marie Doležalová who, as a fifteen-year-old, witnessed Nazi reprisals on the Czech village of Lidice on 9 June 1942 following the assassination of *SS-Obergruppenführer* Reinhard Heydrich by the resistance on 27 May 1942. One hundred and seventy-three adult men were shot, and the 200 women of the village were transported to Ravensbrück concentration camp in Germany. One hundred and eighty-four children were taken and transported to Lodz in Poland. Von Oelhafen describes the experience of Marie Doležalová who was one of the only seven to be chosen for resettlement:

> Once the RuSHA's 'race examiners arrived in Lodz, they assessed each child for signs of Aryan qualities. They 'failed' 103 children, of them; seventy-four were immediately handed over to the Gestapo for onward transportation to the extermination camp at Chelmo, seventy kilometres away. Here they were gassed to death in specially adapted killing trucks. Just seven were selected as suitable candidates for Germanisation. Marie Doležalová was one of them.[31]

Von Oelhafen also described Marie's education at one of the *Heimschulen* where she mixed with other Nordic-looking children from a number of countries who were forced to learn German and punished if they spoke their mother tongue. Following this process of 'Germanisation', she was subsequently adopted by a German couple and encouraged to forget her past in her own country.[32]

In Himmler's futural vision of Nazism, the regeneration of the Nordic gene pool lay not just in the selective breeding but in the 'nordification' of the mind. This was to ensure that, through a programmatic indoctrination of cultural and political Nordicism, the youth would be aware of their Nordic heritage, their attachment to the soil and their duty to refine and expand their bloodline. The RuSHA was one of many SS departments responsible for directing the education of not just the German youth but of the SS Nordic elite who were to have a key role in Himmler's plans to create a new Nordic Order across Europe.

EDUCATING THE FUTURE NORDIC ORDER

From his early political days, Hitler recognised that the task of transforming German society and establishing a thousand-year Reich depended on controlling the 'hearts and minds' of the nation and especially its youth through a Nazified education system. From an early age, racially suitable children were taught the racial principles that would bring about a future generation, sharing a 'hive mind' of Nazi ideology. In *Mein Kampf* Hitler described a future nation of young citizens as 'forged together through a common love and common pride' concluding that 'no boy and no girl must leave school without having been led to an ultimate realisation of the necessity and essence of blood purity'.[33] The Nazi Party's project of recasting the minds of the nation's youth was initiated by a wave of cultural purification or 'culturecide', as it has been termed, when mass book-burning rituals took place across the nation on and around the 10 May 1933. Outside the State Opera in Berlin, Nazi student groups destroyed some 25,000 volumes of academic work considered unsuitable by the regime.[34] These acts of cultural destruction were aimed at purging the German academic sphere of Jewish or Communist influence creating an academic 'scorched earth' on which to rebuild a new culture excluding the Jew as the cultural, political and biological *nemesis* of the Nordic race, a malevolent force that had to be eliminated.

In *Education in Nazi Germany* (2010), Lisa Pine offers a detailed analysis of how, from this academic 'scorched earth', the transformation of the Nazi education system brought about what she terms, 'a root and branch re-engineering of the education system at all levels - from kindergarten, through schools, to universities'.[35] This 're-engineering' of the education system was an essential part of the Nordicist project of bringing about a 'mazeway resynthesis' of 'Nordic thought', a modernist belief system of 'Blood and Soil' through which racially 'awakened' future generations would aspire to bring about the increased purification and supremacy of the Nordic gene pool.

Through the *Nationalsozialistischer Lehrerbund* (NSLB) (National Socialist Teachers' Association), founded in 1929 to promote Nazi ideology in the teaching profession, teachers were retrained in delivering a new curriculum, established by the Reich Minister for Education, Bernhard

Rust (1883–1945). Teachers were trained in racial knowledge, the supremacy of the Nordic/Germanic race, the need to protect the nation's racial purity, the menace of the Jew, the relationship between 'Blood and Soil' and the need to establish *Lebensraum* in the eastern territories. Teachers who were racially unsuitable or who did not follow these reforms were excluded from the profession, and, by 1937, membership of the NSLB reached 320,000 teachers (97% of the profession).[36] Teaching material was strictly censored, and in 1941, the production of textbooks was limited to the *Deutscher Shulverlag*, owned and controlled by the Party. Textbooks were rewritten to reflect the Nazi *Weltanschauung* (world-view) and promote awareness of political, social and racial issues. Images in many schoolbooks favoured the fair-skinned, blue-eyed Nordic type described by Nordicists such as H.F.K. Günther whilst depicting the Jew, as the racial other, an ugly, menacing *Untermensch* to be excluded and progressively eliminated from society.

Children were only admitted to state *Kindergarten* upon proof of racial purity, and the *Law against the Overcrowding of German Schools and Universities* placed a 1.5% ceiling on the number of Jewish allowed within any educational institution. By 1938, an amendment to this legislation excluded Jewish pupils from the Nazi state education system altogether. This purging of the education system allowed the transmission of Nazi ideology to those children destined to become the future generation of 'nordified' Nazi adults whose offspring would regenerate the Nordic/Germanic race. Curriculum subjects were transformed to teach diverse aspects of Nazi ideology such as racial purity, the danger of miscegenation, physical fitness, Germanic and Nordic culture, the necessity of *Lebensraum* and the application of academic subjects to the improvement of the race. One school textbook asked pupils to calculate and compare the cost to the state in Reichsmark of maintaining: 'a cripple, a mentally ill person, a deaf and dumb person, a feeble-minded person, an alcoholic, a pupil in care, a pupil in a special school and a pupil at an ordinary school'.[37]

Alongside this Nazi national curriculum, the *Hitlerjugend* (Hitler Youth, for boys aged 14–18), the *Deutsches Jungvolk in der Hitlerjugend* (for boys aged 10–14) and the *Bund Deutsche Mädel* (for girls aged 10–18) had taken over all youth groups from 1936 onwards. Their role complemented the daytime education of the future Nazi generation through a range of evening and weekend activities such as camping, sports, political instruction and shooting, designed to instil a sense of comradeship, ideological awareness and physical fitness in Germany's youth. It was also established as a 'feeder institution' for elite Nazi educational establishments and organisations such as the SS Recruitement was driven by powerful images of ideal physical types (Fig. 5.1).

The *Hitlerjugend* played a significant educational role in transforming the 'hearts and minds' of the youth by ensuring that the time that pupils spent out of school was closely monitored and kept in line with Nazi ideology. Children whose parents were critical of the Nazi regime were

Fig. 5.1 Hitler-Jugend Deutschlands Zukunft (Germany's Future). Period postcard by Ludwig Hohlwein (1874–1949) based on a recruitment poster for the Hitler Youth showing the ideal Nordic type. These impactive racial images were an integral element of Nordicist indoctrination. Scan from private collection

encouraged to denounce their parents to their leaders who would pass the information to local authorities such as the Gestapo.

Within this state education system, the Nazi regime established three main types of educational institutions tasked with the training of the future elite of the Greater German Reich: the *Nationalpolitische Erziehungsanstalten* (National Political Educational Institutions) or *Napolas*, the *Adolf Hitler Schulen* (Adolf Hitler Schools) or AHS and the *Ordensburgen* (Order Castles). *Napolas* were highly selective, secondary boarding schools whose aim was the creation of a future political, administrative and military leadership. In 1933, the Minister of Education Bernhard Rust founded the first three *Napolas* in Plön, Potsdam and Köslin, and by 1945, forty-three *Napolas* had been opened. In addition to the National Socialist school syllabus, these institutions taught racial science, politics, military tactics and orienteering, placing an emphasis on competitive sports to develop physical and mental toughness. In her description of the *Napolas*, Lisa Pine quotes two former pupils who recalled that 'physical stamina was driven to the limit' and 'if anyone showed weakness he was considered a wet, a weakling, a coward, a disgrace to the whole platoon or company'.[38] Between 1936 and 1939, under a new SS *Napola* inspector, August Heissmeyer, the *Napolas* became increasingly influenced by the Nordicist ideology of Himmler's SS until, in 1940, they came under his direct control. Between 1941 and 1944, new *Napolas* were established in occupied territories to educate those who were classified as 'racially valuable'.[39]

Adolf Hitler Schulen were residential secondary schools in each *Gau* (Party region) designed to produce future members of the Nazi Party to work in its administration and leadership. In a speech to armaments workers on 10 December 1940, Hitler declared the aims and objectives of the AHS:

> We are bringing talented youngsters, the children of the broad mass of our population. Workers' sons, farmers' sons, whose parents could never afford to put their children through higher education [...] Later on they will join the Party, they will attend an Ordungsburg, they will occupy the highest positions.[40]

To apply for a place at an AHS, both parents had to be active party members and prove their Aryan descent back to 1800. Prospective pupils also had to be selected from the *Deutsches Jungvolk* and their application endorsed by the local *Gauleiter*. They had to pass a rigorous selection process including a detailed racial examination and physical endurance tests. Once admitted, students attended sessions on racial science, political instruction, physical training and the Party apparatus, to enable them to become effective 'cogs in the machine'. In her analysis of the organisation, Lisa Pine describes how, in addition to the Nazi national curriculum, imbued with the Nazi *Weltanschauung*, Slavic languages were taught so that AHS students would, in the future, be able to give orders to the subordinated peoples of the soon-to-be conquered eastern territories. All AHS pupils also spent time working in Party offices to gain practical experience of Party administration and to create what Pine describes as 'an administrative corps of enthusiastic and trained Party leaders, with an unconditional belief in the Nazi *Weltanschauung*'.[41]

Following their period of education at an AHS, students who had completed a six-month period of compulsory labour service and two years national service in the army could apply for selection to attend the *NS-Ordensburgen*. These were four 'Order Castles' planned as prestigious institutions of higher education for future high-ranking Party officials and leaders. This project was initiated by Hitler's Head of the Labour Front, Dr Robert Ley (1890–1945), who planned to construct four 'Order Castles' in Crössinsee in Pomerania, Vogelsang in the Eifel mountains, Sonthofen in Bavaria and Marienburg in East Prussia. These were intended to be prestigious, well-appointed centres of excellence, each forming a stage in a four-year programme designed to develop future Party leaders, through rigorous paramilitary and ideological training. Ley envisaged that these prestigious educational institutions would 'open doors to the highest positions in the Party and in the State'.[42] In her analysis of these institutions, Lisa Pine quotes comments by visiting foreign reporters who described how: 'The young men are told that they form a Nordic crusading order like that of the Knights Templar of old' and another who described the students as 'leaders of the Hitlerite Valhalla'.[43] These *Ordensburgen* represented Nazism's futural vision of a Nordic Order rooted in the traditions of German medieval and Nordic history.

Alongside the *Ordensburgen*, Himmler created a number of institutions to train future leaders of his SS order to regenerate the Nordic bloodstock and rule over the subjugated peoples of the east. In 1934, Himmler established the first of these *SS-Junkerschulen*, housed in a prestigious castle at Bad Tolz and a second in Braunschweig in 1934. During the war, three other *SS-Junkerschulen* were established in Posen-Treskau, Klagenfurt and

Prague to train Himmler's Nordic elite to rule over the occupied territories. Like students of the *Ordensburgen*, students were referred to as *Junkers*, an honorific term, derived from Middle High German meaning 'young nobleman' or 'young lord'. In her work, Lisa Pine describes this futural role of the *Junkers* as a Nordic racial aristocracy, united not by their social status but by a bond of blood:

> Himmler's new, elite man was the political soldier of the armed SS who would be trained in the SS-Junkerschulen, the new SS institutions established for that very purpose. Racial selection was the pre-eminent elite characteristic for the SS. The cadets were encouraged to see themselves as future leaders [...] It was at the *SS-Junkerschulen* that Himmler built his elite leadership corps aimed at ruling the 'New Order' Nazi empire. The bulk of the cadets were not of noble birth, but they constituted what the SS regarded as 'an aristocracy of blood'.[44]

To provide this emerging 'Nordic aristocracy' with an ideological focus point and elite training centre, Himmler acquired the derelict castle of Wewelsburg near Paderborn in 1934 and immediately began restoring it at considerable expense.[45] Himmler planned that this castle would eventually form the heart of a complex of structures providing an SS village for staff, residents and senior officers described by Heather Pringle as 'a cross between a monastic retreat and a finishing school for the upper echelons of the SS'.[46] Himmler needed a suitable location to create an ideological training centre and a prestigious retreat for his senior officers. He was guided in his choice of location by one of his closest ideological advisers, Karl Maria Wiligut (1866–1946), also known as *Weisthor* (Wise Thor).

Wiligut was an ultranationalist mystic who claimed to be a descendant of both *Þórr* (Thor) and the Germanic chieftain *Arminius*, a chieftain of the Germanic *Cherusci* tribe who famously led an allied coalition of Germanic tribes to a decisive victory against three Roman legions in the Battle of the Teutoburg Forest in 9 AD. Wiligut had considerable influence over Himmler's plans for Wewelsburg and was appointed by the *Reichsführer-SS* as head of the department for pre- and early history at the RuSHA. In his biography and source book of Wiligut, *The Secret King* (2001), Odinist and occultist Stephen E. Flowers describes him as 'a product of the *Zeitgeist* governing his time and the influences that preceded him'.[47] Wiligut was a mystic who claimed to possess a spiritual connection with his Nordic primordial past and a spiritual knowledge of runology, transmitted to him from his ancient ancestors. During his period of influence, Wiligut created SS marriage and baptismal ceremonies as well as the design of ritual objects such as the SS *Tötenkopf* honour ring worn by senior SS officers.[48] He was a prolific writer of esoteric verse and a regular contributor to esoteric and Nordicist journals such as *Hagel* and was also associated with both the *Edda-Gesellschaft* (Edda Society), founded by Rudolf John Gorsleben, and the *Nordische Gesellschaft* (The Nordic Society), led in part by Alfred Rosenberg and Himmler. Much of his work focused on the power of Nordic runes and the ancient Gods such as this verse published in *Hagel* and quoted by Flowers:

> Rune-Knowledge is pounding in our hearts,
> It whispers and warns us to duty with its pure mouth...
> Once again honour your ancestors' Sal according to loyal Nordic custom,
> Give honour to God! Then his spirit will live in your midst![49]

Wiligut worked closely with Himmler and the chief architect in charge of the castle's restoration and expansion, Hermann Bartels, to develop a centre for a Nordicist cult of the SS from which Himmler could develop and diffuse his own particular synthesis of Old Norse and medieval Teutonic culture as a new religion of the SS elite. The most notable features of this castle are its triangular footprint which has a north-south alignment, often associated with pagan religions, a marble *Sonnenrad* (sun-wheel) inlaid into the floor of what was called the *Gruppenführersaal* (Hall of the Generals) and the crypt with 'an eternal flame' at its centre surrounded by twelve stone pedestals. The top of the domed ceiling of this crypt was also decorated with an extended swastika. This was to be the *inner sanctum* of Himmler's ideological centre and cult of the SS.

The *SS-Schule Haus* at Wewelsburg was developed as a museum of prehistoric artefacts and a library containing some **30,000** titles, including a number of early publications and manuscripts.[50] This education centre would be open to visiting high-ranking SS officers and Nazi scholars who sought to deepen both their knowledge and sense of Nordic spirituality at this prestigious SS academic centre and focus point of the SS cult.

This Nazi education system was designed to create a new Nazi generation of young healthy adults who, unlike many of their parents who did not share their zeal, had been indoctrinated from an early age to believe in their racial superiority and their right to claim and expand the living space in which future generations would flourish. Within this futural project,

Nordicism was a dominant feature presenting the Nordic type as the model of the future German, and within this strand, the SS played a significant role in developing and promoting a cult of the Nordic as a belief system of the racial elite whose gene pool would become increasingly refined.

April 1940: Occupying the North

On the 9 April 1940, Operation *Weserübung* was implemented, and German forces invaded Denmark and Norway, bringing about what Nordicists such as Himmler and Rosenberg perceived to be a historic *Anschluss* between the Germanic and the Nordic peoples. The Scandinavian countries had declared themselves neutral, and, being unable to defend themselves against the overwhelmingly superior German forces, Norway and Denmark were quickly forced to surrender and accept German occupation. Sweden was not occupied, however, and remained neutral throughout the war. This occupation of the North differed from other invasions, in that Germany hoped to establish a peaceful occupation representing itself as a concerned neighbour who was coming to the assistance of Denmark and Norway rather than a foreign aggressor. This was how Nazi propaganda presented it. In a leaflet dropped over the Danish capital of Copenhagen on 9 April, the occupying forces appealed to the public to accept their presence and blamed Britain for violating the neutrality of the two countries to legitimise their occupation as a protective military operation in Norway and Denmark. The text of the leaflet read:

> Germany has decided to anticipate the English attack, and with its military forces take over the protection of the Danish and Norwegian kingdoms' neutrality, and preserve it as long as the war lasts.[51]

In his political diary of the time, Alfred Rosenberg described the negotiations that took place in secret, prior to the invasion, with sympathetic right-wing Norwegian politicians such as Vidkun Quisling (1847–1945) who were preparing themselves for the opportunity to take power following the occupation.[52] In his entry of the 9 April 1940, Alfred Rosenberg expressed his Nordicist viewpoint that this invasion was an *Anschluss*, a historic unification of the Germanic and the Nordic that had been separated for too long. This was a historic occasion described by Rosenberg as 'a great day in German history' who quoted Hitler's response as 'Just as

Bismarck's Reich arose out of the year 1866, the Greater Germanic Reich will arise out of the present day'.[53] Whilst mainstream Nazism saw the strategic advantage to the operation, in military terms, Nordicists within the party regarded the occupation of Scandinavia as the long-awaited opportunity to restore the Nordic gene pool of Germany through direct integration with the people of Scandinavia, established by racial science as the original dispersal point of the pure Nordic race.

During the 1930s, Norway, Denmark and Sweden, like many European countries and the USA, had all seen the emergence of far-right nationalist parties who modelled themselves on the NSDAP. In Sweden, a number of often-conflicting groups associated themselves with Nazism such as the *Sveriges Fascistiska Folkparti*, established in 1926 (named the *Sveriges Nationalsocialistiska Folkparti* after 1929). In 1933, one of its leading members, Sven Olov Lindholm (1903–1998), established the *Nationalsocialistiska Arbetarpartiet*. In occupied Denmark, the *Danmarks Nationalsocialistiske Arbejderparti* (DNSAP) was founded in November 1930 but had only marginal success in state elections under the leadership of its most prominent leader, Frits Clausen (1893–1945), who led the party from 1933 to 1945. At its electoral peak in 1943, the DNSAP only received 2.1% of the vote in the parliamentary elections.[54] Nazism was therefore a minority movement in these countries and was generally perceived as a foreign threat to the independence of the Scandinavian countries who were engaged in developing their own specific cultural and political identities as inter-related but distinct Nordic nations. Denmark in particular had a historic relationship of defending its territory from early Germanic and Frankish tribes, as evidenced by the creation of the *Danevirke*, a protective Iron Age earthwork in Southern Jutland. Denmark had also recently been engaged in battle with Prussian troops and had been forced to cede the Duchies of Schleswig, Holstein and Saxe-Lauenburg to Prussia following its defeat in the war of 1864. The German occupation of Denmark was therefore resented as a foreign occupation and met with varying degrees of resistance, indifference and in a few cases opportunist collaboration. In October 1943, the Danish people showed their collective defiance of Nazi racial policies by organising the hiding and transport of 7742 Jews and 686 of their non-Jewish relatives across the narrow sea to neutral Sweden, following what is now considered to be a deliberate leak from sympathetic German authorities regarding the intended round up of Jews in Denmark.[55] Sweden also played its part by receiving and accommodating the Jewish refugees. This reaction to the

German treatment of their Jewish citizens made it clear to the Nazi regime that the Nordic nations did not support their policy of ethnic cleansing. In his analysis of the events in *Countrymen* (2013), Bo Lidegaard argues that by rejecting Nazi racial policy, Denmark deprived the Nazis of the 'fig leaf they needed to justify discrimination and legitimize the deed'.[56]

In Norway, the Minister of Defence, Vidkun Quisling, founded the *Nasjonal Samling* (National Unity) in 1933. When the German army seized Norway, on 9 April 1940, Quisling proclaimed himself Prime Minister and ordered a halt to all resistance against the invading German forces. With leading members of his nationalist party, he established a government of collaboration supporting the Nazi regime. In his declaration, broadcast to the Norwegian nation, he blamed Britain for violating the nation's neutrality by laying mines in Norway's territorial waters and stating that the German Army was thereafter offering assistance to the Norwegian government to maintain the nation's independence and assure the safety of the Norwegian people.[57] Quisling had been in secret negotiations with Hitler for a number of months prior to the invasion, and although his party was electorally marginal to the point of insignificance in Norway, the *Nasjonal Samling* (*NS*) was handed power by the Germans as a 'puppet government' to enforce the wishes of the Nazi regime over a generally unsupportive public.

Following the Soviet invasion of Finland which began in November 1939 and ended with the signing of a peace treaty in March 1940, in which Finland was forced to cede border areas to the Soviet Union, the Scandinavian nations were aware of the potential threat to their independence and national identity from the anticipated expansion of the Soviet Union. In *Hitler's Vikings* (2011), Jonathan Trigg examined the role of Scandinavian volunteers for the SS and their diverse motives for enlisting in the army of an occupying nation. In this work, he discusses how many Scandinavian volunteers enlisted to fight the perceived menace of Bolshevism from the East. For some, this was not only a political motive, defending sovereignty and independence, but also a racial one to protect the Nordic race from becoming overwhelmed by eastern Slavs. It remained however more a defensive reaction rather than a wish to join the SS in order to create *Lebensraum* for a superior New Nordic SS Order. It was arguably a choice of the lesser of two evils for many who chose to act in defence of their nation. It was therefore more nationalist and political in character than Nordicist although there must be a certain degree of conceptual overlap. In his analysis Trigg argues that:

As for the Swedes, Norwegians and Danes, they were both angry and fearful as they looked east and saw a brutal dictatorship seemingly willing to assault peaceful countries and bring death and destruction to their doorsteps. The Scandinavian Far-Right's answer was to look south to Nazi Germany for salvation.[58]

The Nazi parties in Norway and Denmark drew on this fear of Stalinism to legitimise the occupation and collaborate with Himmler's SS by acting as recruitment bases for the enlistment of volunteers for Scandinavian SS regiments. They also drew on their nations' Old Norse mythology and Viking heritage; many Scandinavian SS recruitment posters represented mythical images of the nation's early history conjuring up images of a perceived 'Golden Age' of national heroism and victory. The recruitment of volunteers to fight in Scandinavian units was, however, far from successful.

In *The Political Misuse of Scandinavian Prehistory in the Years 1933–34* (1996), Michael Müller White draws on research by John T. Lauridsen in Denmark and Lise Nordenborg Myhre in Norway, into the distortion of Scandinavia's prehistory by Scandinavian National Socialists. White describes how the Scandinavian Nazi parties used images of a mythologised Viking past to evoke the concept of a new 'Nordic Order' unified by a shared gene pool and common ancestral heritage. Both the DSNAP and NS used images of Viking ships, barrows, runes and Nordic warriors in their propaganda, and in Norway, the NS used the impressive Viking barrow cemetery at Borre near Oslo for their annual party gathering (Fig. 5.2).

At the 1942 meeting, held at the Borre cemetery amongst the burial mounds, Quisling spoke of the significance of this sacred site as a link to the nation's once glorious past:

> We gather here at Vest-Viken [Borre], because the people who united Norway in one kingdom were buried here. These people carried the name of Norway all over the world. It was these people who founded the states in Russia and, in a certain sense also the British Empire.[59]

In his speech, Quisling evokes a mythologised image of the ancient Norwegian Viking warrior as the founder of the civilised world drawing on the powerful sensation of being gathered at this ritual site where these Viking chieftains were buried, to create a sense of awe and collective transcendence. This political misuse of the past links political, cultural and

Fig. 5.2 The impressive Borre cemetery in Vestfold, Norway, where the *Nasjonal Samling* held party gatherings surrounded by the burial mounds of Old Norse chieftains. Photo taken during a visit to the site in 2014

biological Nordicism into a means of generating a form of transcendence where the individual only counts as part of a greater over-arching Nordic meta-narrative.

The occupation of the North was a significant strategic operation in military terms but was also viewed by influential Nordicists, such as Himmler, as an ideal opportunity to boost the Nordic gene pool by encouraging sexual relations between his SS troops and the native Nordic population. This was formally organised by the establishment of a number of *Lebensborn* centres in Denmark and notably Norway, where many children of German fathers were born during the war. The occupation of the North was therefore a significant step for Nordicists towards the 'renordification' of the German people, in biological, cultural and political terms, expanding German territory into a greater Nordic Germania.

LEBENSRAUM FOR THE NORDIC: THE EAST

The brutality of the German forces' push into Poland on 1 September 1939 and the Soviet Union on 22 June 1941 contrasted strongly with their aim to create a peaceful protectorate in Scandinavia. The push to the East was a war of brutal annihilation of a political and racial enemy and for Nordicists such as Himmler, whose SS troops played a major role in the genocidal ethnic cleansing of the occupied territories. It was the time for the expanding Nordic empire to claim the essential living space that it required for the propagation of a new Nordic European order. The *Blut und Boden* (Blood and Soil) geo-political movement had laid the pseudo-scientific foundations of the concept of *Lebensraum*; the need to reclaim land for the future expansion of the Nordic race to create a people united with the land through an eternal bond of ancestral heritage.

In an address to his senior officers in 1931, Himmler had emphasised the historic importance of what he perceived to be the ultimate struggle for existence between the superior Nordic and the racially inferior *Untermensch* of the East. Himmler described this final battle in apocalyptic terms as a fight to the death to protect Nordic civilisation:

> Shall we, by filtering out the valuable blood through a process of selection, once again succeed in training and breeding a nation on a grand scale, a Nordic nation? Shall we once again succeed in settling this Nordic people in surrounding territory, turning them into peasants again and from this seed-bed create a nation of 200 million? Then the earth will belong to us! But if Bolshevism is victorious then this will mean the extermination of the Nordic race, of the last valuable Nordic blood, and this devastation would mean the end of the earth.[60]

This was, therefore, far from a simple occupation of enemy territory as during the invasion of France and Holland in May 1940, this was intended to be a fight to the death between deeply opposed races and political ideologies. The aim of occupying the eastern territories was not to relocate civilian refugees or capture enemy troops; the only plan for occupation of the east was the enslavement and annihilation of the sub-humans inhabiting these territories and the communist armies that defended them.

In May 1941, as part of the plans for *Operation Barbarossa*, special task forces called the *SS-Einsatzgruppen* were formed from the personnel of the SS, the SD, the *Gestapo* and other police units. Under the direct control of Himmler and Reinhard Heydrich, these specially formed task forces operated behind the lines in occupied territories in Poland and the Soviet Union. Their role was to carry out operations of political and ethnic cleansing ranging from individual killings to the mass murder of large groups of the local population such as the operation at Babi Yar near Kiev between 29 and 30 September 1941 where 33,771 Jews were killed in two days.[61] Stripped naked, the victims were led into a ravine where each man, woman and child was shot in the back of the head or neck. The massacre continued without interruption for two days, and new victims were forced to lie on those already dead. Similar incidents also took place at Kharkov in the Ukraine where an estimated 21,600 Jews were murdered and in the Rumbala forest near Riga, Latvia, where an estimated 25,000 were killed.[62] Any children deemed Nordic enough in appearance were saved from these executions for assessment before being handed over to the *Lebensborn* organisation for 'nordification'.

This slaughter of civilians was matched by the brutal treatment of Polish and Soviet prisoners of war, in comparison with British and later American POWs. Figures vary but in *Total War* (1972), Peter Calvocoressi and Guy Wint estimate that out of approximately 5.5 million Russian prisoners captured during Operation *Barbarossa*, more than 3.5 were dead by the middle of 1944. It has been estimated that nearly 2 million died in camps, another million died in military custody in the USSR and a quarter of a million disappeared or died in transit. Another further 473,000 died or were killed in military custody in Germany or Poland. The authors of these statistics conclude that 'the assumption must be that they were either deliberately killed or done to death by criminal negligence'.[63]

These were not military actions, necessitated by operational or strategic demands; they were a means of clearing the occupied territories of racially inferior inhabitants to create the *Lebensraum*, the living space, for the foundation of a new Nordic Empire. The SS units of the *Einsatzgruppen* and police units, together with local nationalist volunteers, were tasked with the extermination of a race that had endangered the Nordic race through miscegenation and whose lands were needed for the expansion of the future Nordic *Ubermensch*. To justify these actions, Nordicism had constructed its own moral and ethical framework, creating a narrative of the Nordics' struggle for existence against a sub-human enemy that threatened their survival and whose victory would mean the end of their civilisation. Nordicist myth-making therefore played a significant role in the Holocaust by creating a 'mazeway resynthesis', fusing science and myth to create a Nordicist *nomos* through which the mass-murder of women and children could be rationalised, not as a crime, but as a biological necessity to ensure the survival of the Nordic race.

In *Ordinary Men* (2001), Christopher Browning's vivid descriptions, drawn from witness testimonies of Police Battalion 101, deployed in Poland, illustrate how each man dealt with the executions of Jewish men, woman and children in different ways and discuss how such ordinary men, from mixed backgrounds, were transformed into killers. Although, as Browning points out, it is impossible to develop generalised conclusions about so many individuals' personal motives, their actions were nonetheless the result of orders aimed at the realisation of the Nordic visions of the SS leadership who commanded them. Willing or not, they were to be the agents of Himmler's racial blueprint and the implementation of his Nordicist visions.

In his analysis, Browning discusses the research of American social psychologist Stanley Milgram (1933–1984) during the 1960s. To examine the psycho-dynamics of the Holocaust, Milgram conducted a series of experiments to explore the conflict between obedience to authority and personal conscience. During these experiments, the subjects were led to believe that they were inflicting a series of increasingly painful electric shocks on a subject. Milgram concluded that individuals were more willing to inflict pain if they could not see or hear the effects of their actions. This corresponds with Browning's descriptions of the relative ease with which the members of the Battalion rounded up Jews for transport to Nazi death camps such as Treblinka rather than being directly involved in shootings. Milgram also concluded that, together with peer pressure, ideological training played a key role in transforming these ordinary men into the instruments of the mass killings that took place throughout the conquered eastern territories. In his discussion of their rationalisation of their actions, Browning quotes Milgram's argument that: 'Ideological justification is vital in obtaining willing obedience, for it permits the person to see his behaviour as serving a desirable end'.[64] It could, therefore, be argued that Nordicist ideology and the systematic indoctrination of SS and police units played a role in conditioning the men to deal with a population that was deemed unworthy of life by providing legitimisation and attenuation for their actions.

Conclusion: Ragnarǫk

The outcome of Nazism's racial policies, the final death count of the T4 programme, the brutal regime of the concentration camps, mass executions in the field by *SS-Einsatzgruppen* and later industrial-scale genocide in purpose-built death camps are some of the best-documented and most debated aspects of modern history. The process of eliminating the 'other', planned with bureaucratic efficiency at the Wannsee conference of December 1942, was refined as the war turned against Hitler's armies, to create the death camps in which millions were put to death as part of the *Endlösung*, the final solution to the Jewish Question, designed and implemented mainly by Himmler's SS.

The course of the war following Germany's costly defeat at Stalingrad in February 1943 and the subsequent counter-attacks of the Soviet Army prevented the permanent relocation of the *Untermensch* and the expansion of the future Nordic Order into the mythical 'promised land' of the conquered territories. The final solution to protect the Nordic race was therefore implemented by Himmler's SS troops. In a speech to his senior officers on the 4 October 1943 in Posen, Poland, Himmler discussed the role of the SS in carrying out a brutal mission of racial cleansing that could never be written into their history:

> I am talking about the evacuation of the Jews, the extermination of the Jewish people. It is one of those things that is easily said. "The Jewish people is being exterminated", every party member will tell you, "perfectly clear, it's part of our plans, we're eliminating the Jews, exterminating them, a small matter" [...] Most of you know what it means when 100 bodies lie together, when 500 are there or when there are 1000. And to have seen this through and, with the exception of human weakness, to have remained decent, has made us hard and is a page of glory never mentioned and never to be mentioned.[65]

The true extent of the Holocaust was discovered, nonetheless, as Allied and Soviet soldiers liberated the concentration camps that had been abandoned by fleeing SS troops and found evidence of the massacres that had taken place. The mass graves, full crematoria, stacked corpses, documentary evidence and witness accounts were evidence of the results of Nordicism being unleashed without the legal or moral constraints of a democracy that would otherwise have prevented it.

As the Nazi regime finally collapsed in the ruins of Berlin, so did the Nordicist project of protecting and purifying the Nordic race. Many, unable to face the failure of their utopian dreams or aware of their guilt and the consequences, committed suicide; others were tried for their crimes against humanity at Nuremberg and later trials where many were imprisoned or hanged. Some, such as H.F.K. Günther, whose ideological participation did not constitute a crime against humanity escaped the law, were acquitted but remained academically discredited and socially isolated in a post-war society that condemned their theories as being contributory to the Holocaust. Their myth of Nordicism as a futural project of regeneration had been totally discredited by its own outcome as the world became aware of the extent to which the Nordicist strand within Nazism had contributed to this elimination of the 'other'.

The increasingly extreme eugenics measures, implemented by the Nordicist strand within the Nazi regime, had failed to bring about the regeneration of a mythologised past as an alternative to the Weimer Republic from which they had felt alienated. As a revitalisation movement, they rejected modernity, viewing it as a path to racial degeneration and eventual destruction and attempted to create an alternative modernist vision of racial regeneration and purity in which the Nordic race would rule over the racially inferior. To bring about this vision meant winning a battle to the death to assert their racial predominance over the 'other'. In 1942, Quisling presented the Manichean struggle he witnessed between the world's disintegration into cultural and racial chaos and the process of regeneration fought for by the Nazis and her allies arguing that:

> These currents of corruption are all closely linked with each other and finally merge in the mighty stream which we call Anglo-Jewish world capitalism. That is the Midgard snake which wraps itself round the world and gnaws at the roots of the Nordic tree of life. To remove Anglo-Jewish, capitalist influence from every area, dynastic, political, social, economic and cultural is the premise for the resurrection of Norway and hence the principal goal of our movement for national unification.[66]

The war against Nazism and the defeat of the Axis powers was a victory for pluralism and multi-culturalism over the cult of racial purity and the demonisation of the Jew. The Nordicist attempt to banish the culture eroding liquidity from modernity by building the culture-regenerating solids of a thousand-year Reich had failed. Yet ideologies and movements that aim to re-establish temporal fixity and provide a new cultural or ethnic rootedness for the future can never completely disappear, since the *nomic* crisis that engendered them continues in different forms. Inevitably, aspects of Nordicism and the mythologisation of the Nordic can still be found in our modern society like the flotsam of a wrecked vessel. The final chapter of this work will examine how these fragments have resurfaced in both Northern Europe and the USA as a reaction to our current state of rapidly evolving modernity, driven by information technology and globalisation, which sociologist Zygmunt Bauman described in 2000, as a state of 'liquid fluidity'.[67]

NOTES

1. Remak, Joachim (1957) *Friends of the New Germany: The Bund and German-American Relations.* The Journal of Modern History. The University of Chicago Press. Chicago, Vol. 29, No. 1 pp. 38–41. http://www.jstor.org/stable/1872584 (Accessed: 19/07/18).
2. Taylor, Alan *American Nazis in the 1930s - The German American Bund.* https://www.theatlantic.com/photo/2017/06/american-nazis-in-the-1930sthe-german-american-bund/529185/ (Accessed 25/07/17).
3. Ibid 2.
4. *Anti-Semitic Legislation.* ushmm.org. https://www.ushmm.org/wlc/en/article.php?ModuleId=10007901 (Accessed 20/07/17).
5. Rosenberg, Alfred (Trans. Bird V. 1993) *The Myth of the Twentieth Century.* Noontide Press, California p 146.
6. *Euthanasia Program.* ushmm.org. https://www.ushmm.org/wlc/en/article.php?ModuleId=10005200 (Accessed 24/10/17).
7. Pringle, Heather (2006) *The Master Plan - Himmler's Scholars and the Holo*caust. London, Harper Perennial p 38.
8. Longerich, Peter (2012) *Heinrich Himmler - A life.* Oxford University Press, Oxford p 271.
9. Ibid. 8 p 123.
10. Ibid. 8 p 123.
11. Ibid. 8 p 127.
12. Weale, Adrian (2010) *The SS - A New History.* Little Brown, London p 66.
13. Ibid. 12 p 41.

14. Höhne, Heinz (2002) *The Order of the Death's Head: The Story of Hitler's SS.* Penguin Books, London p 52.
15. Source of translated document: *SS Marriage Order.* GHDI. http:// germanhistorydocs.ghi-dc.org (Accessed 28.07.17).
16. Ibid. 15.
17. Ibid. 7 p 3.
18. Ibid. 7 p 3.
19. Ibid. 7 p 141.
20. Weale, Adrian (2010) *The SS - A New History.* p 122.
21. *The Lebensborn Program.* www.jewishvirtuallibrary.org. http:// www.jewishvirtuallibrary.org/the-quot-lebensborn-quot-program. (Accessed 28.07.17).
22. Hagen, Louis (2011) *Ein Volk, Ein Reich: Nine lives under the Nazis.* The History Press, Stroud (Digital edition) p 4652.
23. Hagen, Louis *Ein Volk, Ein Reich.* p 4652.
24. Ibid. 22 p 4653.
25. Ibid. 21 p 4653.
26. Ericsson, Kjersti and Simonsen, Eva (2005) *Children of World War Two: The Hidden Legacy.* Bloomsbury, Oxford p 22.
27. Von Oelhafen, Ingrid and Tate, Tim (2016) *Hitler's Forgotten Children.* Dutton Caliber, Canada, p 126.
28. Von Oelhafen, Ingrid and Tate, Tim. *Hitler's Forgotten Children.* p. 128.
29. Dyck, Brent Douglas (2016) *Hitler's Stolen Children.* http://warfarehistorynetwork.com (Accessed 2/08/17).
30. Ibid. 29.
31. Ibid. 28 p 130.
32. Ibid. 28 p 130.
33. Hitler, Adolf (Trans. Manheim, R. 1995) *Mein Kampf.* Pimlico, London pp. 388–389.
34. *List of Banned Books.* library.arizona.edu. http://www.library.arizona.edu/exhibits/burnedbooks/documents.htm (Accessed (23/10/17).
35. Pine, Lisa (2010) *Education in Nazi Germany.* Berg Publishers, Oxford (Digital edition). p 957.
36. Pine, Lisa *Education in Nazi Germany.* p 406.
37. Ibid. 35 p 1440.
38. Ibid. 35 p 2144.

39. Ibid. 35 p 2197.
40. Ibid. 35 Quoted by Pine, L. p 2260.
41. Ibid. 35 p 2322.
42. Ibid. 35 p 2322.
43. Ibid. 35 p 2364.
44. Ibid. 35 p 2500.
45. See the models of the expansive complex in Cook, Stephen and Russell, Stuart (1999) *Heinrich Himmler's Camelot*. Kressmann-Backmeyer, USA pp. 27–33.
46. Ibid. 7 p 48.
47. Flowers, Stephen E. (2001) *The Secret King - Karl Maria Wiligut Himmler's Lord of the Runes*. Dominion Press, USA p 11.
48. See the record of Wiligut's name giving rite in Flowers, Stephen E. Appendix C p 122.
49. From Runic exhortation by Wiligut quoted in Flowers, Stephen E. p 11.
50. Cook, Stephen and Russell, Stuart (1999) *Heinrich Himmler's Camelot*. Kressmann-Backmeyer, USA p 126.
51. Hong, Nathaniel (2012) *Occupied - Demarks Adaptation and Resistance to German Occupation 1940–1945*. Danish Resistance Museum Publishing, Copenhagen p 31.
52. Matthäus, Jürgwen and Bajohr, Frank (2015) *The Political Diary of Alfred Rosenberg and the Onset of the Holocaust*. Rowman and Littlefield, Maryland p 191.
53. Matthäus, Jürgwen, Bajohr, Frank *The Political Diary of Alfred Rosenberg*. p 191.
54. Ibid. 51 p 154.
55. Lidegaard, Bo (Trans. Maass, R. 2013) *Countrymen: The untold story of how Jews escaped the Nazis*. Atlantic books, London (Digital edition) p 5634.
56. Ibid 55 p 5945.
57. *Recording of a speech of Quisling of 9th April 1940*. https://www.youtube.com/watch?v=v5nuooEl1QQ (Accessed 19/10/17).
58. Trigg, Jonathan (2011) *Hitler's Vikings: The History of the Scandinavian Waffen-SS: The Legions, the SS Wiking and the SS Nordland*. The History Press, London p 211.
59. Quisling quoted by Müller-Wille, Michael et al. (1996) *The Waking of Angantyr: The Scandinavian Past in European Culture*. Arhus University Press, Arhus p 157.

60. Himmler quoted by Longerich, Peter Ibid. 8 p 123.
61. *1941 Mass Murder.* http://www.holocaustchronicle.org/staticpages/270.html (Accessed 23/10/17).
62. Ibid 61.
63. Calvocoressi, Peter and Wint, Guy (1989) *Total War.* Penguin Books, London p 50.
64. Browning, Christopher R. (2001) *Ordinary Men.* Penguin Books, London p 176.
65. *Himmler's Posen Speech.* http://www.jewishvirtuallibrary.org/himmler-s-posen-speech-quot-extermination-quot (Accessed 11/10/17).
66. Quisling, Vidkun (1942) *Nationaler Verfall und nationale Wiedererhebung* (National decay and national resurgence) in *Quisling ruft Norwegen!* Franz Eher Verlag, Munich pp. 134–6.
67. Bauman, Zygmunt (2000) *Liquid Modernity.* Polity Press, Cambridge.

BIBLIOGRAPHY

PRINTED WORKS

Calvocoressi, P., & Wint, G. (1989). *Total War.* London: Penguin Books.
Cook, S., & Russell, S. (1999). *Heinrich Himmler's Camelot.* Kressmann-Backmeyer.
Ericsson, K., & Simonsen, E. (2005). *Children of World War Two: The Hidden Legacy.* Oxford: Bloomsbury.
Flowers, S. E. (2001). *The Secret King - Karl Maria Wiligut Himmler's Lord of the Runes.* Dominion Press.
Hagen, L. (2011). *Ein Volk, Ein Reich: Nine Lives Under the Nazis.* Stroud: The History Press.
Hitler, A. (1995). (Trans Manheim R.) *Mein Kampf.* London: Pimlico.
Höhne, H. (2002). *The Order of the Death's Head: The Story of Hitler's SS.* London: Penguin Books.
Hong, N. (2012). *Occupied - Demarks Adaptation and Resistance to German Occupation 1940–1945.* Copenhagen: Danish Resistance Museum Publishing.
Lidegaard, B. (2013). (Trans. Maass, R.) *Countrymen: The Untold Story of How Jews Escaped the Nazis.* London: Atlantic Books.
Longerich, P. (2012). *Heinrich Himmler - A Life.* Oxford: Oxford University Press.
Matthäus, J., & Bajohr, F. (2015). *The Political Diary of Alfred Rosenberg and the Onset of the Holocaust.* Maryland: Rowman and Littlefield.

Pine, L. (2010). *Education in Nazi Germany*. Oxford: Berg Publishers.
Quisling, V. (1942). *Nationaler Verfall und nationale Wiedererhebung (National Decay and National Resurgence) in Quisling ruft Norwegen!* Munich: Franz Eher Verlag.
Roesdahl, E., & Sorensen, P. M. (1996). *The Waking of Angantyr: The Scandinavian Past in European Culture*. Arhus: Arhus University Press.
Trigg, J. (2011). *Hitler's Vikings: The History of the Scandinavian Waffen-SS: The Legions, the SS Wiking and the SS Nordland*. London: The History Press.
Von Oelhafen, I., & Tate, T. (2016). *Hitler's Forgotten Children*. Dutton Caliber.
Weale, A. (2010). *The SS - A New History*. London: Little Brown.

WEBSITES AND DIGITAL PUBLICATIONS (WITH DATE ACCESSED)

Anti-Semitic Legislation. Accessed 20/07/17, from https://www.ushmm.org/wlc/en/article.php?ModuleId=10007901
Dyck, B. D. (2016). *Hitler's Stolen Children*. Accessed 2/08/17, from http://warfarehistorynetwork.com
Euthanasia Program. Accessed 24/10/17, from https://www.ushmm.org/wlc/en/article.php?ModuleId=10005200
Himmler's Posen Speech. Accessed 11/10/17, from http://www.jewishvirtuallibrary.org/himmler-s-posen-speech-quot-extermination-quot
List of Banned Books. Accessed 23/10/17, from http://www.library.arizona.edu/exhibits/burnedbooks/documents.htm
Recording of a Speech of Quisling of 9th April 1940. Accessed 19/10/17, from https://www.youtube.com/watch?v=v5nuooEl1QQ
25 Mass Murder. Accessed 23/10/17, from http://www.holocaustchronicle.org/staticpages/270.html
Remak, J. (1957). Friends of the New Germany: The Bund and German-American Relations. *The Journal of Modern History, 29*(1), 38–41. University of Chicago Press, Chicago. Accessed: 19/07/18, from http://www.jstor.org/stable/1872584
Rescue in Denmark. Accessed 23/10/17, from https://www.ushmm.org/outreach/en/article.php?ModuleId=10007740
SS Marriage Order. Accessed 28.07.17, from http://germanhistorydocs.ghi-dc.org/sub_document.cfm?document_id=1505
Taylor, A. *American Nazis in the 1930s - The German American Bund*. Accessed 25/07/17, from https://www.theatlantic.com/photo/2017/06/american-nazis-in-the-1930sthe-german-american-bund/529185/
The Lebensborn Program. Accessed 28.07.17, from http://www.jewishvirtuallibrary.org/the-quot-lebensborn-quot-program

CHAPTER 6

The Flotsam of Nordicism in Our Liquid Modernity

'Liquid modernity' describes our current state of constant change that offers no sense of fixity from an endless stream of fast-flowing progress. From his first hit single, as the astronaut Major Tom in *Space Oddity* (1969), floating away in the emptiness of infinity, to his haunting final album *Blackstar* (2016), the audio-visual art of David Bowie (1947–2016) epitomised the constantly evolving and increasingly 'liquid' nature of our current state of modernity. Throughout his long career, Bowie never stood still long enough to become associated with any established style, genre or look, continuously absorbing and resynthesizing sound and image to create a unique ever-shifting stream of creativity, where change was the only identifiable constant. Bowie never let his artistic work solidify before melting it down, to recast it again, in another new form, which represented in itself, yet another transient state.

The concept of reality's 'liquefaction' under the impact of globalising modernity was introduced by sociologist Zygmunt Bauman in his seminal work *Liquid Modernity* (2000), as an alternative term for post-modernity, a phase of post-war change described by sociologists and cultural theorists such as Jürgen Habermas (1929–present), Jean-François Lyotard (1924–1998) and Jean Baudrillard (1929–2007). Bauman developed this term to describe his interpretation of our current state of modernity, which he views as an evolution of late modernity into something even more elusive and transient. 'Liquid modernity', and its concomitants 'liquid times', 'liquid love' and 'liquid fear', describe the heightened state of flux and

© The Author(s) 2020   215
G. E. Forssling, *Nordicism and Modernity*,
https://doi.org/10.1007/978-3-030-61210-8_6

ephemerality that material, cognitive and emotional realities have entered under the impact of increasingly rapid technological and social (and now ecological and demographic) change.[1] Subjectively, this new human condition is reflected in the compulsive need that many members of modern societies experience to constantly adapt and transform their lives, proliferating new personae in order to make sense of the increasingly fragmented plural realities of which they consist. The 'liquefaction' of existential and social reality has, of course, been intensified by the revolution in social media and the exponential growth for the younger generations in virtual realities.[2]

In a socio-political context, post-modernity and liquid modernity have been described as reactions to the impact of globalisation, industrialisation, urbanisation, the melting of traditional religious certainties and the growth of multi-cultural, multi-faith societies in which no single theology or creed can maintain its authority or hegemony. In this context, the totalitarian and authoritarian societies of the twentieth and twenty-first centuries can be seen as various attempts to put an end to modern 'liquefaction' by creating a society based on a single, absolutist, hegemonic truth system that fixes reality again for its citizens.[3] It is within this context that the absorption of cultural, political and biological Nordicism into racist creeds makes sense as part of a rebellion against the threat of relativism, nihilism and ephemerality in the same way that the massive stone edifices of totalitarian architecture expressed the will to permanence and the monumental.

In *Modernism and Fascism* (2007), Roger Griffin characterises such initiatives as 'modernist' reactions to modernity. These crystallised into ideologies that sought to create alternative political, economic and social structures. Firstly, as the foundation of a new vision of the world that re-established a sense of transcendence, hope and *nomic* certainty (e.g. Romanticism) and later as the basis of a utopian socio-political 'new order' which used state power to embrace planned progress banishing what was seen as chaotic flux and atomising individualism and decadence. Bauman refers to these counter-modern, regenerative, artistic, ethical, social and ideological structures as 'solids', human constructs created to replace older out-dated structures that have become eroded and rendered obsolete by the continuous flow of modernity.

In this context, the emergence of Nordicism as a 'solid', rooted in a deeply mythicised or pseudo-scientised structure in the late nineteenth and early twentieth centuries, both in its Romantic and racist or totalitarian manifestations, was a reaction against the increasingly *anomic* mood of the time. Appropriated by Nazi and Aryan racial theorists, Nordicism was instrumentalised to ward off the perceived threat to the established *nomos* of Northern European racial superiority and purity. To counter this erosion, Nordicists sought to develop an alternative modernity or new 'solid', through a resynthesis of the ancient and the modern legitimising their project of regenerating a pure Nordic nobility to rule over inferior racial types. Through this synthesis, racial Nordicists aspired to create a more durable 'solid', the *Thousand Year Reich*, which would resist the erosion of modernity and eventually achieve their *telos* of the *Ubermensch*. This ideal was no longer the spiritually gifted, transcendent higher self of Nietzsche, but a new evolutionary phenotype, the racially and culturally superior human being, master and hegemon of a new civilisation. The victory of capitalist modernity over both Nazi and Soviet experiments in creating what Bauman called in *Modernity and Ambivalence* (1991), 'the gardening state', has ensured that, except in pockets of socio-political 'solidity', artificially maintained at great human cost (e.g. North Korea, Iran, Saudi Arabia), the Nietzschean 'rope over an abyss' has no final mooring point on *terra firma*.[4] We are forced to remain on a constant journey across an abyss of almost constant *anomie*, tantalisingly faced with the ever-receding cliffs on the other side of the ravine. All truly modern human beings suffer new variants of the fate of *Tantalus*.[5]

According to Bauman's theory, modernity no longer offers the concept of any ultimate *telos*, and society is in a constant state of 'becoming', rejecting the failed projects of twentieth-century programmatic modernism as redundant or utopian. Modernity no longer allows 'solids' to develop into any firm structure before they are melted away and replaced with other temporary structures which in turn will be melted and remolded into new temporary 'solids'. In Bauman's words:

> To be 'modern' means to modernize—compulsively, obsessively; not so much 'to be', let alone to keep its identity intact, but forever 'becoming', avoiding completion, staying underdefined. Each new structure, which replaces the previous one as soon as it is declared old-fashioned and past its use-by date is only another temporary settlement—acknowledged as temporary and 'until further notice'.[6]

To be 'modern' is therefore to exist in a constant state of *anomic* flux in which any structure offering shelter from the constant state of change is temporary and will soon be replaced by another which in turn will be but a brief respite.

In *Retropia* (2017), Bauman develops his existing theories of 'liquid life' by examining the concept of nostalgia. In his discussion of our reactions to 'liquid modernity', Bauman refers to the publication of Svetlana Boym, *The Future of Nostalgia* (2001), in which she describes a present-day 'global epidemic of nostalgia'. On an individual level, Boym describes this phenomenon as 'a sentiment of loss and displacement' and 'romance with one's own fantasy'.[7] On a societal level, she views this as a protective shield against our *anomic* state of existence, a search for forms of collective transcendence to replace those that have broken down:

> [...] a longing for a community with a collective memory, a longing for continuity in a fragmented world [...] a defence mechanism in a time of accelerated rhythms of life and historical upheavals.[8]

The term nostalgia originally derives from the ancient Greek *nostos*, meaning to return home, and *algos* meaning pain. Today's nostalgia can therefore be perceived as a deep-rooted longing to return home to an imagined, idealised past to escape the eroding forces of modernity. In her work, Boym describes this reaction as the 'promise to rebuild the ideal home', a process that draws on emotion rather than rationalism which, she argues, can be observed in 'national and nationalist revivals all over the world, which engage in the anti-modern myth-making of history by means of a return to national symbols and myths [...]'.[9] This process aligns with Griffin's theory of 'palingenesis' (rebirth and regeneration) through which he examines how forms of fascism emerged in the 1930s as myth-making nationalist revitalisation movements, to counter the 'disenchanting' effects of modernity. It also aligns with Bauman's theories of society's attempts to construct 'solids' to replace those which have become eroded and redundant. In this context, earlier 'solid' forms of Nordicism and the current fragments which can be found in our modern nostalgia can be interpreted as an attempt to ease this pain of longing for an 'ideal Nordic home' away from the stress and uncertainty of contemporary modernity.

Since the downfall of the Third Reich, Nordicism has become conceptually associated with Nazism and its murderous project of regenerating a mythical 'Master Race'. Applying Bauman's theory, the failure of this project signifies its lack of viability as a 'solid', washed away by the dominant current of modern thought and liberal pluralism that judged it not just incompatible and obsolete but indefensibly evil within a modern humanitarian society. Assigning the term Nordicism to a particular phase of history fails, however, to recognise its extended and protracted history, emerging from the Romantic quest for new forms of *nomos*, or that 'solids' such as Nordicism do not completely dissolve. Instead, they remain as dispersed, marginal fragments in later societies and are still relevant to our understanding of the dynamics of certain strands of far-right-wing thought in Northern Europe and the USA.

This final chapter will not attempt to identify any cohesive international neo-Nordicist movement capable of providing 'fixity' and 'solidity' in the way it did at the height of the nineteenth-century cult of rootedness and mythic ancestries or the twentieth-century cult of racial essences. It will, however, consider how certain aspects of this ideology and its aims are still prevalent in small groups and individuals in society. It will also avoid the process of attempting to 'make the subject fit the mould' by using the term 'Nordicist' to label any individual or group but examine the aspects of their 'world-view' which fall within the definition of Nordicism that this work has proposed. This section will, therefore, examine a number of contemporary examples that demonstrate how fragments of the shattered 'solid' of Nordicism are still prevalent in far-right thought and a longing for a retreat from what Walter Benjamin called the 'storm of progress'.

Modern Nostalgia for the Old Norse in Popular Entertainment

In his concluding chapter of *Thor—Myth to Marvel*, Martin Arnold argues that our current nostalgia for Old Norse culture is largely dominated by today's mass-market, consumer-led society seeking diversion and a sense of adventure away from the daily concerns and worries of everyday life. This trend is comparable in many ways to the nineteenth-century fascination with the Old North across Northern Europe and North America, as Arnold observes:

> From Longfellow to Lee, and, so, from myth to Marvel, ideas about Thor and Scandinavian antiquity have generally involved a shift away from the purview of scholars, polemicists and the literati [...] and into mass-markets, where entertainment substitutes for aesthetics and unbridled imagination substitutes for serious analysis and accuracy.[10]

Although our current academic climate seeks, through the evidence provided by modern archaeological methods, to provide a more balanced and accurate cultural image of Old Norse material and spiritual culture, Arnold argues that the popular received image of Vikings and Old Norse mythology still lies more in the hands of modern myth-makers than scholars. Arnold suggests that the dominant trend is towards what he describes as the 'irreversible decline into the *ersatz*, the kitsch and the lowest common denominator'.[11] He further argues that this modern representation of the Old North could be viewed as a post-war reaction against Nazism's appropriation of Norse mythology and its continued use by some far-right individuals and organisations:

> Doubtless the taint of Nazi ideology and the continued promulgation of Nordic supremacist ideas by far-right groups have done much to provoke a counter-balancing trivialization of Norse mythology.[12]

This current trivialisation of Norse mythology and the Viking is evident in the popular representations in Marvel comics and later cinematographic works representing *Þórr* as a global superhero waiting to come to the rescue of a world from cosmic powers of evil and destruction. In a consumer-led society, where net profit serves as an indicator of public opinion, the box office popularity of the Marvel *Thor* feature films, starring Christopher Hemsworth as *Þórr* and Anthony Hopkins as *Oðinn*, demonstrates the appeal of Old Norse culture as part of our global trend of nostalgia.[13] This current mass-market appeal is comparable with the popularity of the tales of Norse mythology, adapted from the *Eddas* and *Icelandic Sagas* that were published during the nineteenth century to an eager readership who were more excited by the image of the noble warrior and adventurer than the research of historians. Marvel's modern representation of *Þórr* does not, however, attempt to create any serious form of modern myth-making during the nineteenth century. Critics of Marvel Studio's recent *Thor* project, *Ragnarok*, have discussed the self-deprecating, humorous moments in the film in which the characters do not take themselves seriously, demonstrating at times the post-modern rejection of cultural Nordicism described by Arnold.[14]

Another example of the role of modern cinema in Nordic myth creation and its diffusion on a mass scale is the global success of the stunning cinema adaptations of J.R.R. Tolkien's (1892–1973) *The Hobbit* and *The Lord of the Rings* trilogy by director Peter Jackson. These global box office hits recreate the world of Nordic and Northern European mythology described by Tolkien in his best-selling novels, originally published between 1937 and 1949. The significance of the global impact of these printed works is evident in the sales figures for *The Hobbit* of over 100 million copies worldwide, in over 50 languages.[15] From his extensive academic knowledge of early Northern European languages and mythology, Tolkien created a detailed and expansive world of mythology from a synthesis of a wide range of Northern European historical and literary sources. Tolkien's works are now considered classics of modern mythology that demonstrate how, in a modern society where science attempts to answer everything, there is still a constant need for myth to explore and explain the dynamics of human experience. A number of critics have, however, claimed that some themes of Tolkien's work could be interpreted as examples of cultural Nordicism and the debate between these critics and those who oppose this view illustrates the permeable membrane that separates academic and popular interest in the Nordic, from what could be interpreted as cultural Nordicism.

In an article on the Tolkien Society web site, entitled *Taboo Tolkien: The Nordicist Claim on Middle-earth Refuted*, Tolkien scholar Michael Martinez defends the work of Tolkien against interpretations from academics such as Stephen Shapiro who have argued that themes of cultural and biological Nordicism can be recognised in *The Lord of the Rings*. In an interview in 2003, Shapiro claimed that 'Tolkien was not a Nazi but he was a Nordicist in that his works hark back to England's original culture before the Norman invasion'.[16] In Tolkien's defence, Martinez quotes letters from the author in which he claimed that: 'I know better than most what is the truth about this Nordic nonsense' and referred to the Nazi leader as 'that ruddy little ignoramus Adolf Hitler'. In one letter Tolkien criticised Nazism for:

> (…) ruining, perverting, misapplying, and making forever accursed, that noble northern spirit, a supreme contribution to Europe, which I have loved, and tried to present in its true light. Nowhere, incidentally was it nobler than in England, nor more early sanctified and Christianized.[17]

This reaction expresses Tolkien's anger at the process through which nationalist and racial ideologists appropriated Nordic culture into Nordicist thought, adopting the North as their cultural 'ideal home' of racial purity and predominance. Tolkien clearly considered this a distortion of the culture that inspired so much of his academic and creative work. Martinez also quotes an interview with the *Daily Telegraph* in 1967 in which Tolkien complained that the term Nordic had become associated with 'racialist theories' and that he preferred to avoid applying this term to his work.[18] Tolkien's rejection of this term shows how post-war definitions of Nordicism have linked it with Nazism and how post-war writers have sought to distance themselves from this regime, firmly distinguishing their Nordic cultural interest from cultural Nordicism. This debate over the influence of Nordicism in Tolkien's work also illustrates how our contemporary liberal democracy seeks out the development of any identifiable pockets of Nordicism in order to expose and attack them before they can develop into any form of 'solid'. This debate also highlights the ambivalence of popular interest in Scandinavia both in the nineteenth century and today between a benign interest in Nordic culture and the idealisation of this culture into a national or racial myth.

This ambivalence is also evident in the success of the multiple award-winning *Vikings* television series, created by historical novelist Michael Hirst for the *History Channel*, which premiered in March 2013 on Canadian television. Since its premier, six seasons have been produced for a worldwide audience fascinated by this representation of Old Norse culture.[19] *Vikings* was originally inspired by the Icelandic sagas describing the Viking king *Ragnar Lothbrok*, famous for his raids on Britain and France, and his sons who ruled in England and Scandinavia. This series, based on a wide range of historical, archaeological and literary sources, immerses the modern viewer in a Viking world of pagan mythology, passion, loyalty, betrayal, sexual desire, war and peace in much the same way as the Icelandic sagas were translated and packaged for the sensibilities of the Victorian, German, Scandinavian and American readership of the nineteenth century. In keeping, however, with our current historiographical and social trends, this series goes to considerable length to represent the Vikings not just as warriors. They are depicted as settlers, skilful craftsman, expert boat builders, explorers, tradesmen and a deeply spiritual people seeking to survive and prosper in the harsh climatic, social and political conditions of their Scandinavian homeland. It remains, however, a work of fiction, frequently adapting chronology and characters to enhance plot development. There are also more than enough battle scenes, sex and violence to entertain the viewing public in keeping with the received Anglo-Saxon depiction of the Viking as a warrior and barbarian. What *Vikings* has in common with *The Lord of the Rings*, however, is a global popularity measured in many millions of readers and viewers. This points once more to the insatiable appetite of those carried in a sea of 'liquid' modernity for fictional islands of a stable, absolute *nomos* of the kind that, under modernity, can only occur in myth. In these imaginary lands, life can still be lived dramatically and heroically, untouched by existential doubt and a sense of insignificance.

The received stereotype of Vikings as a bloodthirsty warrior caste is most prevalent in the video game market where Viking-inspired games come and go in a rapidly evolving consumer-driven marketplace where any game or genre has a relatively short shelf life. Popular titles which range in style from fantasy adventure to 'hack and slash' include *Saga: Rage of the Vikings* (1998), *The Elder Scrolls V: Skyrim* (2011), *Völgarr the Viking* (2013), *War of the Vikings* (2014), *The Banner Saga* (2014), *Jotun* (2015), *Northgard* (2016), *For Honor* (2017) and *Vikings: Wolves of Midgard* (2017).[20] The industry's latest release, *Assassin's Creed—Valhalla* (2020), immerses the gamer in a Viking world of alliances, battles and raids with stunning graphics and brutal violence. These popular games are not designed to educate the viewer, but to provide a form of audio-visual entertainment which takes the gamer into a fantasy world founded on early medieval civilisations and Nordic myth as a form of escapism from the real world of material concerns and domestic worries.

Our popular interest in Nordic culture through the media of entertainment can, therefore, be viewed with ambivalence both as a benign nostalgic escape from the disorienting pace of our 'liquid modern' culture and as the idealised, romanticised cultural basis for contemporary fragments of Nordicism. In response to consumer demand, Old Norse culture has been turned by the film, fantasy literature and videogame industries into a commodity designed to generate huge sales in mass-market places where innovative entertainment and computer technology are the key to the highest sales at the cinema box office, cable, satellite and online subscriptions. It has also created a popular idealisation of Old Norse culture that bears many characteristics of the foundations of cultural Nordicism of the nineteenth century through its appeal to those seeking a mythologised home of racial beauty and predominance. In a cultural context, television, cinema and the Internet can be considered modern forms of a cultural collective transcendence as individuals are brought together to share an image of an ideal cultural home in the past, a return to an idealised past to shelter from the stresses of contemporary modernity.

The idealisation of the Nordic is a feature of society that has arguably transcended the demise of Nordicism to become a noticeable element of post-war culture. In an article, published in the *Social Semiotics* journal in 2017, Christopher M. Hutton examines the role of visual propaganda during the Third Reich as a means of disseminating the Nordic thought of ideologues, such as H.F.K. Günther, to the general public. Hutton describes how the political rise of Nordicism at the end of the nineteenth century coincided with the emergence of mass media and culture through the ability to mass produce photographic images for use in advertising, the popular magazine, cinema and books:

> Established visual forms such as the photograph and the map took on greater potency as they were diffused through newly popular genres such as the school textbook and national newspapers. The photograph became a key tool of racial theory, as a modality ideal for mediating between race theory and the popular iconography.[21]

Hutton points out that, although the bio-political element of Nordicism moved into the marginal strands of neo-Nazism during the post-war years, the established image of the Nordic in Western culture, as a model of health and beauty and shorn of Nazi connotations, transcended its political context. He argues that, through the mass media, it evolved into a contemporary received image of the Nordic as the role model of the ideal human being and life style:

> In post-war Europe and North America, the Nordicist political movement moved to the neo-fascist fringe. [...] Nordic iconography, in particular the Nordic aesthetic of beauty and health, became key to post-Second World War popular culture in the West, notably mass advertising and the Hollywood film industry. Racial iconography survived the collapse of institutionalised race theory, diffusing through the imagery of the new global media.[22]

Hutton suggests that the image of Nordic type became a popularised stereotype of health and beauty through the influence of the mass media. He proposes that the Nordic ideal of the tall, blond, blue-eyed individual was prevalent in post-war mass culture as frequent representations of Nordic beauty quoting iconic figures such as the Barbie Doll, Hollywood movie stars such as Veronica Lake, Buster Crabbe and the Marvel hero Captain America.[23] According to Hutton, this 'Nordic aesthetic' transcended the Nordicist bio-political context to become what he terms 'part of a global visual vocabulary' transmitted culturally through the visual representation of the Nordic type as a model of health and beauty. This 'Nordic aesthetic' could be considered an enduring aspect of Nordicism that exists both in a benign and a racist form in contemporary culture. Hutton also points out that this idealisation of the Nordic physique and life style is often associated with the natural untamed beauty of the Nordic landscape:

> It is redolent of health, fitness, athleticism, the naked body, as well as unsullied purity and naturalness. It suggests harmony between the aesthetics of the body, the rugged and austere Nordic environment, with its dazzling snow-covered mountains, crystal-clear lakes and blue skies, and the "made world" of design, fashion and architecture.[24]

This association between the physical beauty of the ideal Nordic type and the natural environment of Scandinavia, as an idealised land of untamed beauty, was a notable feature of National Romantic thinkers and artists who considered the northern climate to be a formative element of the superior Nordic man. This attraction to the savage beauty of the Nordic environment is reflected in the current popularity of the literary and cinematographic genre now termed 'Nordic Noir'. In this genre, the development of the characters and the plot are intertwined with the backdrop of the harsh Nordic climate and landscape to explore and express the dark side of human nature. Notable authors of this literary genre are the Swedish novelist Stieg Larsson (Millennium Trilogy) and Norwegian Jo Nesbø (Harry Hole series), whose novels are now international best sellers. Many novels have been made into popular films, set against dramatic landscapes in Scandinavia. Writers such as Ragnar Jónasson draw on the dramatic climatic conditions of Iceland to reflect an intense atmosphere of social claustrophobia in which the characters of his novels interact both with each other and the untameable forces of their hostile setting. In his work, Jónasson explores the interaction of close-knit, isolated communities, exploring human passions and conflict in a way that could in many ways be compared with the Icelandic sagas that became so popular during the nineteenth century.

In conclusion, the idealisation of the Nordic has transcended its sinister wartime associations and remains a cultural phenomenon in contemporary society. It could also be argued that the permeable membrane that distinguished scholarly and popular interest in Nordic culture from cultural and later political and biological Nordicism during the nineteenth century still exists today and that, in our 'liquid culture', one flows with ease into the other.

THE RE-EMERGENCE OF RIGHT-WING THOUGHT IN EUROPE

The re-emergence of right-wing thought and direct action groups across Europe has arguably been boosted by increased immigration into Northern and Western Europe in the years following what has come to be termed the *European Migrant Crisis* of 2015. During this period, rising numbers of migrants arrived in the European Union (EU), travelling across the Mediterranean Sea or overland from Southeast Europe. These included many asylum seekers but also others, such as economic migrants and a few dangerous political and criminal elements, including a small number of suspected Islamic state militants who attracted considerable media attention. This has brought about a significant shift towards protectionist thought and criticism of state and European immigration policies. In Germany, who accepted large numbers of migrants, the populist right-wing PEDIGA group (Patriotic Europeans Against the Islamisation of the West) has grown in influence since its founding in 2014.

In an article entitled, *The Right is Rising and Social Democracy is Dying Across Europe*, published in the Guardian in September 2017, Josef Joffe discusses the rise of right-wing nationalist thought in Europe and the subsequent decline in social democracy. Although his article focuses mainly on the electoral success of the right-wing party, the *Alternativ für Deutschland* (Alternative for Germany), it also considers the increased success of what he terms right-wing 'authoritarian populists' in Europe such as Marine Le Pen (*Front national*), Geert Wilders (*Freedom Party*), the *UK Independence Party* and in the USA, Donald Trump.[25] These figures and parties all succeeded in gaining public support for their nationalist, anti-immigration and protectionist policies.[26] In the USA, this included a travel ban on Muslims in 2017, stricter immigration laws and a controversial wall across the US-Mexican border. The article argues, however, that many voters in European elections, such as in Germany, voted for these right-wing parties as a protest vote, an expression of their feelings of frustration and abandonment by the mainstream parties. It could, however, also be argued that within this trend of populism there is a significant element of nationalist revivals emerging as a reaction to immigration and globalisation.

Although they are still minority parties in Europe, this continuing trend towards nationalist thought is evident in the percentage of votes won by right-wing parties across Europe in their recent general elections. Notable among the European results were Hungary (Fidesz 49.3% and Jobbik 19%), Austria (Freedom Party 16.2%), Switzerland (Swiss People's Party 25.6%), Belgium (New Flemish Alliance 16%), Estonia (Conservative People's Party 17.8%), Finland (The Finns 17.5%), Sweden (Sweden Democrats 12.9%), Italy (The League 17.4%), Spain (Vox 15.1%), Denmark (Danish People's Party 8.7%), France (National Rally 13.2%), the Netherlands (Freedom Party 13.1%) and Germany (Alternative for Germany 12.6%).[27] Although it is a generalisation to view such figures without taking into account overall trends and the electoral process and party politics behind each election, these figures demonstrate, nonetheless, a continued presence of populist right-wing thought from which extremist groups or individuals emerge periodically to take direct action to further their ultra-nationalist aims.

European commentators and journalists have also observed a rise in far-right and neo-Nazi activity. In May 2019, a BBC news article reported that Felix Klein, the German government's anti-Semitism minister, caused public concern when he warned the Jewish community against wearing the kippa 'at all times, everywhere in Germany'. This followed a 10% rise in the number of anti-Semitic offences recorded by the police. Assaults against Jews also rose during this period with sixty-two violent incidents recorded in 2018 compared with thirty-seven in 2017. In an interview, Klein cited the Internet and social media as contributing factors to attacks on their 'culture of remembrance'. Jewish groups also warned that a rise in popularity of far-right groups and organisations is encouraging anti-Semitism and hatred of ethnic minorities throughout Europe.[28]

One of the most significant manifestations of this trend towards populist nationalist revivals was Britain's referendum of June 2016 in which the public voted for the nation's independence from the European Union, commonly known as *Brexit*. This was described by former Labour Minister Lord Adonis in a letter to the Prime Minister Theresa May, as 'a populist and nationalist spasm'.[29] This referendum brought into question the viability of a European Union and sparked calls from right-wing parties in a number of other European countries, for similar referendums to restore national independence from the legal, political and economic control of the European community.[30] This trend towards populist, nationalist policies in Britain was further confirmed in the May 2019 European Elections in which the Brexit Party, established by Nigel Farage following his departure in December 2018 from UKIP, took many conservative and labour seats to gain 31.6% of the vote, emerging as the dominant party.

In his analysis of the currents of populist right-wing thought in British politics, *The Road to Somewhere—The New Tribes Shaping British Politics* (2017), political commentator David Goodhart analyses the populist surges which, in his view, brought about both Brexit and the rise of President Trump. Goodhart describes two groups of individuals who make up Western society: the 'Anywheres' and the 'Somewheres'. He defines the 'Anywheres' as 'a large minority group of the highly educated and mobile' who 'value autonomy and openness and comfortably surf social change' and the 'Somewheres' as a 'larger but less influential group' who are 'more rooted and less well educated, who value security and familiarity and are more connected with group identities'.[31] Goodhart argues that over recent decades the more conservative 'Somewheres' have felt excluded and alienated from the public sphere and that the populist 'backlash', as he describes it, is a manifestation of this social and political discontent. This theory of a large group within the population which yearns for a return home to the security and familiarity of a rootedness in the past aligns with both the emergence of Nordicist nineteenth-century thought, as a populist movement, and the contemporary re-emergence of fragments of Nordicist thought in both Northern Europe and the USA.

FRAGMENTS OF NORDICISM: NOSTALGIA FOR A MYTHICAL RACIAL PURITY

In his analysis of right-wing ideology in Scandinavia, *Racist and Right-Wing Violence in Scandinavia* (1997), Tore Bjørgo discusses the historical misperception of many right-wing thinkers and groups who believe that interbreeding with other racial types is a feature of modernity and globalisation rather than a natural process which has taken place throughout history. In their recreation of an idealised past, many right-wing thinkers have constructed their theories on the core nostalgic belief that there was a period in the past when races lived in separate territories, defended by conflict, founding an essential sense of their rootedness in a particular place and ethnic culture. In his analysis, Bjørgo argues that:

> Some versions of nationalist ideology are based upon the assumption that the 'natural order' of things- before history, modernity or imperialism started to mess things up- was that ethical or cultural groups lived apart in neatly separate territories. Ethnic conflict, racism, war and instability are seen as invariable outcomes when these 'natural' boundaries are over-stepped and different cultural groups become mixed. Stability and peace can only be re-established when the various national (or cultural) groups find a way back to their natural, separate and homogenous societies.[32]

This belief in an ideal, racially pure state of previous existence is a common strand in the 'world-view' and myth-making of many right-wing individuals and groups who believe in a mythical past of racial purity during which the Nordic race, developing in geographic and racial isolation, reached a stage of perfection. Now diminished though interbreeding, this race could still be regenerated through modern programmes of positive eugenics. The following case studies of individuals and groups, whose 'world-views' demonstrate aspects of Nordicism, illustrate this belief in an era of primordial heterogeneity as the foundation for their belief systems and in programmes of Nordic cultural and biological protection and regeneration. They also illustrate how fragments of Nordicism can be perceived as both free-floating and interconnected attempts to recreate temporary forms of 'solidity' in our increasingly 'liquid society'.

Nordicism.com: Online Nordicism

Much of the 'liquidity' of our modern society is driven by the rapidly developing and expanding technology of the Internet. This has allowed the uncensored transmission of ideas to a global readership that has never previously existed. Through privately maintained web sites, blogs, forums and social networking platforms such as Facebook, Twitter, YouTube and Instagram, the dissemination of political and religious ideology has been liberated from the constraints of traditional publishing and news reporting. For mainstream political parties, the astute use of this means of communication has become an essential tool of electoral success. It has also become, however, the platform for many extremist groups to communicate their ideologies and terrorist groups who rely on the near-instant transmission of terrorist incidents around the world to amplify the impact of their actions. This network also provides a number of isolated Nordicist thinkers with the means of communicating, spreading propaganda and discussing their 'Nordic thought' with other like-minded individuals as part of an online community. The Internet, whose servers defend the right to uncensored free speech and self-expression, is therefore a virtual publishing house and meeting place for Nordicist thinkers who use both well-established and short-lived web sites to express and discuss their racial views. Control over such material is difficult to impose, and many sites are short-lived as their authors are blocked by servers or close down their sites to re-emerge elsewhere on the web, an impermanence that is characteristic of its 'liquid' nature. The following sites are examples of current and recent sites where views of political, cultural and biological Nordicism are expressed.

Stormfront.org, established in the early 1990s by former *Ku Klux Klan* leader Don Black, is an international forum site that describes itself as 'a community of racial realists and idealists' and 'white nationalists who support true diversity and a homeland for all peoples'.[33] This site contains millions of posts divided into a range of nationalist and white supremacist subject threads, and a search of the term Nordic or Nordicism reveals numerous posts discussing its relevance historically and in today's society.

Germanic Pride was created in 2015 and displays the *Óðal* rune ᛟ (heritage) over a photo of the *Externsteine* on its home page with the slogan 'No roots = No future'. This natural sandstone rock formation in the Teutoburg Forest, Westphalia, was used as a hermitage during the Middle Ages and attracted the interest of SS scholars and archaeologists who conducted excavations at the site. *Germanic Pride* is devoted to developing a sense of rootedness for those who consider themselves to be of Nordic/Germanic origin. Sections of the site include a YouTube video of Dr Alfred Ploetz, son of the German eugenicist of the same name, recalling how his father referred to the Nordic race as the 'salt of the Earth'.[34] An article about the mythical island of Thule describes it as 'a great empire created and inhabited by the Nordic type of people only' which covered the North Pole, Scandinavia, North Germany, the Baltic area, Siberia, Canada and Alaska in prehistoric times. These Nordic people are described as a perfect physical and spiritual race of human beings that has progressively deteriorated. This site also idealises the Nordic race, celebrating the imagined space of Thule, in which the Nordic race is supposed to have lived in a perfect state of racial purity in isolation from other peoples. An article on the site describes the superior nature of the inhabitants of Thule with a quasi-religious fervour:

> Someone did name them like the "Divine Race" because their soul-level was very close to God's wisdom and their brain was very much evolved.[35]

In another section, entitled *Germanic Roots,* the anonymous author of the site displays a number of images by SS war artist Wolfgang Willrich of ideal Nordic types and argues that the terms Germanic and Nordic are synonymous. The site claims, however, that it does not promote racial hatred but a sense of rootedness in a once great Northern tribe and that the preservation of the Nordic bloodline is 'one of the most high and Holy actions'.[36]

Nordic Anti Semite, closed in 2019, was a private blog by far-right-wing blogger Aidhan, whose articles on the superiority of the Nordic race and the need to protect and regenerate it were filled with vile derogatory terms such as 'brown subhumans', 'ratlike Jews', 'genetic wastage' and 'mongrels'. These blogs were interspersed with images of ideal Nordic physical types contrasted with degrading images of black and Jewish people, including a period photograph of an African American hanging from a tree with a caption by Aidhan that read: 'Sometimes it's the only thing a N****r understands'.[37] These pages also included a number of images of Hitler and members of the Hitler Youth as examples of an ideal Nordic society. Promoting the concept of Nazism, the web site also included a section for the memoires and pro-Nazi anti-Semitic articles of Jerry, a former member of the Hitler Youth and *Reichs Arbeits Dienst* (RAD), the Reich Labour service, during the Second World War.

In his blog, Aidhan called for the geographic segregation of races to protect them from miscegenation especially the Nordic race, which he idealised in his images and descriptions, as the tall, blond, blue-eyed stereotype of the Scandinavian. Amongst the many historical photos of Nordic types from the period of the Third Reich, one image showed a map copied from Madison Grant's *The Passing of the Great Race* of the distribution of the Nordic, Alpine and Mediterranean races in Europe. Aidhan used these images to evidence his opposition to multi-culturalism and his call for racial segregation. Calling for a homeland for a purified Nordic race, Aidhan also demanded the eventual extermination of the Jewish people as a punishment for their destruction of the Nordic race describing what he viewed as an essential racial battle for survival against the Jew:

> The Nordic Race would have a Nordic country, Negroes would have a Negro land/place to go (country is not a Negro concept) and Jews would be blamed for what they have done and forcibly exterminated for their guilt. This is why the Jew seeks to end the Nordic Race.[38]

Nordicantisemite.com expressed the belief that the Nordic race is genetically superior to others and Aidhan's blogs were radically anti-Semitic, attacking both the Jewish people and high-profile individuals who he considered to be the principal enemies of the Nordic race. He also described racial awareness and segregation as survival instincts of the Nordic race:

> Nordicism, and the belief in inherent Nordic racial superiority of the Nordic group, and the consequent will for racial separation is innate to surviving members of the Nordic Race, who the Jews have decimated.[39]

In his blogs, Aidhan also blamed the European Union for an immigration crisis that risked the eventual destruction of the Nordic race arguing that 'they are the ones who set the quotas that allowed the mass swamping in subhuman effluent "refugees" to begin with'.[40] He also argued that powerful Jewish organisations and individuals formed a silent majority supporting Muslim immigration into Europe and that a key function of the EU is the destruction of European nation states, cultures and identities.[41]

Similar in name and views and associated by hyperlink to Aidhan's blog site was that of Trent who hosted the *Anti-Semitic Nordicist* blog site. On this site, Trent claimed that the 'Nordic man or Aryan man is the only species of human biologically capable of forming advanced civilisations' and has been 'poisoned by Jews'.[42] Like his associate Aidhan, Trent's views were radically anti-Semitic, describing the Jewish race as 'demon spawn in human form'.[43] He expressed his sympathy with Hitler's Nazi regime by stating that they lost the war 'trying to free mankind in an effort to save the Nordic race'.[44] Trent also described the physical beauty of Nordic blue eyes and blond hair, supported by images of ideal Nordic types, and his belief that the Nordic race is superior to others both physically and as leaders of empires that have ruled the world:

I believe that Nordics, a zoological subspecies of man Indigenous to Scandinavia are a super race, with their blonde hair and blue eyes they have founded glorious empires that rule the world, and nobody else has, period.[45]

Facebook has also been used as a platform by Nordic interest groups and individuals such as *Nordic Beauty@protectnordicbeauty*, a Facebook page dedicated to the 'beauty, culture and tradition and for the preservation of the Nordic people scattered all around the globe' and to making 'people aware of the problems in Europe and in particular in the Nordic countries'.[46] This Facebook page, now removed, had 118,927 followers at one point.[47] It supported Nordicism by providing a platform for group members to discuss and admire what they considered to be the natural blue-eyed and blond-haired beauty of the Nordic race and view a large gallery of, mostly female, ideal Nordic physical types posted by the site's followers.

Facebook has also been home to the right-wing network of the interconnected *Nordic Defence League* (4,907 followers), Norwegian Defence League (29,691 followers), *Swedish Defence League* (9,835 followers), *Danish Defence League* (12,014 followers) and *Finnish Defence League* (10,639).[48] Whilst not overtly Nordicist, and focusing primarily on social and political issues, these Facebook pages have provided a platform for anti-Muslim and anti-Semitic news reports and political comments aimed at the protection of the Nordic people and opposing globalisation and multiculturalism. As Facebook modifiers regularly monitor these sites for racist or abusive comments, postings must conform to regulations or be deleted, the expression, however, of the belief that the Nordic race is endangered and needs protection is thinly veiled in some postings. The responsibility of these platforms to monitor postings and suspend accounts is an on-going debate. They are, however, increasingly vigilant of racist content in postings.

NORSE PAGANISM AND NORDIC PURITY

Nordic nostalgia and the search to create sacred spaces of collective memory and transcendence based on resynthesised models of the Nordic past have led to the re-emergence of new religions based on ancient pagan worship. Although the practice of Norse paganism has been present on the outer fringes of religion throughout history, the late twentieth and early twenty-first centuries have seen a re-emergence of Norse paganism in Northern Europe and the USA.

The neo-pagan *Ásatrú movement* (translated from Old Norse meaning faith of the *Æsir*) has become one of the most prominent branches of Norse neo-paganism, defining itself as 'the indigenous religion of the Northern European peoples' and 'a religion that reveres nature and ancestry and values honor and nobility'.[49] This movement has no formal universal creed or form of worship and is composed of a number of strands whose beliefs and rituals differ considerably. One group that has attracted considerable media attention is the *Ásatrúarfélagið* (*Ásatrú* Fellowship) of Iceland, founded in 1972, which has seen its membership steadily increase to 4,126 members in 2018.[50] It regularly celebrates pagan days of worship and its Facebook site has 14,638 followers.[51] Permanent temples have now been built in both Iceland and Denmark reflecting the extent to which *Ásatrú* has become established as an alternative faith to Christianity. In Sweden the *Samfundet Forn Sed Sverige*, originally founded in 1994 as the *Sveriges Asatrosamfund*, has also increased in popularity.

Another popular strand of Norse paganism is Odinism, which shares many similarities with *Ásatrú* but remains distinct as an organisation and form of worship. Odinist groups include *The Odinist Fellowship* and *Odinic Rite* (London) and *The Troth* (USA). These groups promote the worship of the Norse pantheon and the celebration of Old Norse traditions and festivals. These neo-pagan groups draw on the texts of thirteenth-century Icelandic scholars, to recreate forms of worship connecting their followers with their Old Norse spiritual heritage. It is therefore a faith that is attractive to those who wish to celebrate their Nordic identity and historic culture but also to those who form a discreet strand that draws on Norse mythology as a foundation for their racial and nationalist beliefs. These groups are often described as the *völkisch* strand of Norse heathenry. One online group called Odinist.org describes itself as 'a gathering place for Nordic Folk' and hosts a number of articles celebrating the Norse pantheon alongside radical anti-Semitic and anti-immigration articles. This fusion of Norse mythology with a political and racial agenda of racial purity can also be seen in the actions, writings and videos of Norwegian Varg Víkernes.

On 20 January 1993, the Black Metal musician behind the solo project *Burzum*,[52] known as Varg Víkernes (1973–), came to public notoriety when one of Norway's leading newspapers, *Bergens Tidende*, published an article entitled *Vi tente på kirkene* (We burned down the churches).[53] In this article, Víkernes and his associates claimed responsibility for the arson of a number of wooden medieval stave churches. This was intended as an attack on the foreign faith of Christianity, historically imposed on the pagan peoples of Norway. On this same date, Víkernes was arrested by police for the arson of four churches and later released on bail. On 19 August 1993, Víkernes was further arrested for the murder of Black Metal collaborator Øystein 'Euronymous' Aarseth, and the subsequent trial received considerable media coverage, raising the profile of Black Metal as a serious social concern in Norway. At the conclusion of his trial in May 1994, Víkernes was found guilty and sentenced to twenty-one years for the murder of 'Euronymous'. He was also further convicted of the arson and attempted arson of Åsane Church and Storetveit Church in Bergen, the arson of Skjold Church in Vindafjord and the arson of Holmenkollen Chapel in Oslo. Víkernes was, however, acquitted by the jury of the arson of Fantoft stave church, dating from the twelfth century, despite protests from the judge.[54] The burnt ruins of this ancient church were provocatively used as the cover photo of Burzum's 1992 EP, *Aske* (Ashes).

It has been suggested that it was during his period of imprisonment that Víkernes further developed his political ideology away from the Satanist 'hype' of the Black Metal scene, which had attracted increasing media attention and which, whilst advantageous as a means of promoting his music, detracted from any credible socio-political agenda inspiring his work and actions. In *Black Sun* (2002), Nicholas Goodrick-Clarke points out this shift, commenting that during this period, 'Vikernes began to formulate his nationalist heathen ideology using materials from Norse Mythology combined with racism and occult National Socialism'.[55] During this time, Víkernes also became associated with the *Allgermanische Heidnische Front* (German Heathen Front) and the *Norsk Hedensk Front* (Norwegian Heathen Front), who both promoted the neo-pagan faith of *Óðalism* as a form of 'Blood and Soil' ideology.[56]

Víkernes served fifteen years of his sentence and was released on probation, on 22 May 2009. Following his release from prison, Vikernes left Norway to live in an isolated location in France with his family, out of the eye of the media where he has continued writing and publishing. In 2013, he began his blog and YouTube channel (which was closed in 2019); both called the *Thulean Perspective—For Blood and Soil* and, through his writings, promoted an ideology called *Óðalism* based on an adapted form of 'Blood and Soil' nationalism. In 2013, Víkernes posted his definition of his *Óðalic* belief system fusing Old Norse religion with a modern political agenda based on racial purity and the need to regenerate lost traditions, customs and religions that have been lost to the progress of Christianity and globalisation:

> Óðalism is in the strictest sense an ideology based on blood (of the native population) and soil (the homeland of the native population); protecting, promoting and if necessary reviving the customs, traditions, world view, values and religion that naturally came from each particular population in their homeland.[57]

In this article, Víkernes explains his belief in racial and cultural diversity, arguing that each unique culture should remain in their own territory where their blood attaches them to the soil. Víkernes does not promote the expansion of his Nordic race into other territories but promotes its protection on its own soil against what he describes as the threat of miscegenation and what he terms the 'genocidal politics of feminism and colonialisation'.[58] He further argues for the segregation of the races calling for the exclusion of non-Europeans and the return of pure-blooded Europeans from former colonies to preserve the Nordic race:

> Óðalism is advocating the repatriation of all non-Europeans in Europe as the solution to the genocidal politics lead by most European nations today— and also repatriation of all unmixed Europeans from the former European colonies. Óðalism is not nationalism in a modern sense: each and every modern nation is a modern construct based on geography (where the borders have been drawn) and ethnicity (i.e. languages spoken) instead of racial—or if you prefer tribal—identities. The Óðalic nationalism is based on race.[59]

Víkernes defines his form of nationalism as a return to primordial tribalism, claiming that race is not confined by what he sees as the 'modern construct' of national borders. Víkernes' nationalism, promoted through the modern technology of the Internet, is both forward-looking and nostalgic. In his numerous YouTube videos, he calls for a return to a rural lifestyle as an alternative to modernity, the rejection of Christianity as a foreign form of faith and the exclusion of Jews and Muslims from European soil. Opposing globalisation he argues that religion, culture, traditions and all that forms a racial 'world-view' cannot be made universal, as they should grow out of a historic relationship between blood and soil. He also promotes the re-establishment of native European values and belief systems such as traditional forms of Norse paganism, which he claims are rooted in Northern European racial identity. In addition to his YouTube video blogs and web site, Víkernes has published a number of printed works, *Sorcery and Religion in Ancient Scandinavia* (2011) and *Reflections on European Mythology and Polytheism* (2015), and in 2017, he co-authored *Paganism Explained* (Parts 1 and 2) with Marie Cachet with accompanying YouTube videos. These works celebrate the Old Norse pantheon as an alternative belief system to Christianity.

In his modernist belief system, Víkernes has created a 'sacred space' connecting the past with the present and future. This consists of a resynthesised form of ancient paganism, rejecting of our current state of modernity, which he perceives as bringing about the weakening of existing races through miscegenation. Like a number of geographically isolated Nordic thinkers, Víkernes makes constant use of the Internet to promote his religious and racial ideology and once had 214,729 subscribers to his YouTube channel *The Thulean Perspective*.[60] YouTube deleted his channel in June 2019 as part of a crackdown on racist material on their site, but he is still present on the web.

MODERN VÍNLAND

During the late nineteenth century, the record of America's discovery by Leifr Eiríksson, set down in the Iceland during the thirteenth century in the *Grœnlendinga saga* (The Saga of the Greenlanders) and *Eiríks saga rauða* (*Eirík* the Red's Saga), became a foundation myth for many descendants of Nordic and Germanic settlers in the USA. Although based on events that actually took place, the discovery of Vínland became a mythologised original homeland for Germanic and Scandinavian Americans, where the original Viking settlers first set foot on American soil and became a focal point of Northern European nationalism in the USA. This myth of Vínland is still present in a number of right-wing groups in America who strive for white supremacy to defend their race from perceived annihilation through immigration and interbreeding between races.

In 2007, an American prison inmate, Dr. Casper Odinson Cröwell (1963–), established the *Vinland Folk Resistance*, as a breakaway group of the *Aryan Brotherhood*, with the aim of creating an organisation devoted to the purity of the Nordic/Aryan race in America and the promotion of an adapted version of the Old Norse faith of Odinism. *The Aryan Brotherhood* was originally founded in 1964 in San Quentin Prison,

California, as a white supremacist, neo-Nazi prison group that defended the interests of white prisoners from black and Mexican gangs. Since this date, the organisation has grown and become increasingly involved in organised crime both within and outside the prison system.

On leaving the *Aryan Brotherhood* and giving evidence against them in 2007, Cröwell, with the support of his wife Linda, and Ron McVan (1950–), a white supremacist and Odinist, founded the *Vinland Folk Resistance* web site from inside prison. In his introduction to the group, he states that: 'Our mission goal is to awake our race to the detrimental and ultimately catastrophic reality of racial extinction which we face [...] Our intention is to promote awareness and pan-Aryan Tribalism and solidarity among our dwindling people'.[61] On his welcome page, Cröwell describes the USA and Canada as Vínland, rejecting the term America as Latin and referring to Christopher Columbus as a 'fraudulent hero'. On his site, Cröwell states that:

> Vinland is the name our Nordic-Aryan Ancestors gave to this land and it too is the name by which we call it with great affection and respect for those hearty and stalwart Ancestors. We are Patriots of our Aryan Folk and this land, our Odal/Othal land, which our Ancestors found and centuries later established and built upon.[62]

In his writings, Cröwell makes no distinction between the terms Aryan and Nordic and roots the foundation myth of his modern-day Aryan/Nordic tribe in the belief that Vínland is an ancestral homeland that they must defend. In his blog, Cröwell describes the process of deterioration of the white European population in the USA, providing figures showing that in 1967 the racial composition of the USA was 76% white, whereas in 2007 it stood at 50%.[63] Cröwell blames this on the US government's immigration policy, which he claims is weakening the white race, calling for an awakening of the people to protect the Aryan/Nordic folk:[64]

> We resist and defy the Government sponsored program of 'Passive Genocide' of the White Race, and we seek to incite a revolution in thought to first awaken the lethargic and complacent minds of our people and then educate those minds towards the welfare, existence and survival of our race and thereafter, the advancement of our folk.[65]

To counter this trend towards the erosion of Northern European white supremacy and the eventual extinction of his race, Cröwell cites the slogan originally credited to white supremacist David Lane (1938–2007), known as the 'fourteen words'. The number 14 is often used on tattoos of the Aryan Brotherhood and other white supremacist groups and has become a nationalist slogan. These fourteen words are: '*We must secure the existence of our people and a future for white children*'.[66] To secure this future, Cröwell and McVan call for a return to family values, racial segregation and stricter immigration laws to protect the Aryan/Nordic race that founded Vínland. They also call for a return to Old Norse paganism, the indigenous religion of the original Viking settlers.

Cröwell and the principal contributors to his site, such as McVan, root their beliefs in a resynthesised strand of Odinism, creating a brotherhood of priests (*Gothar*) and warriors (*Einherjar*) who collectively form the *Sacred Order of the Sons of Odin 1519*. This pagan group use the ancient Norse *Valknut* design as a symbol of their devotion to *Oðinn* and to represent their 'honor and reverence to all our ancestors who chose to die horrible deaths at the hands of the Christian missionaries'.[67] Like many neo-pagans, Cröwell presents Christianity as a foreign faith, often brutally imposed on the Old Norse pagans and aims to regenerate this faith. Cröwell describes their mission as:

> Our primary purpose is the defence, advancement and promotion of all aspects of our native and indigenous Pagan/Heathen religion called Odinism. This religion and way of life was indigenous to the peoples of Northern and Western Europe and so it remains so of their descendants today, "us"![68]

Through a series of periodicals entitled *Gungnir* (the spear of *Oðinn*), Cröwell and his collaborators discuss their Odinist beliefs, rules and conditions of membership, their spiritual objectives and the significance of runes. They also encourage their readers to take part in pagan ceremonies to celebrate the Norse pantheon and passing of the seasons. Cröwell has also published two works entitled *Ek Einherjar: Hammer of the Gods* (2009) and *Vor Forn Sidr* (Our ancient religion, 2012) in which he discusses his faith, the Norse pantheon, and provides advice on conducting ceremonies and rituals, with sections attributed to both Ron McVan and David Lane. McVan has also independently published a number of works on Norse mythology and Odinism such as *Creed of Iron* (2012) *Wotan's Holy Rites and Ritual* (2012) and *Book of Wotan* (2016).

Through their writings, Cröwell and his associates draw on Old Norse mythology and the settlement of Viking explorers in Vínland to create a modern myth of Nordic predominance and pagan heritage in the USA. This is a reaction to the current state of modernity, which they perceive as destroying the Aryan/Nordic race through immigration and miscegenation. For these Odinists, the Vikings' discovery of Vínland provides a sense of rootedness and historical purpose for their belief system aimed at regenerating the Nordic gene pool in the USA.

Another American far-right group that draws on ancient paganism and the myth of Vínland is a small group, based in Virginia, called the *Wolves of Vinland*. This group, which has been associated with white supremacist organisations in the USA, has established a small community on private land in Virginia called *Ulfheim*, from Old Norse, meaning the home of the wolves. This community, which has been described as more as a biker gang than a serious political or religious movement, uses the site for pagan celebrations, weight-lifting, wrestling, boxing matches and rituals involving animal sacrifice to honour the Norse pantheon. For some time, the group regularly published photos of these events on Instagram and Twitter, using social media to promote and recruit members to their group. [69] Through their creation of *Ulfheim*, this group has established a small piece of a mythical Vínland where they can practise a modern resynthesis of the lifestyle and rituals of their Nordic ancestors.

THE NORDIC RESISTANCE MOVEMENT

The *Nordiska Motståndsrörelsen* (Nordic Resistance Movement) is a neo-Nazi organisation founded in Sweden in 1997, which is also active in Finland, Norway and Denmark.[70] Actual membership figures are not published, but it has an active web site called *Nordfront* and has had a number of groups on Twitter.[71] An organised march in Gothenburg, in September 2017, was attended by some 500 sympathisers and attracted media attention.[72] It is therefore a small but prominent National Socialist organisation, active both within and outside the parliamentary system. It declares that it is engaged in a battle against international Zionism and the threat of Muslim mass immigration aiming to create a global caliphate. The NRM seeks to create a racially pure, unified Nordic region as a National Socialist State as detailed in its political manifesto *Our Path—New Politics for a New Time*, published in English on the Internet in 2016. Their presence on the streets at marches has also raised their public profile (Fig. 6.1).

In its manifesto, the NRM claims that, since 1945, the destructive forces driving multiculturalism, Zionism, Islam and Marxism, have 'continually conducted political genocide against the Nordic and ethnic peoples of Europe'.[73] It declares that National Socialism 'delivers a strategy of survival for our race and has succeeded in providing a modern political form that reflects the eternal laws of nature'.[74] In its manifesto, the NRM blames Zionism, Marxism and liberalism for a process of globalisation and mass immigration that threatens not only the Nordic people but also the stability and existence of Western culture. It claims that:

> The current goal of the global Zionist elite is not only to promote the state of Israel, but also to contribute to long-term instability in all nations who

Fig. 6.1 NRM supporters in Stockholm in 2016 showing the combined *Týr* and Inguz runes of their flag. According to the NRM website, the *Týr* rune represents courage, self-sacrifice, struggle and victory and the *Inguz* rune fertility, creative energy, purposefulness and focus. The green represents the ecological aims of the party. Photo by Frankie Fouganthin—CC BY-SA 4.0, https://commons.wiki-media.org

may pose a threat to their power structure. This includes, not least, the ethnically homogenous countries of the Western world. Therefore, all global Zionists work towards not only multiculturalism and mass immigration, but also other socially disintegrating ideologies such as liberalism and norm-dissolving cultural Marxism.[75]

The core policy of the NRM is the protection and progressive regeneration of the Nordic gene pool that is threatened by multi-culturalism, mass immigration and miscegenation. The group aims to prevent the further dilution of the Nordic bloodline in Scandinavia to avoid what it considers to be the ultimate 'racial genocide' of the Nordic people:

> Our racial survival and freedom is the most important goal of the political efforts of the Nordic Resistance Movement. Against this goal there are many threats, including the most alarming and urgent today which is the mass immigration of foreign races to the Nordic countries. This, in combination with the current lower birth rate of Nordic women in comparison to immigrants, and the fact that the immigrated foreigners sometimes conceive with Nordic women and men, result in the diminishing of the ethnically Nordic population in relation to the non-Nordic population. The so-called multiculturalism and mass immigration is in actuality a physical displacement and genocide of the Nordic people.[76]

The manifesto further argues that the Nordic people have historically developed in isolation from the biological and cultural influence of other races and that this uniqueness is reflected not only in their physical appearance but also in noble, admirable characteristics that have been refined and perfected by millennia of racial separation:

> Historically, the Nordic people have lived separated from the involvement of foreign races and have therefore, preserved a unique gene pool, culture and sense of society and community. Unique attributes that differ from other races can be found not only in the physical appearance of the Nordic people, but on a level that goes much deeper. Traits such as cooperation, ingenuity, sense of order, devotion to duty, and altruism have been the societal result of thousands of years of racial separation.[77]

This myth of racially unique, pure and noble Nordic people, which once existed in biological and cultural isolation, was disseminated by many Nordicist thinkers and groups of the late nineteenth and early twentieth centuries who proposed a range of positive and negative eugenics measures to remedy the decline of civilisation. To protect and re-establish the Nordic gene pool, the NRM proposes a range of positive eugenics solutions such as the immediate repatriation of those who are not racially identifiable as being of Northern European descent and an immediate halt to mass immigration leading to a racially selective Nordic immigration policy. Its means of racial selection echoes the physical criteria of Himmler's SS fused with modern science when it declares that, 'in reality, it is in most cases quite obvious who is of Nordic or closely related descent. In more uncertain cases we could use modern genetic profiling to determine which people are predominantly of Nordic racial descent'.[78]

THE NORDIC TERROR OF ANDERS BREIVIK: OSLO AND UTØYA 22/7

On 22 July 2011, Anders Behring Breivik (1979–), a seemingly ordinary thirty-two-year-old Norwegian citizen who was assessed as fit to stand trial by a court psychiatric report, planted a bomb in Norway's capital before going on a shooting spree on the island of Utøya, leaving a total of 77 dead and over 240 injured. In court, Breivik calmly and remorselessly accounted for the actions which he insisted were undertaken 'out of goodness, not evil', explaining that 'the aim of the killings was for racial purity and to change the direction of multi-cultural drift'. Breivik further stated that: 'The only way I could protect the white native Norwegian was through violence'.[79] Breivik stood before the court with no remorse and offended both the judges and his victims with his initial insistence on saluting the courtroom each day with a raised clenched fist, the salute of the Knights Templar described in his manifesto.[80]

During the trial, the court heard how this act of resistance against multi-culturalism in Norway had taken years of planning and preparation. Breivik also discussed his political manifesto, *2083: A European Declaration of Independence*, in which he details his preparations for that day, his criteria for potential targets, and explains the political and racial motivations for his actions. That morning, shortly before his attacks, Breivik emailed this manifesto to approximately a thousand recipients, many gathered from his Facebook page and posted a YouTube video denouncing multi-culturalism, entitled *Knights Templar 2083*, to publicly present his rationale for the terrorist acts he was about to commit. In court Breivik also explained that, in keeping with what he termed 'a great European tradition', he gave names from Norse mythology to his weapons. He named his rifle '*Gungnir*' after the magical spear of *Oðinn*, and he named his handgun '*Mjǫllnir*' after *Þórr's* hammer, giving his weapons a mythical significance as defenders of his racial *Miðgarðr*.[81]

The court also heard that, during 2007, Breivik spent up to sixteen hours a day playing the online early medieval mythological game *World of Warcraft* which contains many visual and thematic references to Northern European myth and legend.[82] Even more significantly, in order to play this game, he created the avatar 'andersnordic', a heroic double which doubtlessly informed the persona which murdered sixty-nine people on the island of Utøya in the name of awakening his fellow Norwegians to the need to preserve the purity of their country's unique Norse-Christian culture. Breivik considered himself a soldier, fighting for his race, an image that he presented in a self-portrait in his manifesto and video (Fig. 6.2).

Fig. 6.2 Anders Breivik posing as a modern-day Nordic warrior with his Ruger Mini 14 rifle. This image was posted in an appendix to his manifesto and was included in his video posted on the Internet on the morning of the attacks. Image published by Breivik, Anders. *2083: A European Declaration of Independence* (2011)

Breivik's manifesto, *2083: A European Declaration of Independence*, could in many ways be considered a mind map of Breivik's radicalisation and the blueprint both in practical and ideological terms for his actions of July 2011. In his manifesto, composed mainly of a compendium of articles copied and adapted from a range of sources, such as Wikipedia, nationalist web sites and anti-Islamic 'Eurabia' bloggers such as Fjordman, Breivik protests against Cultural Marxism, the threat of Islam, mass immigration, globalisation and multi-culturalism.[83] He defines Cultural Marxism as the belief among right-wing ideologists that Marxists are attempting to erode traditional Western values from within by breaking down social inequalities and establishing what they term, a culture of 'political correctness'. In his work, Breivik, who describes himself as a 'cultural conservative', claims that, during the post-war years, cultural Marxists have seized control of the world's media as a platform for silencing critics of the globalisation and multi-culturalism that he perceives as a threat to the existence of his race. In Breivik's words:

> The mainstream media has been hijacked by cultural Marxists/ Multiculturalists who are not acting in the interest of Europeans and Europe. There is no freedom of speech in Europe. If you don't cheer and embrace your own annihilation you are a racist bigot, an enemy of the establishment and must be suppressed, ridiculed, undermined and persecuted. This policy of oppression and persecution has been ongoing since the creation of multiculturalism in the 50s, 60s and 70s.[84]

Breivik attacks the European Union for dismantling border controls, undermining national stability and weakening Europe's culture. He accuses multiculturalists of the 'cultural genocide' of the European people by exposing them to increasing harassment, assault, rape and other forms of violent crime committed by immigrants. In a section dealing with crimes committed by Muslim immigrants, Breivik states that: 'European cultural Marxists/multiculturalists are collectively held responsible for all criminal acts committed by Muslims against indigenous Europeans in Europe'.[85]

Discussing the spread of Islam and his planned reaction to it, Breivik describes a European Civil War divided into three phases: 1999–2030, 2030–2070 and 2070–2083. During these periods, he projects the spread of Islam from 2–30% of the population to 30–50%. He also describes the development of European resistance to this spread of Islam through the formation of clandestine cells, resistance groups and future *coup d'états* to overthrow regimes supporting Marxism and multiculturalism including the executions of the movements' prominent figures. To bring about this counter-attack for European culture, Breivik claimed an association with a newly founded clandestine order of the *Knights Templar*, originally established in 1119.[86] According to Breivik, this group is called *The European Military Order and Criminal Tribune* whose aims are the seizure of political control and punishment of leading multi-culturists and other 'traitors'.[87]

Breivik also describes the role and function of various ranks and structures within the organisation as part of the three phases of the European civil war including the use of 'terror as a method of waking up the masses'.[88] He also provides a detailed 'manual' of methods and techniques necessary to carry out a range of terror attacks, drawing on his personal experience of planning the attacks of July 2011. He includes a categorisation of potential targets and details of the eventual acquisition and deployment of weapons of mass destruction such as anthrax.[89]

Although Breivik discusses the battle against multiculturalism in Pan-European terms as a modern-day crusade of the historic order of the *Knights Templar*, his discussion of the future of the Nordic people draws on many aspects of pre-war Nordicism. Referring to the Nordic type as defined in Madison Grant's *Passing of the Great Race* and drawing on demographic maps and statistics contained in that work, Breivik predicts that the Nordic type will be largely destroyed through interbreeding with other races within 150 years. To preserve the Nordic gene pool, Breivik describes a racial struggle that would only be won through resistance and direct violent action:

> [...] within 4–5 generations (if the current development is allowed to continue) the Germanic/Nordic race in several countries will be diluted or annihilated to such a degree that there will be no one left with Nordic physical characteristics; blond hair, blue eyes, high forehead, sturdy cheekbones. As such Nordic tribes will become extinct if we do not resist and seize political and military control of our countries. To illustrate the ongoing demographic annihilation of the Nordic peoples; in 1900 there were 50% Nordics in the US (blonde hair, blue eyes). But now, as a result of primarily non-European immigration, there was in 2008 ONLY 16%.[90]

Breivik describes the Nordic people, not just in physical terms but also as a European ethnic tribe who are threatened with biological and cultural extinction through multiculturalism and immigration. To defend Nordic interests, Breivik suggests the establishment of a Nordic League of Scandinavians, Germans, the British, Americans, Polish, Swiss, Dutch, Belgians and Balkans with the aim of 'propagating Nordic interests'.[91]

Discussing the dilution of the Nordic gene pool through interbreeding, Breivik explains that the 'Nordic genotype' is recessive in comparison with the African, Arab or oriental genotypes and Nordic characteristics have been therefore weakened through interbreeding; he describes children of mixed race as 'cut off forever from their extended ethnic family'.[92] To counter this process of 'racial annihilation', Breivik suggests the implementation of positive eugenics policies through the modern science of bioengineering to protect and even potentially enhance the Nordic race:

> The key to our survival is to liberalise the strict bio-technology laws and to commercialise and glorify repro-genetics while there is still a sustainable selection of Nordics of 99% purity left (this window of opportunity will be forever lost in 150 years). Not only will we have the option to secure our survival but we will be able to purify our tribe and add several IQ points to our off-spring in the same process.[93]

Breivik also proposes to encourage the birth rate and improve the biological health of the Nordic through measures to reduce the influence of feminism, reduce promiscuity and greatly restrict divorce, contraception and abortion in Nordic territories.[94] He also proposes a system very similar in aims and selection methods to the SS *Lebensborn* project. Breivik describes what he terms a network of 'surrogacy facilities' in low-cost countries to 'outsource breeding' through a commercial program of egg/sperm donation and in vitro fertilisation with the state caring for and educating the children in large boarding homes divided into five developmental age groups.[95] As Breivik describes, there would be of a process of careful racial selection of the potential candidates:

> All egg and sperm donors must be screened according to high pre-defined standards including genetic diseases. Optimally the donors should score high in interpersonal, verbal-linguistic, logical-mathematic, intrapersonal and visual-space intelligence tests and be of the indigenous group.[96]

In his elaboration of his ambitions for this programme, Breivik projects that this plan would initially need to create 30,050 Nordic-type children per year to counter-balance Norway's annual birth deficit.[97] He even refers to the potential development of artificial womb technology in these surrogacy centres.[98] Breivik insists, however, that just having children is pointless unless they are educated to believe in the dangers of Islam, multiculturalism and the basics of what he terms 'our patriotic struggle', describing in detail, a process of education of all Nordic children in his 'world-view'.

In his social visions for a futural Nordic state, Breivik differs from many Nordic nationalists through his lack of interest in the revival of ancient forms of pagan faith. Breivik points out that being a Christian is a rule of the Knights Templar and describes himself as a militant Christian who is influenced by his secular surroundings and environment. Despite this mixture of a secular outlook and Christian affiliation, Breivik describes pagan Odinists as 'brothers in our common fight' arguing that 'Odinism, as a religious movement, does not have the potency to unite us against such a devastating force as Islam, cultural Marxism/multiculturalism and capitalist globalism'.[99]

Breivik, much like his manifesto, is a composite of right-wing extremist thought in which a strand of Nordicism can clearly be identified as part of his radicalised 'mazeway resynthesis'. In this psychological construct, he perceives himself as a Nordic warrior fighting against globalisation and multiculturalism which he sees as a threat, not only the Norwegian state but to the future of the Nordic race. Breivik was sentenced to Norway's maximum sentence of twenty-one years of imprisonment and has remained, to date, in solitary confinement despite his legal protests. Although it would be an over-simplification of Breivik's complex psychology to label him simply as a Nordicist, it could be argued that aspects of cultural, biological and political Nordicism formed a significant aspect of his 'world-view' and rationale for his actions of July 2011. Breivik saw the events of this day as an important act of resistance in a war against globalisation and the threatened extinction of the Nordic race.

In his analysis of Anders Breivik, within the historical and contemporary context of populist and extreme-right views in Norway, social anthropologist Sindre Bangstad argues that Breivik is a product of what he describes as 'dark undercurrents' of historical racist ideology in Norway and other Western countries which have re-emerged today in the form of Islamophobia.[100] In his work, Bangstad describes how, from his youth, he was taught the 'hegemonic narrative' of Norway's fight against fascism in which 'heroic blond and mainly male Norwegians' took refuge in the countryside to continue their resistance against the German troops who had invaded Norway in 1940.[101] Bangstad also challenges the enduring myth of Norway as a racially pure racial model arguing that the 'utopian fantasy of Norway as an ethnically "pure" and "homogenous" country is a recurrent theme in Norwegian history'.[102] In his analysis, Bangstad positions himself amongst the revisionists of this established version of Norwegian history, highlighting the extent to which a number of Norwegians collaborated with the occupying German forces. Bangstad proposes that 'by the 1980s the first cracks in the hegemonic narrative of Norway's role in the Second World War began to appear' suggesting that academia has previously 'sanitised' Norwegian history.[103] Bangstad argues that Norway suffers from the same racial tensions as many other European states and is in no way immune to forms of populist racism emerging across Europe. He adds that the current revision of right-wing thought in Norway 'will be provocative, even intolerable, for Norwegians long accustomed to seeing themselves—and being seen by others—as the embodiment of all that is good and virtuous in the world'.[104] In his conclusion, Bangstad also warns that the overlap between racial extremism and populist right-wing thought in Europe remains a significant threat to the integration of immigrants into Western culture and society:

> The greatest material threats to equal rights to citizenship, inclusion and participation in contemporary liberal democracies in western Europe remain those emanating from the exclusionary discourses and from the mainstreaming and sanitising of extreme right-wing discourses and rhetorical tropes by the populist right wing in Norway and other Scandinavian and western European countries. As the horror of 22/7 slowly, painfully but surely fades into the historical past, that challenge remains with us for the foreseeable future.[105]

Although Bangstad does not refer to Nordicism in his work, it could be argued that his analysis reveals many points which suggest that elements of Nordicist thought are still emerging as a reaction to globalisation and when radicalised can still produce horrific crimes against humanity. The attack on a mosque near Oslo on 10 August 2019 and the murder of his Chinese stepsister, by Norwegian neo-Nazi Philip Manshaus, is a sign of racial tensions still present in Norwegian society and in Europe as a whole.[106] According to Bangstad, Manshaus once applied for membership of the Nordic Resistance Movement and drew inspiration from Anders

Breivik and New Zealander Brenton Tarrant who murdered fifty-one people in two mosques in 2019. He was sentenced to twenty-one years in prison and showed no remorse at this trial.

CONCLUSION: LIQUID NORDICISM

Like flotsam carried in the currents of our 'liquid modern' society, manifestations of Nordicism can still be found in contemporary society, no longer in the form established by the failed project of Nazism, but in new adapted forms emerging as a reactions against our current state of twenty-first-century modernity. In this contemporary state of 'liquid modernity', where globalisation and multiculturalism have become seemingly unstoppable forces, Nordicist elements appear from time to time as small revitalisation movements or lone wolves, attempting to regenerate an idealised, imagined state of primordial racial purity. These constructs are, however, generally short-lived, unstable 'temporary solids' that fail to last or combine with others to form any cohesive movement. Some re-emerge in new far-right organisations, others fade away into obscurity and a few extremists are imprisoned for racially motivated crimes earning brief moments of notoriety in the media. Despite a cultural climate which arguably still idealises both the past and present in Scandinavia, our dominant current of contemporary thought rejects racism as a crime against humanity and seeks to limit, marginalise and eliminate Nordicist elements through the media, public disapproval and anti-racist legislation. This however is not a guarantee of defence against the potential threat of Nordicism, which can still emerge under certain conditions and pose a dangerous threat to society.

This work has attempted to shed new light on Nordicism by examining it as single entity, with its own cultural dynamics and historical narrative and as a reaction to the unstoppable progress of modernity. From its emergence out of late eighteenth-century Romanticism, Nordicism has evolved through its interaction and fusion with diverse aspects of modernity, most notably the rise of National Socialism, when it evolved into its most evil, malignant form of racial selection and elimination of inferior 'others'. Through this process, Nordicism developed from a Romantic, nationalist yearning for national identity and sense of rootedness in Old Norse culture, into a cultural, political and biological agenda of programmatic modernism. At the conclusion of the Second World War, this 'solid' of Nordicism was left shattered like the smouldering ruins of Berlin as the

Soviet forces broke through the last defences of the capital to end the regime that had planned and overseen the industrial-scale genocide of millions of those considered racially threatening to the purity of the Nordic race.

Like fragmented remnants of the failed projects of late nineteenth- and early twentieth-century modernism, designed to bring about a mythologised ideal state of human existence, the threat of Nordicism is still present as an active force in today's society. This emerges as the 'Somewheres' in society attempt to create pockets of 'solidity' and 'fixity' as existential anchors in today's 'liquid universe'. This analysis has highlighted how various strands of Nordicism can stem from the same modernist impulse to generate and realise myths to re-establish and maintain a sense of transcendence, hope and *nomic* certainty. Contemporary society is abandoning futural visions of ultimate perfection as it struggles to come to terms with the constant sense of 'liquid fear' permeating our existence. Nordicism will never again be able to 'solidify' on the scale of its previous murderous form but the continued idealisation of the Nordic and the permeability of the membrane separating this phenomenon from the fragments of Nordicism, floating like flotsam in our 'liquid modernity', mean that this narrative is still incomplete. The horror of 22/7 was a poignant reminder of this.

NOTES

1. These are all titles and themes of subsequent publications by Bauman.
2. *Liquid Life and Social Media*. InvisibleStudio.it. http://www.invisiblestudio.it/new/blog/liquid-life-and-social-media/ (Accessed 20/04/18).
3. Griffin, Roger (2015) *Fixing Solutions: Fascist Temporalities as Remedies for Liquid Modernity*. Journal of Modern European History. 13. pp. 5-23.
4. Nietzsche, Friedrich (Trans. Common, T. 1917) *Thus Spoke Zarathustra*. The Modern Library, New York p 7.
5. For offending the Gods with his crimes, the Greek God Tantalus was sentenced to spend eternity standing in a lake with fruits hanging out of his reach so that he was unable to satisfy his thirst and hunger.

6. Bauman, Zygmunt (2012) *Liquid Modernity*. Polity Press, Cambridge (Forward to the 2012 edition).
7. Bauman quotes Boym, Svetlana (2001) *The Future of Nostalgia* in *Retropia*. Polity Press, Cambridge p 2.
8. Ibid. 7 p 2.
9. Ibid. 7 p 2.
10. Arnold, Martin (2011) *Thor – Myth to Marvel*. Continuum Books, London p 159.
11. Ibid. 10 p 159.
12. Ibid. 10 p 159.
13. *Thor - Ragnarok* (2017) reached a worldwide box office total of $843,376,522 in December 2017. http://www.boxofficemojo.com/movies/?id=marvel2017.htm (Accessed 22/12/17) This figure does not include income received through Internet downloads or DVD sales.
14. Rose, Steve (2017) *Thor - Ragnarok Review*. https://www.theguardian.com/film/2017/oct/19/thor-ragnarok-review-chris-hemsworth-cate-blanchett-taika-waititi (Accessed 25/02/18).
15. *Tolkien's Hobbit celebrates 75th anniversary*. https://www.usatoday.com/story/life/books/2012/09/20/hobbit-tolkien-75-anniversary-corey-olsen/1576943/ (Accessed 25/02/18).
16. Hari, Johann (2003) *The wrong Lord of the Reads*. http://www.independent.co.uk/voices/commentators/johann-hari/the-wrong-lord-of-the-reads-82201.html (Accessed 25/02/18).
17. Quotes taken from a letter dated 9th June 1941. Quoted by Martinez Michael (2015) *Taboo Tolkien: The Nordicist Claim on Middle-earth Refuted*. https://www.tolkiensociety.org/blog/2015/11/taboo-tolkien-the-nordicist-claim-on-middle-earth/ (Accessed 25/02/18).
18. Ibid. 17.
19. *Vikings renewed for sixth season*. http://ew.com/tv/2017/09/12/vikings-renewed-season-6/ (Accessed 22/01/18).
20. *Top 10 Viking games on PC*. http://www.gamersdecide.com/pc-game-news/top-10-viking-games-pc (Accessed 22/12/17).
21. Hutton, Christopher M. (2017) *Racial ideology as elite discourse: Nordicism and the visual in an age of mass-culture*. Social Semiotics, 27 (3): p 339.
22. Hutton, Christopher M. *Racial ideology as elite discourse*, p 344.
23. Ibid. 21 p 335.

24. Ibid. 21 p 335.
25. Joffe, Josef (2017) *The Right is Rising and Social Democracy is Dying Across Europe.* https://www.theguardian.com/commentisfree/2017/sep/29/right-social-democracy-dying-europe-afd-far-right-germany (Accessed 09/01/18).
26. In his recent work on the French New Right, Stéphane François refers to the influence of Nordicism as part of its attack on Judeo-Christianity, globalization, anomic modernity and multicultural democracies. François, Stéphane (2018) *Paganisme, écologie et identité.* Taylor and Francis, Paris.
27. Statistics correct on 16/08/20.
28. *German Jews warned not to wear kippas after rise in anti-Semitism.* https://www.bbc.co.uk/news/world-europe-48411735 (Accessed 26/05/19).
29. *Lord Adonis in a letter of resignation to the Prime Minister as government infrastructure advisor.* http://www.bbc.co.uk/news/uk-42515637 (Accessed 30/12/17).
30. *Brexit sparks calls for other votes.* http://www.bbc.co.uk/news/world-europe-36615879 (Accessed 09/01/18).
31. Goodhart, David (2017) *The Road to Somewhere: The New Tribes Shaping British Politics.* Penguin, London. Introduction.
32. Bjørgo, Tore (1997) *Racist and Right-Wing Violence in Scandinavia* Tano Aschehougs Fontenserie, Norway p 67.
33. *Stormfront Homepage.* https://www.stormfront.org/forum/index.php (Accessed 04/01/18).
34. *Germanic Pride Homepage.* https://cometa9a.wordpress.com/about/ (Accessed 10/01/18).
35. *Thule Island.* https://cometa9a.wordpress.com/91-2/ (Accessed 10/01/18).
36. *Germanic Roots.* https://cometa9a.wordpress.com/germanic-roots-2/ (Accessed 10/01/18).
37. *Nordic Anti-Semite Blog Homepage* https://nordicantisemite.com (Accessed 04/01/18). I have placed the asterisks.
38. Ibid. 37.
39. Ibid. 37.
40. Ibid. 37.
41. Ibid. 37.

42. *Anti-Semitic Nordicist Blog Homepage.* https://antisemiticnordicist.wordpress.com (Accessed 07/01/18).
43. Ibid. 42.
44. Ibid. 42.
45. Ibid. 42.
46. *Facebook Profile Page.* https://www.facebook.com/protectnordicbeauty/ (Accessed 04/01/18). This page has now been removed from Facebook.
47. Figures correct on 04/01/18.
48. Figures correct on 01/11/19.
49. Puryear, Mark (2006) *The Nature of Ásatrú.* iUniverse, Lincoln, USA p xv.
50. *Ásatrú membership.* https://asatru.is/felagafjoldi (Accessed 1/ 11/18).
51. Figure correct on 18/04/20.
52. Burzum was founded by Víkernes as a solo project in 1991 and is still releasing albums available as cds or for download on popular web sites such as amazon.com and Apple's iTunes. The term Burzum originates from JRR Tolkien's *The Lord of the Rings* in which the followers of Sauron speak the 'Black Speech'. In this fictional language Burzum means darkness and is inscribed on the 'One Ring'.
53. *Twenty years since the Church Burnings.* http://www.bt.no/ nyheter/lokalt/20-ar-siden-kirkesjokket-2932446.html#. UlnFZxa89UM (Accessed 12/10/13).
54. *A Burzum Story.* http://www.burzum.org/eng/library/a_burzum_story02.shtml (Accessed 12/10/13).
55. Goodrick-Clarke, Nicholas (2002) *Black Sun. Aryan Cults, Esoteric Nazism and the Politics of Identity.* University Press, New York p 204.
56. In an interview entitled *And Thus Spake Varg*, Vikernes stated that he wrote a political article for the organisation http://www.burzum.com/burzum/library/interviews/varg/   (Accessed 30/12/17).
57. Vikernes, Varg. *Why Óðalism?* https://thuleanperspective. com/2013/07/31/why-odalism/?wref=tp (Accessed 23/12/17).
58. Ibid. 57.
59. Ibid. 57.
60. Number of subscribers on 30/12/18.

61. *Vinland Folk Resistance Blog Homepage.* http://vinlandfolkresistance.blogspot.co.uk/2007/03/welcome-to-vinland-folk-resistance.html (Accessed 06/01/18).
62. Ibid. 61.
63. Ibid. 61.
64. This concept of a racial awakening was a significant element of early Nazi ideology that used the slogan *Deutschland erwacht.*
65. Ibid. 61.
66. Ibid. 61.
67. *Sons of Odin - 1519.* http://sonsofodin1519.org/node/2 (Accessed 06/01/18).
68. Ibid. 67.
69. *Wolves of Vinland Newsfeed.* http://twitter.com #wolvesofvinland (Accessed 05/01/18).
70. On 30 November 2017, a Finnish court banned the movement for encouraging crimes of racial violence.
71. Nordfront Sweden had 1,112 followers on Twitter on 15/08/20.
72. *We expect chaos.* https://www.express.co.uk/news/world/860686/nazi-demonstration-protest-Sweden-Gothenburg-police-arrests-Nordic-Resistance-Movement-NRM (Accessed 28/07/20).
73. *Our Path - New Politics for a New Time.* https://www.nordfront.se/wpcontent/uploads/2016/12/Our-Path.pdf p.10. (Accessed 15/03/18).
74. Ibid. 73 p 10.
75. Ibid. 73 p 16.
76. Ibid. 73 p 12.
77. Ibid. 73 p 12.
78. Ibid. 73 p 13.
79. *Breivik's testimony of 17th April 2012.* http://news.sky.com/home/world-news/article/16210390 (Accessed 18/04/12).
80. Breivik, Anders (2011) *2083: A European Declaration of Independence.* http://www.deism.com/images/breivik-manifesto-2011.pdf (Accessed 20/03/18).
Military salutation of the Knight's Templar. p 1102.
81. *Testimony of Anders Breivik: Day 4.* http://www.telegraph.co.uk/news/worldnews/europe/norway/9213218/Norway-killer-Anders-Behring-Breivik-trial-day-four-as-it-happened.html (Accessed 29/04/12).

82. *The life of a mass murderer in World of Warcraft.* https://kotaku. com/5903501/the-life-of-a-mass-murderer-in-world-of-warcraft (Accessed 08/01/18).

83. Peder Are Nøstvold Jensen (born 11 June 1975) is a prominent Norwegian blogger who writes under the pseudonym Fjordman and whose articles are far-right and anti-Islamic. His web site can be found at http://gatesofvienna.net

84. Breivik, Anders *2083: A European Declaration of Independence.* p.801. (Accessed 04/11/12).

85. Ibid. 84 p 153.

86. Breivik claimed that the *Pauperes commilitiones Christi Templique Solomonici* (the poor Fellow-Soldiers of Christ and the Temple of Solomon) was re-founded in London in 2002 by representatives of eight European countries. Ibid. 84 p 817.

87. Ibid. 84 p 817.

88. Ibid. 84 p 836.

89. Ibid. 84 p 961.

90. Ibid. 84 p 1153.

91. Ibid. 84 p 1155.

92. Ibid. 84 p 1158.

93. Ibid. 84 p 1159.

94. Ibid. 84 p 1179.

95. Ibid. 84 p 1182.

96. Ibid. 84 p 1184.

97. Ibid. 84 p 1184.

98. Ibid. 84 p 1187.

99. Ibid. 84 p 1361.

100. Bangstad, Sindre (2014) *Anders Breivik and the Rise of Islamophobia.* Zed Books, London p 151.

101. Bangstad, Sindre *Anders Breivik and the Rise of Islamophobia.* p 140.

102. Ibid. 100 p 151.

103. Ibid. 100 p 151.

104. Ibid. 100 p 197.

105. Ibid. 100 p 219.

106. Bangstad, Sindre *The 2019 mosque attack and freedom of speech in Norway* https://www.aljazeera.com/indepth/opinion/norway-manshaus-case-freedom-speech-200525102742004.html (Accessed 15/08/20).

BIBLIOGRAPHY

PRINTED WORKS

Arnold, M. (2011). *Thor – Myth to Marvel*. London: Continuum Books.
Bangstad, S. (2014). *Anders Breivik and the Rise of Islamophobia*. London: Zed Books.
Bauman, Z. (2012). *Liquid Modernity*. Cambridge: Polity Press.
Bauman, Z. (2017). *Retropia*. Cambridge: Polity Press.
Bjørgo, T. (1997). *Racist and Right-Wing Violence in Scandinavia*. Norway: Tano Aschehougs Fontenserie.
Boym, S. (2001). *The Future of Nostalgia*. New York: Basic Books.
François, S. (2018). *Paganisme, Écologie et Identité*. Paris: Taylor and Francis.
Goodhart, D. (2017). *The Road to Somewhere: The New Tribes Shaping British Politics*. London: Penguin.
Goodrick-Clarke, N. (2002). *Black Sun - Aryan Cults, Esoteric Nazism and the Politics of Identity*. New York: University Press.
Griffin, R. (2015). *Fixing Solutions: Fascist Temporalities as Remedies for Liquid Modernity*. Journal of Modern European History, *13*, 5–23.
Griffin, R. (2007). *Modernism and Fascism – The Sense of a Beginning Under Mussolini and Hitler*. Basingstoke and New York: Palgrave Macmillan.
Hutton, C. M. (2017). *Racial Ideology as Elite Discourse: Nordicism and the Visual in an Age of Mass-Culture*. Social Semiotics, *27*(3), 1–13.
Nietzsche, F. (1917). (Trans. Common T.) *Thus Spoke Zarathustra*. New York: The Modern Library.
Puryear, M. (2006). *The Nature of Ásatrú*. Lincoln: iUniverse.

WEBSITES AND DIGITAL PUBLICATIONS (WITH DATE ACCESSED)

A Burzum Story. Accessed 12/10/13, from http://www.burzum.org/eng/library/a_burzum_story02.shtml
Anti-semitic Nordicist Blog Homepage. Accessed 07/01/18, from https://antisemiticnordicist.wordpress.com
Ásatrú Membership. Accessed 15/01/18, from https://asatru.is/felagafjoldi
Breivik, A. (2011). *2083: A European Declaration of Independence*. Accessed 20/03/18, from http://www.deism.com/images/breivik-manifesto-2011.pdf
Breivik's Testimony of 17th April 2012. Accessed 18/04/12, from http://news.sky.com/home/world-news/article/16210390
Brexit Sparks Calls for Other Votes. Accessed 09/01/18, from http://www.bbc.co.uk/news/world-europe-36615879

Capon, F. *Neo-Nazi Activity on the Rise in Europe.* Accessed 02/01/18, from http://www.newsweek.com

Family from Hell: The Rise of the Aryan Brotherhood. Accessed 05/01/18, from http://www.independent.co.uk/news/world/americas/family-from-hell-the-rise-of-the-aryan-brotherhood-8563520.html April 2013

Hari, J. *The Wrong Lord of the Reads.* Accessed 25/02/18, from http://www.independent.co.uk/voices/commentators/johann-hari/the-wrong-lord-of-the-reads-82201.html

Germanic Pride Homepage. Accessed 10/01/18, from https://cometa9a.wordpress.com/about/

Germanic Roots. wordpress.com. Accessed 10/01/18, from https://cometa9a.wordpress.com/germanic-roots-2/

Joffe, J. (2017) *The Right Is Rising and Social Democracy Is Dying Across Europe.* Accessed 09/01/18, from https://www.theguardian.com/commentisfree/2017/sep/29/right-social-democracy-dying-europe-afd-far-right-germany

Liquid Life and Social Media. Accessed 20/04/18, from http://www.invisiblestudio.it/new/blog/liquid-life-and-social-media/

Lord Adonis Letter of Resignation to the Prime Minister. Accessed 30/12/17, from http://www.bbc.co.uk/news/uk-42515637

Nordic Anti-Semite Blog Homepage. Accessed 04/01/18, from https://nordicantisemite.com

Nordic Beauty - Facebook Profile Page. Accessed 04/01/18, from https://www.facebook.com/protectnordicbeauty/

Our Path - New Politics for a New Time. Accessed 15/03/18, from https://www.nordfront.se/wp-content/uploads/2016/12/Our-Path.pdf, p. 10.

Rose, S. (2017) *Thor - Ragnarok Review.* Accessed 25/02/18, from https://www.theguardian.com/film/2017/oct/19/thor-ragnarok-review-chris-hemsworth-cate-blanchett-taika-waititi

Sons of Odin - 1519. Accessed 06/01/18, from http://sonsofodin1519.org/node/2

Stormfront Homepage. Accessed 04/01/18, from https://www.stormfront.org/forum/index.php

Taboo Tolkien: The Nordicist Claim on Middle-Earth Refuted. www.tolkiensociety.org. Accessed 25/02/18, from https://www.tolkiensociety.org/blog/2015/11/taboo-tolkien-the-nordicist-claim-on-middle-earth/

Testimony of Anders Breivik: Day 4. Accessed 29/04/12, from http://www.telegraph.co.uk/news/worldnews/europe/norway/9213218/Norway-killer-Anders-Behring-Breivik-trial-day-four-as-it-happened.html

The Life of a Mass Murderer in World of Warcraft. Accessed 08/01/18, from https://kotaku.com/5903501/the-life-of-a-mass-murderer-in-world-of-warcraft

Thor: Ragnarok. Accessed 22/12/17, from http://www.boxofficemojo.com/movies/?id=marvel2017.htm

Thule Island. Accessed 10/01/18, from https://cometa9a.wordpress.com/91-2/

Tolkien's Hobbit Celebrates 75th Anniversary. Accessed 25/02/18, from https://www.usatoday.com/story/life/books/2012/09/20/hobbit-tolkien-75-anniversary-corey-olsen/1576943/

Top 10 Viking Games on PC. Accessed 22/12/17, from http://www.gamersdecide.com/pc-game-news/top-10-viking-games-pc

Twenty Years Since the Church Burnings. Accessed 12/10/13, from http://www.bt.no/nyheter/lokalt/20-ar-siden-kirkesjokket-2932446.html#.UlnFZxa89UM

Vikernes, V. *Why Óðalism?* Accessed 23/12/17, from https://thuleanperspective.com/2013/07/31/why-odalism/?wref=tp

Vikings Renewed for Sixth Season. Accessed 22/01/18, from http://ew.com/tv/2017/09/12/vikings-renewed-season-6/

Vinland Folk Resistance Blog Homepage. Accessed 06/01/18, from http://vinlandfolkresistance.blogspot.co.uk/2007/03/welcome-to-vinland-folk-resistance.html

We Expect Chaos. Accessed 28/07/19, from https://www.express.co.uk/news/world/860686/nazi-demonstration-protest-Sweden-Gothenburg-police-arrests-Nordic-Resistance-Movement-NRM

Wolves of Vinland Newsfeed. http://twitter.com #wolvesofvinland. Accessed 05/01/18.

World Happiness Report 2018. Accessed 30/03/18, from http://worldhappiness.report

INDEX

© The Author(s) 2020
G. E. Forssling, *Nordicism and Modernity*,
https://doi.org/10.1007/978-3-030-61210-8

261

9 783030 612092